THE VIKING

Philip Thiel 1985

THE VIKING

This work is the result of comprehensive team-work by scientists and specialists from a number of countries.

BERTIL ALMGREN
Professor at Uppsala University, Sweden, archeologist and specialist in Ancient History, has been the chief contributor to and advisory expert for this work.

CHARLOTTE BLINDHEIM
Norway. Curator, Museum of Antiquities, University of Oslo.
YVES DE BOUARD
France. Professor at the University of Caen.
TORSTEN CAPELLE
Germany. Ph. D. University of Göttingen.
ARNE EMIL CHRISTENSEN JR. M. A.
Norway. Curator, Museum of Antiquities, University of Oslo.

KRISTJÁN ELDJÁRN
Ph. D. Iceland. National Custodian of Icelandic Antiquities, Reykjavik.
RICHARD M. PERKINS
Iceland. Lecturer at Reykjavik University
THORKILD RAMSKOU
Denmark. Curator, National Museum of Antiquities, Copenhagen.
PETER SAWYER
Great Britain. Lecturer in Early Medieval History. University of Leeds.

Contributors;
INGA HENNING
Sweden. B. A. Uppsala.
SUNE LINDQVIST
Sweden. Prof. Em., University of Uppsala
KJELL LUNDHOLM
Sweden. M. A. Uppsala.
T. R. NICHOLSON
Great Britain. M. A. (Oxon.). Supervising editor of the English text.

KERSTIN PETTERSSON
Sweden. M. A. Uppsala University. Institution of Scandinavian Archeology.
JAMES STEWART
Sweden. Lecturer at Uppsala University.

Main illustrations;
ÅKE GUSTAVSSON

*Copyright © 1975
by AB Nordbok, Gothenburg*

*All rights reserved including
the right to reproduce this book
or portions thereof in any form.*

This edition published by
CRESCENT BOOKS
distributed by Crown Publishers, Inc.
by arrangement with
AB NORDBOK
b c d e f g h

*Library of Congress Catalog
Card Number:
63-18428*

Printed in Italy, 1984, by New Interlitho S.P.A.

ISBN: 0-517-445530

THE VIKING

CRESCENT BOOKS
New York

CONTENTS

SOUTH TO THE MEDITERRANEAN AND EAST TO ASIA — THE VIKINGS CARRY WAR, COMMERCE, AND NEW PEOPLE INTO OLD EMPIRES

The Vikings attacked the empire of Charlemagne and established the Duchy of Normandy in northern France. Their traders went down the rivers to the heart of Russia and to Byzantium.

THE POWER OF WORDS — MAGIC RUNES, THE HEROIC SAGAS, POEMS OF LOVE, HATE, TRIUMPH AND TRAGEDY

Before the Latin alphabet came north with Christian missionaries the Vikings used runic symbols which were generally carved on stones. The Vikings regarded the runes with mystic awe and attributed magic powers to them. The history and legends of the Vikings are found in the sagas and eddas and in the elaborate poetry of the scalds. Viking literature is rich, heroic but often grim, reflecting the hard life of Viking Scandinavia.

THE FAMOUS VIKING LONGSHIP — HOW IT DEVELOPED FROM ITS EARLIEST BEGINNINGS TO ITS GREATEST DAYS

The discovery of the burial ships at Gokstad and Oseberg have provided the materials for our greatest insights into the Viking way of life. In 1893 a replica of the Gokstad ship was built and satisfactorily crossed the Atlantic. The construction of these boats remains unsurpassed for ships of their class. Other ships have been found since, but none so rich with Viking archaeological material as those of Gokstad and Oseberg.

VIKING VALUES — THE OLD GODS AND THE NEW, THE CLASSES AND PROFESSIONS, CUSTOMS AND MORALS

The Vikings worshiped the teutonic pagan gods. The early Viking communities knew no national boundaries, but were divided into classes according to wealth and property into earls, peasants, and thralls. Women and children were important in Viking society, but the infirm old were generally regarded with disfavour.

DAILY LIFE — DOMESTIC ARTS, TOOLS, CLOTHES, AND CRAFTSMANSHIP FOR PEACE AND WAR

Archaeological excavations have provided a full picture of the Viking way of life. In their large timber houses the earls prepared for war, the women cooked and wove; the peasants farmed the land and hand-crafted tools, utensils and weapons. The thralls carried out the heavy unskilled work. Metal work and woodwork were highly developed; cooking utensils varied and ingenious. Fine gold jewellery and inlaid silver work show a high degree of craftsmanship. Beautifully made sledges and wagons have been reconstructed from the Oseberg and Gokstad excavations.

THE MAPS

The text is illustrated and amplified throughout by an abundance of clear and detailed maps compiled by the many archaeologists and historians who have collaborated in the writing of this book. Four important colour maps show the extent of the Viking voyages of adventure, plunder and commerce:

On page 283 there is a complete index of the maps.

A brief glossary of places and persons mentioned in this book may be found on page 285.

A CONVENIENT NAME

"Vikings" and "Viking Age" are words which will appear on countless occasions in this book, because they have come to be the common designations of the Scandinavian peoples and a particular three-century period of their history. However, the Northmen never used the word to describe their whole race, and neither did neighbouring peoples who were exposed to their attacks. The Franks, who gave their name to present-day France, called the Vikings "Normans", meaning simply, "the men from the north". What else should they call them? They all spoke the same language, which was very different from that of the Franks, and they all came from the same cold corner of the world. The precise origin of the world *viking* is a mystery. Some scholars believe that it meant "creek-men", but in spite of much learned speculation, the problem still remains unsolved. Whatever its origin, its significance was definite enough, in that it was exclusively used to describe pirates and people who, for economic reasons, sailed on predatory expeditions and then returned home to settle down on their farms again.

THE "PICTURE-STONES" OF GOTLAND

On the Baltic island of Gotland are a number of monuments called "picture-stones", dating from the sixth to the eleventh century A.D. They are large upright slabs of stone set in the ground. On one side of each are carved various symbols and scenes. These are very difficult to decipher, for they refer to episodes in Scandinavian history and literature which are now lost. Among the most common things illustrated are ships filled with armed men; but it is very uncertain what they represent. The symbols at the head of each chapter in this book are taken from different Gotland picture-stones. The one on this page shows a Viking ship under sail.

At all times, people have learned to adjust themselves to the physical conditions that surround them. The geographical character of the countries of Scandinavia is at the root of the historical events which were of such great importance, particularly to western Europe, during the period that goes by the name of the Viking Age. The harsh northern sea dominated old Scandinavia. Land communication was obstructed by deep sea inlets, mountains, and trackless forests which here and there opened out to allow room for cultivated areas around the villages. The ubiquitous sea, however, suggested its own possibilities for communication. The west coast of Norway is battered by the Atlantic, but a multitude of islands protects the mainland so well that from very ancient times, navigation has been possible inside the archipelagoes. The islands formed a " corridor " along the coast favoured by fair winds and small waves. Along the Norwegian coast it is called *Leden* — literally " the lead " — a passage that leads the ships behind the island shield against the wild Atlantic waves. So effective is this shelter that people going to the coast to look at the sea are often very disappointed. Instead of a vast, glittering prospect of open sea, they find a stretch of water no wider than a big river, frequently hemmed in by tree-covered islands lying so close to each other that they look like an unbroken land-mass. Along the deep fjords a population of farmers settled down; people who were just as familiar with the sea as those living out among the islands. Traffic overland had to follow the valleys, or laboriously climb mountain passes.

If ships were convenient for communication in Norway, in Denmark they were indispensable. The country is split up into more than 500 islands of all sizes, each divided by creeks and narrow sounds. The peninsula, Jutland, is the only part connected to the European continent. Without ships, there could have been little mutual contact. The same applies to Sweden, where the rivers and the lakes were the most important means of communication. In Sweden at this time there was no clear line of demarcation between the dense network of islands and skerries off the east coast and the innumerable creeks around the present-day Lake Mälar, then still a brackish bay. These provided an easy passage for large rowing-boats that could also be brought up rivers, in Russia as well as Sweden. And for Swedes the passage to Russia was made easier by the Åland archipelago (still one of the world's leading ship-owning areas); a series of island stepping-stones which leaves only about twenty miles of really open sea to be crossed. In the middle of the Baltic, too, lay Gotland, which, although an island, was never culturally isolated, obviously thanks to its ships, which from the year 400 onwards are handsomely depicted on stone monuments. Lacking good natural harbours, the Gotlanders clearly had use for shallow-draught ships like those used by the early Greeks.

Islands breed seafarers. The first sailor to be immortalized in human memory was Odysseus from the island of Ithaka, who sailed the Mediterranean for years from island to island. The Greeks are still one of the world's leading sea-going nations, together with other island-dwellers like the Scots, the Norwegians and the inhabitants of the Åland archipelago. To the early Greeks, the islands of the Aegean formed a bridge to the rich civilizations of the Near East. It was no great thing to try to cross from the mainland to the nearest island and so on to the next and the next. The demands of nature made the Scandinavians not only farmers and sailors, but also shipbuilders. Experiments with new boat types, and especially with sails, would be dangerous on the open sea, but were encouraged by the quieter waters behind the island barriers. A brilliant nautical invention — the keel — made the Scandinavians masters of the sea. It is not known when or how they evolved the keel, but the significance of this detail of construction is clear. With it they could make their ships broad and flat. Keels gave them seaworthiness and stability, and at the same time made them easier to propel. This stability in turn permitted the use of mast and sail on the open sea, thereby increasing range and speed. The construction below the waterline was strong, and at the same time so elastic that it could yield and still resist the powerful pressure of the waves. However seaworthy they were, these craft were still open and without comfort of any sort. When the ships headed out to sea, the deck was filled with barrels of provisions and drinking-water. Every man had his own sea-chest, but what they brought with them in the way of trade-goods must have been stowed in piles on the deck. Everyone on board worked, slept and ate in the same exposed, cramped place, perhaps under some stretched tent-canvas. It

SHIPS IN WOOD

Above, a high-prowed fleet sails out to sea in a Norse wood-carving. The ship below was carved by a thirteenth-century Scandinavian on his walking stick, but its design had hardly changed from Viking times. An inscription on the stick reads: "Here goes Sea-Darer."

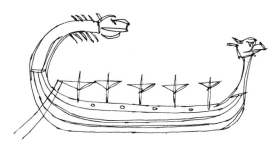

A VIKING SHIP REBORN

The largest and most well-preserved of all the Viking ships yet discovered (right) was found in 1880 at Gokstad, on the western shore of the Oslo Fjord. The ship has been completely rebuilt, with the exception of the stems, which are thought to have had a higher rise. It is now kept in the Viking Ship Museum at Bygdøy, in Oslo.

THE DANGEROUS ROAD

In the drawing above, a small fleet of Viking ships has shipped oars and set its sails, as the last of the sheltering islands of the North Sea coast of Scandinavia are left behind. The crews are resting, while they can. The sea in its fierce moods was always the Vikings' enemy, especially off rocky shores like those of western Sweden, shown in the colour photograph on the next pages. The Saga of Torfinn Karlsevne *tells of a battle lost to the sea. " ... Because of the tempest, Bjarne Grimolfsön drifted with his ship to the Irish Sea, and they met a breaker, and the ship began to go down. They had a small boat greased with tar which protects against the seaworms. They entered the boat but realized that it could not carry all of them. Then said Bjarne, 'Whereas the boat cannot carry more than half of our men, it is my advice that lots should be cast to settle who shall go into the boat, because this cannot be settled by rank.' They all thought this very fair, so nobody objected. So they drew lots, and it fell to Bjarne's share to go in the boat with half of the men, because the boat could not carry any more. "*

could be bitterly cold, and two men would lie together in the same sleeping-bag in order to keep warm. Everyone relieved himself over the rails. "Going to board", it was called, when less polite expressions were not used. Knowledge of navigation was just as necessary as knowledge of seamanship. Justifiably, the Norse discoveries in the North Atlantic have excited much admiration. The Vikings were, in fact, the only sailors of early medieval Europe prepared to sail far away from landmarks. The original discoveries in the North Atlantic are remarkable enough, but they are not miraculous. In the spring the existence of land far away is betrayed to those with keen sight by the flight of nesting sea birds. Sailors who observed the pattern of flight of birds like gannets each evening would know where land probably lay. The regular navigation of the Atlantic did not, of course, depend on sea birds. On starry nights the Vikings used the North Star, but astral navigation was difficult in the light northern summer nights. At night in the summer, therefore, they navigated by the sun. They could do this because, thanks to countless observations taken during the year, just before dawn and after sunset, they knew the motion of the sun across the sky. A table compiled by a man called Stjerne-Oddi (Star-Oddi) and who lived at Flatey in Iceland, has been preserved. It gives the altitude of the sun for the whole year, and also a table showing the direction of dawn and twilight; that is, of the light on the horizon at the sun's going up and down. All the measurements of angles were made in what was called a "half wheel", a kind of half sun-diameter, which corresponds to about sixteen seconds of an arc. This was something which was known to every skipper at that time, or by the "long-voyage pilot" or "kendtmand" (man who knows) who sometimes went along on voyages when the skipper was himself unfamiliar with the route. When the sun was in the sky, it was not, therefore, difficult to find the four points of the compass, and the determining of latitude did not cause any problems either. For establishing the altitude of the sun, and thereby latitude, Norse writing indicates there was a "solbrädt" (sun-board) divided into "half wheels", though an example of these has unfortunately never yet been found. However, a bearing-plate or pelorus similar in principle to those used today has been discovered. It was used partly for coastal navigation, and partly to find the four points of the compass, which could be done because the position of the sun was known at sunrise and sunset.

In bright weather, it was thus possible to keep a pretty straight course on a voyage along a latitude. The course could be regulated every noon by means of the "sun-board". If the angle to the sun had grown larger, the ship had drifted southwards; if it was smaller, the course had slipped too far north. But

11

on cloudy or foggy days, the situation was dangerous, and in a storm the shipmaster often had to concentrate solely on keeping his vessel afloat until the weather was clear enough to let him see where wind and sea had carried him. It was more difficult to determine distance travelled; the degree of longitude. This was not achieved until the chronometer was invented in the eighteenth century. During the Viking Age the distance covered could only be roughly reckoned. An experienced skipper would be able to guess his speed from the size of the bow-wave, or else he observed the ship's heeling in relation to the force and direction of the wind. There were no other means.

It is certain that directions for other sailors, including observations and estimates of distance, were drawn up. They are not mentioned in the sagas, but they were essential if the Vikings were to find their way back to the places said to have been discovered by chance, Iceland and America for example. All this has mostly to do with navigation on the expeditions of Norwegians into the Atlantic. Danish and Swedish Vikings must mainly have had to concern themselves with coastal navigation, sailing in their own waters or along the North Sea shores to Friesland and northern France. The voyages of the Swedish Vikings, who preferred the Baltic, did not demand any knowledge of astronomy. Neither did crossing the North Sea from Denmark to England — though this latter run did often require great seamanship. No one knows if the Vikings were familiar with the compass, the first use of which, in any case, cannot at present be positively fixed earlier than 1300 A.D. However, some sagas mention a mysterious instrument called a "sun-stone." One saga, for instance, tells how the Holy King Olaf and his chief Sigurd Syr were on board their ship when ". . . it was foggy and it was snowing heavily. The king asked a man to take a look outside and the sky was cloud-covered. He then asked Sigurd to tell him where the sun could be and he [Sigurd] told him. Then the king picked up the 'sunstone' and he then saw how the stone was radiating and out of that he made the conclusion that Sigurd was right." Sigurd's instrument was a remarkable one, but if the "sun-stone" was a primitive compass, *i.e.* a piece of magnetic stone floating on a piece of wood in water, and if Sigurd had no doubt about the time of day, it would not have been difficult for him to tell where the sun was. How the stone could radiate is another question, but presumably the story-teller has furnished it with some specially mystifying qualities to embellish the story.

Thus equipped with swift ships and tools for deep water navigation, the Vikings were ready to embark on what was to become the Viking Age — the romantic, violent and troubled period which caused such upheavals not only in Scandinavia but all over western Europe.

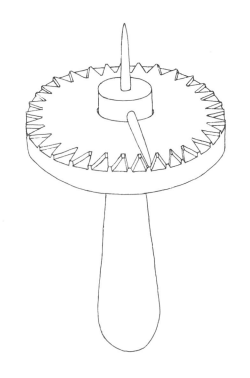

A VIKING NAVIGATIONAL INSTRUMENT

A reconstruction of a ship's bearing plate, of the type which the Vikings probably used. The navigator could find north at sunrise or sunset by means of a shadow cast by the vertical shadow pin. The horizontal pin is the course indicator.

Kaupang

Birka

GOTLAND

Hedeby

POPULATION DISTRIBUTION

The shaded areas on this map show the distribution of population in Viking-Age Scandinavia. They emphasize the extensive settlements throughout southern Sweden (except for heavily-forested districts), in Norway (except the high mountain areas) and in Denmark (except for the sandy moors of Jutland). Viking-Age grave finds are very rare in parts of Denmark and south-east Sweden, but abundant in most of Denmark, east-central Sweden and Norway. As a result the map has been largely based on the distribution of Viking-Age coin-hoards and rune-stones.

15

The illustration from a picture-stone at the top of the page shows a cross-section of a house, with two people sitting in log chairs in deep conversation. To the left the roof is extended to make a shelter for the watchdog.

THE ISLAND SHIELD

The maze of islets seen on the left, which are in the Skagerak off Sweden's west coast, are typical of the long barrier of islands which provided the Vikings with sheltered sea routes along the Atlantic coast of Scandinavia and encouraged them to become masters of seamanship and boat design.

From archaeological discoveries and from Viking literature and placenames, it can be established that during the Viking period, Denmark, Norway and Sweden were mainly farming countries. People had always settled down where they found the best land, easily accessible, and not too covered by forest. As a result the settlements acquired a different character in each of the three countries because the land was different in each. In Norway, though there were a few solitary farms in fertile spots in the mountains, most settlements were along the fjords and in the valleys. In all three countries generally, the same areas populated then are still inhabited today. But whereas in Norway there was soon a shortage of good land — which was partly responsible for the colonization of the Atlantic islands — in Denmark the supply of virgin soil did not run out so swiftly, and Danish settlements were still growing throughout the Viking Age. Placenames ending in, for example, *by*, *toft* and *torp* (all meaning a type of settlement) reveal that these places were settled in Viking times. The same type of name is found in the Danish-occupied areas of England, where the Danes used the names they were accustomed to at home. A typical example are the names consisting of a personal name plus the ending *by*, where we probably have the name of the man who founded the settlement. In Sweden and in Finland scholars have tried to date the beginnings of a settlement — before, after or during the Viking Age — by measuring the rise in the level of land on an inhabited site. In Sweden, too, we have to look for Viking settlements in accessible and fertile places. In Skåne in the south they are of the same type as in Denmark — not surprisingly, as Skåne belonged to Denmark during the latter part of the Viking period. In the rest of Sweden settlements are found around the big lakes and along rivers running through broad valleys.

It is natural that in these agricultural countries, the farm settlements should be scattered singly, not concentrated together, so that none should be too distant from its furthest fields. At first, towns did not exist. At most, there would be small villages; that is, a few farms united in a group. Real towns were not necessary, as the farms were largely self-supporting, and there were no craftsmen or traders to buy anything. The same was true of all northern Europe: towns only existed in areas which had been dominated by the Roman Empire. They grew up spontaneously around the garrisons, which required not only traders to handle the wide variety of products needed, but also a staff of skilled craftsmen. What has always distinguished a town from a village is that most of the inhabitants of a town were traders and craftsmen, to whom agriculture was only of secondary importance. They made their living by selling their goods, instead of consuming them themselves. The inhabitants of a village were mainly subsistence farmers, and the craftsmen they needed were no more than those necessary in everyday life, for example a blacksmith and a potter. Authenticated town-like societies do not begin to crop up until about 700 A.D., when western European and Frisian trade with Scandinavia gathered momentum. They were found in places which were easy to reach both by sea and by land, not only for the traders, but also for the customers; that is, for those who wanted to buy and sell. Some people probably came to seek the stimulating company of foreigners from strange places. At the same time, their founders tried to place the markets at strategic points, where it would not be too difficult to defend them, for all the desirable articles that were amassed at market time might be tempting. Norway's Kaupang and Denmark's Hedeby are both hidden at the bottom of a fjord, and Sweden's Birka and Helgö are on small, easily defended islands in Lake Mälar. The traders had to go around with their scales in one hand and their swords in the other.

DENMARK THE FERTILE

Adam of Bremen, writing about 1076 A.D: The first part of Denmark is called Jutland. Its soil is little fertile. From there is the shortest passage to Norway. Funen is quite a considerable island, and from Jutland the distance to Funen is very small in all directions. Funen has a big town, Odense, and in a circle round it are small islands, all very fertile. There are two places from where to go to Zealand, one from Funen. Zealand is an island, widely known both for its brave inhabitants and for its rich crops. Its largest town is Roskilde, the royal residence of the Danes. From Zealand there are many passages to Skåne [then part of Denmark; now of Sweden], the shortest one at Hälsingborg. Skåne is the most beautiful part of Denmark, well supplied with inhabitants, fertile and rich in goods, and now full of churches, twice as many as in Zealand, that is 300 churches, whereas Funen has one third [100]. Skåne is almost an island, as it is surrounded by the sea on all sides except the frontier between Denmark and Sweden, where there are deep forests and trackless mountains.

A BLEND OF LAND AND WATER

The view on the right of Limfjorden, near Ålborg in Denmark, shows flat country, intersected by a waterway like those which were the Danes' principal means of communication in Viking times.

A HAVEN FROM THE ATLANTIC

Lying glass-still between high, snow-tipped mountains, and rimmed with fields and fir trees, the fjord of Skei i Jölster is one of thousands that indent the Atlantic coast of Norway. Vikings farmed these lands a thousand years ago just as a handful of Norwegian farmers do today, and rowed in from the stormy sea to shelter here. But good land, then as now, was scarce. And the long, narrow waterway which led the longships in became the sea road over which Viking families migrated to find homes in England and Iceland.

21

Most of the towns that perished during the Viking period or shortly afterwards have been located and more or less thoroughly excavated. Other towns proved more vigorous, and many modern towns can trace their history back to Viking days. This is not the case with the settlements in the country. Only a few Viking farms and outbuildings have been found. One reason may be that the present villages are placed on top of the old ones, so that the foundations of early Viking buildings lie too deep to find. Other archaeological finds, especially the burials, have helped locate Viking settlements. Men and women were buried with their most valued possessions around them, so that they should be properly equipped for their journey into the next world. The great majority of graves found so far seem to be quite modestly furnished. They represent the broad middle classes, the farmers, who were the nucleus of the population. The graves of the thralls or slaves have not been found, as it is hardly likely that they were provided with grave-goods of a durable sort. Finally, there are a few very rich interments, which must belong to members of the small ruling class. These include the famous ship-burials, which have been found in all the Scandinavian countries. Another kind of find, which also helps to throw light on the question of settlement, is buried treasure. Most Viking treasure consists of fortunes which were buried during a period of heavy fighting and then abandoned for one reason or another. They suggest that many people were far richer than the burials seem to indicate. A third kind of relic are the rune-stones, standing stones which were inscribed with characters in the old Norse (runic) alphabet. Most of them were erected in connection with an interment, and are really, therefore, tombstones. But some rune-stones were set up in memory of certain notable events or good deeds. Finally, the churches should be taken into account, for the majority of them are situated in areas which were inhabited in the Viking period.

The material at our disposal is not often derived from systematic investigation. This, indeed, would be impossible. The most numerous finds are the tombs, which are found under flat fields, and have nearly always been revealed by accident during agricultural work. Only when this is finished may the archaeologist come and make his investigations. The same is true of the treasure. Only rune-stones and grave mounds are always to be seen and recognized for what they are. And yet there is no doubt that even if a lot more material is found in the future, it will not affect the assessments which have been made so far. Archaeology is a science of long standing in Scandinavia, and the existing material is sufficient to map out the settlements in all essentials.

FOREST, LAKE AND RIVER

There was probably little cultivation of land in the wilder parts of Finland in Viking times, but otherwise the picture at left, showing the Kuopio district, gives a good idea of the country which favoured Viking expansion into the land east of the Baltic, with its innumerable waterways.

WHY THE VIKINGS LEFT HOME —
THE POLITICS, POVERTY AND OVERCROWDING
THAT FORCED THEM OUT INTO THE WORLD

People at the time were hardly aware that several different forces were driving the Scandinavians out into the world. They probably distinguished only between the peaceful Norse traders and the rest of the Vikings, who brought war and destruction with them. At times, however, the traders were not as peaceful as all that. They themselves had to beware of pirates, and were therefore armed to the teeth. If they came across a smaller ship with an attractive cargo, it was tempting to throw away the scales, grab the sword, make a quick assault and thus augment their own cargo. When acting in this way, the trader placed himself in the other category: that of the real Vikings who undertook occasional predatory expeditions with the sole purpose of enriching themselves, but who otherwise usually spent their lives on their home farms. Of course a freebooter's life is sometimes pleasantly habit-forming, and many Vikings settled down abroad in the new places they had found, where they would be surrounded by other Scandinavian colonists. Such people came to make up a third Viking category.

The traders are known to us from the story of a Norwegian called Ottar, or Ohthere, who came from Hålgoland in the northernmost part of Norway, where the Lapps lived. He described his life to King Alfred of Wessex, and Alfred had his story written down. "He [Ottar] was very rich in those things that their [i.e. the Scandinavians'] riches consist of, that is, wild animals. When he came to the King [Alfred], he still had 600 unsold tame animals. He called those animals reindeer, and among them were six bait reindeer, which are very expensive among the Lapps, as they are used for catching wild reindeer. He was one of the greatest men in that neighbourhood, and yet he only had twenty oxen, twenty sheep and twenty pigs, and the little he ploughed, he ploughed with horses. And most of his income came from the taxes that the Lapps pay

The little scene on the picture-stone above, left, shows how the Vikings looked to the people they encountered in the world when they left their own countries. Swinging their newly-sharpened swords, their appearance alone terrified their enemies.

A VIKING TRADER

In spite of his outlandish dress, the man shown here is a Viking. He has adopted the clothing of the eastern country in which he is trading, perhaps Persia, so as not to appear too strange to his customers. He holds a portable balance for weighing silver currency. The Viking voyages eastwards and westwards made Scandinavia a part of the vast trading network which already embraced the Mediterranean countries and the areas of Asia accessible by the caravan routes. Bargaining, of course, knows no frontiers. Even if two merchants could not understand a word of each other's languages, they could see and judge the merchandise, and they could both see the means of payment, the silver, and weigh it. A Swedish Viking had no difficulty in buying Chinese silk from Arab merchants at Bulgar on the Volga, any more than oriental merchants had trouble haggling over goods in the market towns of Denmark, Sweden and Norway.

him, and which consist of hides, birds' feathers, whale-bones and ropes made from whale-skin and seal. Everyone pays according to his station in life. Those of the noblest descent have to pay fifteen martens and five reindeer and one bearskin and ten bundles of feathers and one bearskin or otter kirtle and two ship's ropes each of twenty feet, one made of whaleskin and the other of sealskin." In another place we are told of Ottar's expeditions to the White Sea, on Norway's northernmost shores, where he got hold of walrus tusks, which, like the articles mentioned, fur, feathers and ropes, were in great demand in southern Europe. Every year he left Norway with his precious cargo to go to the trading town of Hedeby in Denmark, a voyage of about 1600 miles each way. In Hedeby he met traders from other countries — mostly western Europe — in order to take home attractive luxury articles such as wine, silk and other costly materials, gold, and silver.

Equally long and difficult voyages were made by Swedish traders on the Russian rivers, all the way to Byzantium, capital of the Byzantine Empire. There is a contemporary description of the difficulties of this route, written by the Emperor Constantine Porphyrogenitus. He tells of the traders' voyages on the river Dnieper with their cargoes, and how they negotiated the dangers of the cataracts. They passed the smaller cataracts by making the crews jump into the water and tow the ships carefully past the dangerous places. But the fifth cataract had to be passed in the following way: "At these falls, all the ships stop with the stern pointing towards the shore, and those of the crews who have been chosen to have the watch, go ashore and remove themselves to their posts, and they keep a sharp look-out because of the Pechenegs [a tribe of robbers in southern Russia]. But the others put the goods ashore and also the slaves, who are chained, and walk six miles until they have passed the cataract. Then they take their boats past the falls, partly by towing them, partly by carrying them on their shoulders. There they embark and continue their voyage." The route was of about the same length as the voyage from the north of Norway to Hedeby, but far more exhausting and dangerous, because it led through regions with hostile populations. The Emperor Constantine talks of another article besides the ones already mentioned: slaves. We do not know from where, or how, Viking traders got hold of this much-coveted article. It can be assumed that they either took them as war captives, or caught them in slave hunts. At that time, Hedeby had an internationally-known slave market, where Christian missionaries sometimes had the grief of seeing their co-religionists displayed for sale. At a very early date, Swedish settlements had been planted in the Baltic countries and in Russia. These were trading stations, which functioned as links in the chain of eastbound traffic. In this area traders became settlers simply because their trade required it, and not primarily to colonize a new land. The want of new land was, however, the reason why so many Norwegian colonists went to the Atlantic islands. Some fled from the strict regime of King Harald Fairhair (860 - 930 A.D.), but most of them left their own country because land was desperately short in Norway. They left with all their movable possessions and cattle and tried to make a living as settlers abroad. But even abroad history repeated itself. The land problem often caught up with them again. On Iceland, for example, serious colonization began about 874 A.D. and emigrations continued until 930. In this short time, however, all the useable land was possessed. This forced many to go on to Greenland.

In western Europe, that is in the British Isles and France, the Vikings — especially Danes and Norwegians — played their three roles simultaneously. To a modern eye, it may seem surprising that commercial traffic could continue in spite of military operations, and even more surprising that the Franks sold the Vikings the arms with which they could be sure they would be attacked. At a Frankish assembly held by the Emperor Charles the Bald at Pître in June 864, Franks had to be officially prohibited, on pain of death, from selling arms and horses to the Norsemen. In the year 871, another instance occurs of business taking precedence over defence. The Vikings had for many years frequented the island of Noirmoutier at the mouth of the river Loire. The Franks had found that they could divert the river into another bed, stranding the enemy's boats and rendering them open to attack. This frightened the Vikings so much that they surrendered, and for once it was they who paid Charles the Bald to raise the siege and let them go away with a safe-conduct. Nevertheless, they asked for, and received, permission to stay until February in order to do business, as they had planned. Charles gave his permission, and then, of course, the Vikings stayed where they were. If they were not welcomed as traders, the Vikings were usually at least tolerated. As warriors, however, they were feared for their cruelty: "Free us, O Lord, from the outrages of the Norsemen," they prayed in Frankish churches; "They ravage our land and kill women and children and even old people." Indeed, they did kill and ravage, but what army has not done that, at any stage of history? It was natural that the Christians should see it as a punishment from God when their churches and monasteries were suddenly devastated and plundered by pagans, who came like a bolt from the blue. There was a good reason why these lightning raids were able to terrorize the nations of Western Europe for so long. Although Viking ships were of approximately the same size as a modern small schooner, their keels were usually less than forty inches below the water-line. In ships like these, landing on beaches or penetrating far up inland waterways presented no difficulties. Not many

ANIMALS OVER THE SEA

Norwegian settlers bound for Iceland, Greenland and Vinland took their domestic animals with them.

At the time such animals were much smaller than they are today, so that ships, small by present-day standards, could accommodate them as well as the settlers with all their gear. In time of war, however, the Vikings seldom took their horses with them: it was easier to find them in the foreign country. The settlers probably brought their horses ashore in the manner shown here. The ship is turned parallel to the beach so that the animals can jump into shallow water. Their weight would press down the side of the ship, so the jump would be relatively easy.

minutes need have elapsed from the time a Viking ship was first sighted through the North Sea haze to the time when the pirates were ashore in the coastal towns and villages, plundering and killing. By the time the defenders had assembled, the raiders would be well away with their booty, rowing for all they were worth against the strong head-wind which made such sailing vessels as their pursuers might have had quite useless.

Shallow-draught ships also helped the Vikings when they wanted to make a long stay in hostile territory. Proof of this was the location of Viking winter camps on islands with shelving beaches like Mersea, Thanet and Sheppey in England. Here the deeper-draught craft of the local powers could never get in close enough to drive away the Scandinavian menace. The marauding Vikings were in the rare position of being invulnerable on their island bases. They calmly occupied islands in the Seine, in the very heart of the Frankish Emperor's own territory. The use of such tactics was still common in the tenth century, as can be gathered from the account of the famous battle of Maldon in Essex, described later in this book. The Vikings had landed on the island of Northey, which because of its shelving shores is still harbourless today. The Anglo-Saxon army could not reach them by sea and was forced to invite them to come ashore on the mainland so that fighting could begin. It will

WARRIORS LAND ON AN ENEMY COAST

In the reconstruction shown here, the longships have been driven straight up onto a beach. The manoeuvre was possible, if the sea was reasonably calm, because of the ships' shallow draught. The fighting-men jump confidently over the side at the stem, knowing that the water here will not be deeper than three feet at the most. If they were making a quick raid, they would pull the ship only a little way up the beach, so it could quickly be pushed off again. If they wanted to stay longer, or if the sea and the weather looked threatening, the ship was hauled up on dry land on rollers carried on board.

be seen, too, how the Vikings were able to take another advantage of the remarkable features of their ships. Alfred the Great, king of Wessex, attempted to drive away the Danish ships by building larger, longer and taller vessels. The result was that his ships also needed deeper water to sail in and, when nine English men-of-war engaged six Danish longships, the former ran aground ignominiously. On almost every occasion, however, that the Vikings met compact and well-organized resistance, they were defeated, both in the British Isles and in France. If they won, it was often due rather to weakness and disagreement among their enemies than to their own skill. In the latter half of the ninth century the Vikings organized what historians now call "the great army", which under different leaders ravaged in England and France in its search for land. In England, serious colonization began about 874 A.D. when a part of "the great army" came to York. Its leader, Halfdan, distributed land among his men, and in the north and east of England the Vikings became peasants who lived according to their own Danish customs. A similar colonization took place in France. Among the Vikings who arrived in France was a battle-leader named Rolf, who in 911 received from King Charles the Simple the nucleus of the area today known as Normandy, a name which it got from the Norsemen who settled here. Neither in the British Isles nor in France were the settlers unfamiliar with the culture they met in their new homes. Also, the natural surroundings were more or less similar to those of the places they came from.

BATTLE TACTICS

In this scene, a small party of Vikings raiding England have been cut off from their comrades and their ship. Under attack by a superior English force, they have ranged themselves on the favourable ground offered by a small hill to make a defensive stand. They have formed a "shield-wall", with shields meeting or overlapping for extra protection. The favourite weapons of the Vikings were the battle axe, the sword and the bow. The action was often opened by archers, but the real battle was fought out man to man with axe and sword. By way of armour, the Vikings had conical helmets with nose-protectors. A few wealthy warriors owned a mail-coat, but most could only afford padded leather jackets.

The colonists in England had their ups and downs, partly because they were, of course, attacked by the English themselves, and partly because they also had to fight rival Norwegian Vikings, who came from Ireland. In 920 the Viking colonists had to recognize the English king, Edward the Elder, as their sovereign. In fact, the early spirit of conquest and colonization seems to have left the settled Danes. They no longer had a strong man around whom to rally, as they had rallied to Halfdan. It should be added that by this time many already belonged to the second generation, and no longer even thought of themselves as Danes. They had been anglicized, and probably did not care much whether it was one of their countrymen or an Englishman who sat on the English throne. They were happy if they could till their land in peace. Later, however, England was conquered by the Danish king Cnut the Great, but here again the Christian, Anglo-Saxon culture of the English eventually proved superior. Cnut soon came to look upon himself as king of England rather than as king of Denmark. Development in Normandy followed the same general lines. Here, too, the native culture proved to be the stronger. Nothing but a number of placenames now shows that there was Scandinavian settlement. Second-generation colonists no longer spoke Danish, either at the court of the duke of Normandy or in the villages. They spoke French because they themselves married Frenchwomen and had French-speaking children and servants. One Norman chronicle tells us that in 942 Duke William Longsword sent his son to Bayeux from the court in Rouen, in order that he might there "learn the language of his ancestors". For some reason Danish was still spoken in Bayeux.

At first it seems strange that wherever the Vikings succeeded in conquering and colonizing an area, they were ultimately assimilated by their new culture and surroundings. The explanation, however, is that they were vastly outnumbered, having conquered — through a combination of skill, better tactics and the desperation which drove them from their northern homes in the first place — more peoples and territories than they could control. Even the Swedish colonies and trading centres in the East disappeared, although there the Vikings did not meet a superior culture. It is easier to understand why they succumbed to Christianity too, for at the end of the Viking period they had no faith to compete with the new one.

The town of Birka was possibly the greatest trading centre of the Viking world. It was as large as medieval Stockholm, and the range of its contacts with the rest of the known world was far wider. Unfortunately, though it was the first of the Viking towns to be excavated, less is known about Birka than about Hedeby or Kaupang. The excavations were careful but early, made without benefit of modern methods and machinery. Besides, only a tiny part of the town area was investigated. Birka was located on the island of Björkö in Lake Mälar, about eighteen miles west of Stockholm. What was once a famous town is now known as the Black Earth, an area of twenty-two acres with a depth of eight feet, so called because the soil has been made dark by intensive occupation. A small part of this was first excavated in the nineteenth century. Many objects such as coins were found, together with traces of buildings both of timber and of wattle and daub (mud-plastered wooden frame).

Much knowledge of the town derives from the *Life of St. Anskar*, a treatise written by Anskar's pupil Rimbert before the year 875. Anskar was a Frankish missionary who made two visits to the island, the first about 830, the second about twenty years later.

Describing the missionaries' arrival in Birka, Rimbert writes:

"With great difficulty they accomplished their long journey on foot, traversing also the intervening seas, where it was possible, by ship, and eventually arrived at the Swedish port called Birka. They were kindly received here by the king, who was called Björn, whose messengers had informed him of the reason for which they had come. When he understood the object of their mission, and had discussed the matter with his friends, with the approval and consent of all, he granted them permission to remain there and to preach the gospel of Christ, and offered liberty to any who desired it to accept their teaching.

The illustration from a picture-stone at the top of the page is thought by some scholars to represent a Viking town in an abstract form.

BIRKA

This map shows the islands in Lake Mälar. One trade route went towards Uppsala, and others east and south to the Baltic sea. A winter view from the air (right) clearly shows how well the existing terrain was used in building Birka's hill fort. Towards the island and town, in the foreground, the slope is slight. There, a wall had to be built. Towards Lake Mälar, on the other hand (out of sight to the right) the cliffs fell a full hundred feet straight down into the water.

Accordingly the servants of God, when they saw that matters had turned out propitiously as they had desired, began eagerly to preach the word of salvation to the people of that place. There were many who were well disposed towards their mission, and who willingly listened to the teaching of the Lord. There were also many Christians who were held captive amongst them, and who rejoiced that now at last they were able to participate in the divine mysteries. It was thus made clear that everything was as their [the Swedes'] messengers had declared to the king, and some of them desired earnestly to receive the grace of baptism. These included the prefect of this town, named Herigar, who was counsellor of the king and much beloved by him. He received the gift of holy baptism and was strengthened in the Catholic faith. A little later he built a church on his own ancestral property and served God with the utmost devotion. Several remarkable deeds were accomplished by this man, who afforded many proofs of his invincible faith."

In his account, Rimbert also notes many significant details about Birka, such as the fact that it was governed by an assembly or *thing*, and establishes that Birka merchants had contacts with the trading town of Dorestad in Holland. Rimbert also tells of an attack on Birka, during which the citizens and merchants sheltered in a nearby fortification.

The remains of this fort are easily located today. It stands in a commanding position about a hundred feet above the lake's edge to the south of the town. From the fort's summit it is possible to see great distances along the waterways that lead to the island. The position of this fort in relation to the town is very reminiscent of the arrangement at Hedeby, another Viking town, and a further similarity is the wall that surrounds the site. The walls were late additions at both Hedeby and Birka, and the Birka wall can be roughly fixed in time by the discovery under it of a coin dated 925 A.D. This wall originally enclosed all of the landward side of the town that was unprotected by the fort. There were a number of gaps in it, probably for entrances, which would have been important because some of the anchorages lay beyond the town.

The east end of the wall is nowadays quite a long way from the water's edge, but this was not always so. Since the Viking Age the water level in this part of Sweden has dropped by about eighteen feet, and this has greatly altered the shape of the island. In the ninth and tenth centuries it was very much smaller than it is now, and the anchorages and beaches for landing small boats were better than they seem today. Two of the anchorages have names that go back several centuries and are probably survivals from the days of Birka's existence as a town. They are Korshamn and, opposite the end of the wall, Kugghamn (see the illustration on pages 38-39). The latter may preserve a memory of the

A RELIC OF AN EARLY CHRISTIAN CONVERT

The oldest known crucifix found in Sweden was unearthed in a grave at Birka which dates from about 900 A.D.

Frisian cogs or merchant ships which, with their greater draught, needed deeper water than the local boats. In front of the town the ground shelved gently into the water, and timbers which have been discovered in this part of the lake are probably the remains of jetties. Another shelving beach beyond the fort to the south of the town may also have been used.

Present-day knowledge of Birka and its trade connections depend mainly on the graves that surround the town. There are at least 2000 of them, and over 1100 have been excavated. There are four main types. First, a number of richly furnished burials of the ninth century contain objects from western Europe — glass and pottery from the Rhineland, Frankish jewellery, Anglo-Irish bronzes — and therefore confirm the impression given by the *Life of St. Anskar* that the western trade routes of the town were important. This view is further strengthened by the rare "Birka coins", a few of which seem to have been minted in the town during the ninth century. They are modelled on Carolingian coins, the currency of the empire of the Franks.

There is little evidence of trade connections with the west in the tenth-century graves. Some are richly furnished, but their contents come from the region of the middle Volga in Russia, and beyond. Apart from these rich graves, there are a great many more modest ones that are typical of the Viking Age in this part of Sweden, and also a number of graves that, being sparsely furnished, are difficult, if not impossible, to date. These graves of uncertain date make it difficult to be certain when Birka began to function as a trading centre. It is possible, however, to be more confident about the date of Birka's end. This is determined by the complete absence of any English coins of the reign of King Ethelred (978-1016 A.D.) or of contemporary German coins. Both are so common elsewhere in Scandinavia that their absence from Birka makes us believe that the town ceased to exist before the end of the tenth century, possibly before 980 A.D.

A HOLY MAN FROM FAR AWAY

This bronze statuette of Buddha, which dates from about the fifth century, was brought more than 5000 miles — from northern India to Helgö, the trading centre which flourished before its neighbour, Birka, rose to importance (see page 44).

The main town area of Birka — the part now called the "Black Earth" — consisted of a busy waterfront and behind it a tight jumble of buildings crowding in on dirty, perhaps wood-paved streets, all jammed with goods, people and domestic animals. But on the outskirts, just inside the wall, there was a row of large houses set down in notable isolation. Outside the town wall, which was connected with the fort (see colour picture on page 33), the large graveyards were located. There are a surprising number of openings in the town wall, and it has been assumed that these were filled by defensive wooden gates, though no remnants of them have survived. Birka had no regular harbour, because the shallow-draught Viking ships that made up most of its traffic did not require one. But outside the city area, in the upper part of picture, three tiny harbours can be seen. From the left they are Kugghamn, just outside the wall, which no doubt derived its name from the rather deep-draught Frisian trading ships, known as cogs; Korshamn, in old sources sometimes written Kornhamn; and finally the Salviks pit, now drained, which was nearly rectangular, and was no doubt excavated by the Vikings as a harbour basin.

Grave finds made during recent excavations between the fort and the town indicate that the garrison was located in that area. This assumption is supported by the fact that in these particular spots no definitely "female" articles, like weaving equipment, turned up.

BIRKA'S OLDEST FORTIFICATION

Seen in summer and from the north-east, Birka's hill fort looks peaceful and unassuming. The town wall, built later, and connected with the fort wall, at one time extended over the field in the middle distance, but has now disappeared under cultivation. One of the 2000 grassy grave mounds around Birka can be seen in the foreground.

Birka was not forgotten. It was remembered in the Archbishopric of Bremen as the focus of its missionary endeavours in the north, and it was also remembered in Scandinavia in the so-called Law of Birka, *Björköarätt*. There can be little doubt that this was originally the law of a place called Birch Island (Björkö), and the wealth and importance of the Birka in Lake Mälar makes it hard to believe that it is named after any other place. The *Life of St. Anskar* makes it clear that in the ninth century Birka had already developed a characteristic form of urban organization and a code of law for a trading community. A new, special sort of law was particularly necessary in Sweden, where, on the basis of the oldest Swedish laws from Västergötland, men from the next province were cheap to kill — that is to say, the compensation which murderers, or those guilty of manslaughter, had to pay to the victim's relatives was low. As for complete strangers under the old law, they had no protection at all. Foreign merchants were therefore particularly vulnerable, so to prevent murder for profit, special protection had to be provided by the king and by the scales of compensation laid down in the new law of Birka. All this, of course, was essential to trade.

Such a town law could only have been introduced by a king in an area where he had complete control. This was certainly so in the case of Björkö, because that island was situated between two great estates of the king of the Svea people. Even so, the *Life of St. Anskar* shows that the townspeople as well as the king had considerable influence in questions of law. Even for the king, it must have been difficult to change the law, which existed as an age-old word-of-mouth tradition among the inhabitants.

When, therefore, it came to founding a town for the purpose of trade, for which one of the conditions was the radically new principle that even a foreigner from far afield would enjoy the full protection of the law, it must have been very important to look for a site where the current legal tradition was as vague as possible. From that point of view, Björkö was extremely suitable. It was a small island with very few inhabitants, located, not only between three different hundreds — that is, three different local courts (*thing*) — but also at the junction of two of the three districts (*folkland*) into which the central province of Sweden, Uppland, was divided. Each of these seems to have had its own law to begin with, and perhaps still had it at the time in question. In any case, Birka, centrally situated in Lake Mälar, lies so near the border between two provinces (Uppland to the north of Lake Mälar and Södermanland to the south) that there must often have been doubt as to which of the laws of these provinces

PLUNDER FROM IRELAND

This head from a bishop's crozier, of Irish workmanship, was found at Helgö near Birka.

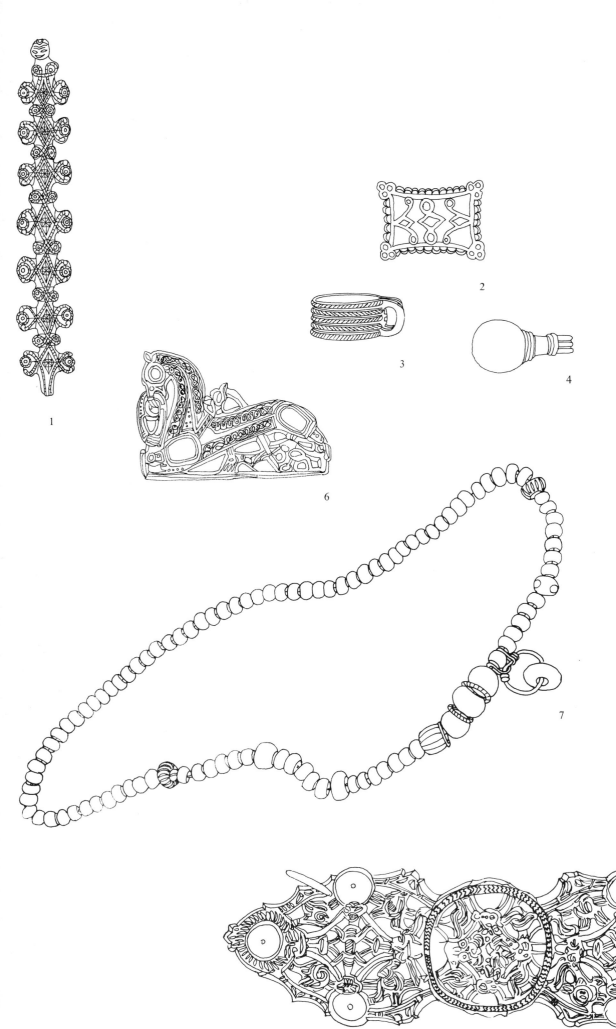

The grave of the woman found at Birka (right) contained a number of precious ornaments which suggest that the Vikings maintained a very high level of workmanship and design.

1. Delicately-carved gilt bronze ornament, found together with another in the neck region of the dead woman. The ornaments were sewn on the hem of a garment — probably the dress.

2. One of a pair of gilt bronze brooches, decorated with blue, red and green enamelling.

3, 4. Two silver ornaments — pendants worn as earrings, or worn on the necklace (see below).

5. A square-armed brooch of gilt bronze, ornamented in the typical Nordic animal style of the early Viking Age. The brooch probably fastened the dead woman's tunic at the neck.

6. Horse-shaped silver gilt ornament. This is also one of a pair, originally made as a pair of brooches, but sewn on the dead woman's dress.

7. A finely wrought necklace consisting of four silver rings and eight beads of rock-crystal and glass with gold and silver foil.

A BIRKA WOMAN'S GRAVE

Judging from the contents of the Birka graves, some women at least must have enjoyed a high position in the community. A reconstruction of one of the most important is seen here. It contained the well-preserved skeleton of a woman, placed in a wooden chamber built in a large burial pit: a so-called "chamber-grave". She must have been buried fully dressed, but only small pieces of silk, undoubtedly imported, have been preserved. This luxurious detail corresponds very well with the abundance of beautiful beads (eighty-one altogether) and silver and gilt bronze ornaments found near her neck. A Frisian-style jug, a glass beaker of Rhineland manufacture, a bronze cauldron of Anglo-Irish origin, all luxurious objects, were found in the grave. So were two wooden buckets and a small wooden box containing a comb of horn. The many imported articles suggest that the dead woman was a rich merchant's wife. She must have lived in the early or middle part of the ninth century.

applied there. It was there, at what was, legally speaking, a virtual no-man's-land, that the king founded his trading town. As it was so near his own properties, he could guarantee military protection, and Birka was further safeguarded by being so far from the sea, behind a sheltering archipelago.

What did the king gain in return? The Birka law stated that the king, through his bailiff, had the right to purchase newly-imported goods three days in advance of everyone else. In other words, he controlled the market in quality products. The king of the Svea people in the Viking Age undoubtedly became such a rich man that he was able to gather power effectively into his own hands, whereas his immediate predecessors certainly had to share that power with their chieftains.

If the exact date of the rise of Birka is uncertain, recent excavations at a site nearer the outlet of Lake Mälar have, nevertheless, thrown new light on the town's origins. On this site, an important trading centre seems to to have existed long before Birka was founded.

On the small island of Helgö (Holy Island), the remnants of a settlement have recently been discovered which for centuries maintained an extensive trade with Europe and the British Isles. Inside and outside the remains of a series of buildings of various sizes, an enormous number and variety of articles have been found, ranging from unique objects like the figure of Buddha (page 35) and a bishop's crozier (page 34) to slag left over from local iron production. Of special interest are many fragments of glass vessels, testifying to stable contacts with glass-producing centres in Europe and Britain from the fourth to the ninth centuries.

There must have been a strong organizing power behind trade on the scale demonstrated in the Helgö finds. No Black Earth has so far been found on the site. Some authorities are inclined to think that the settlement was organized rather as a single commercial house than as a market town like Birka. But it seems quite clear that Birka was founded directly from Helgö. Taken together, the finds from Helgö cover a period of about 600 years from the fourth to the eleventh century, and most objects date from between 400 and 800 A.D. — that is, just up to the time when Birka first began to flourish as a trading centre. The archaeologists are still left with problems. If Helgö was really only a commercial house and not a town, how did it compete with its rich, well-protected neighbour Birka during its later centuries of existence? Such puzzles as this are commonplace difficulties for the scholar.

A BIRKA WARRIOR'S GRAVE

Though most of the graves at Birka were covered by mounds, many of the richest burials were found in the "chamber-graves" (see page 43). A reconstruction of one of the most famous is seen here. The chamber was found in the western part of the cavity. The position of the skeleton gave the impression that he had been sitting in the grave, rather than laid out. His two shields are at his head and his feet and a heavy two-bladed sword was found at his left-hand side. A beautifully decorated dagger, an axe, twenty-four arrows and a spear with silver and copper decoration on the socket were placed at the right-hand side of the body. The equipment indicates that this is a warrior's grave rather than that of a merchant. The skeletons of two horses found in the eastern side of the grave outside the actual "chamber", and the presence of stirrups, make clear that he was a horseman. The date of a silver coin, found underneath the skeleton of the dead man, provides a fairly good idea of the date of the grave: 913 - 980 A.D.

TOWN WALLS

It is a remarkable fact that only the two easternmost Viking towns, Birka and Hedeby, were protected by walls. Kaupang to the west, in Norway, never had a defensive wall; nor, it seems, did Dorestad on the Rhine. On the other hand, there is plenty of evidence of town walls of earth and timber all over eastern Europe, not only at Staraja Ladoga, which the Vikings visited, but also in Estonia and among the Slavs generally. These walled towns seem to have been at least contemporary with the Viking period, perhaps even earlier. In view of how late and scrappily towns and other population centres in Western Europe came to be fortified — quite frequently in the years around the turn of the tenth century in the case of the English "boroughs" — it is possible that the town fortifications of the Slavs influenced the evolution of the fortified Viking towns of Scandinavia. The oldest written record mentioning the subject, the Frankish Royal Annals, describes how in 808 A.D. the Danish king Godfred transplanted to Hedeby the inhabitants of a Slav town, Reric, which he had recently destroyed. The early medieval towns of Sweden dating from the twelfth century and after, which had a mostly immigrant German population, were developed in a similar way. In both cases Viking chiefs and traders seem to have found it necessary to use, exploit and even import people who had long experience in the organization of town life. The emergence of towns in Scandinavia in Viking times, therefore, though obviously the result of west European influence, owned a great deal to Viking initiative.

However, it may not have been only foreign influences that caused the fortification of Viking towns, and it may have come about later. One theory holds that at first Scandinavian trading centres had no need of such defences. In the early Viking Age and before it, Scandinavia was not so plagued by internal strife as it was later on. Town walls were less necessary than they were towards the end of the ninth century and the beginning of the tenth, when the Scandinavians took to fighting each other on a large scale. These internecine struggles might have helped to bring about the fortification of the towns.

AN ARAB DESCRIBES A SLAV FORT

The eleventh-century Arab geographer Al-Bekri describes a typical Slav fort, of the kind which the Vikings probably saw beyond the Baltic, and which may have influenced the building of their own town walls:

" In such a manner do the Slavs build most of their forts: they go to meadows, rich in water and undergrowth, and lay out a round or square place according to the form and extent of the fort, as they foresee it, dig around it and shovel the loose earth up, and this is secured with planks and posts in the manner of ramparts, until the wall reaches the intended height. The fort is given one gateway, on whatever side it pleases [the builders] . . . "

Kaupang in Vestfold, not far from Oslo, was Norway's only known trading town of the Viking Age. Looking at the site today, it is difficult to believe that it was ever an important harbour and centre of trade. The bay is shallow, the surrounding land is marshy, and the area suitable for habitation is severely limited, being squeezed in between craggy hills. In Viking times, however, the shoreline in the bay stood some six feet higher, while at the port of Kaupang at the head of the bay there was a broad and sheltered pool offering excellent harbour facilities for shallow-draught Viking ships. The innumerable islands and shoals of the archipelago which stretches across the mouth of the bay made it difficult for intruders to find their way through the channels without the assistance of a pilot. The hills flanking the bay provided not only shelter from storms and some protection from sudden attack, but also a vantage point from which to keep watch over the sea. Excavations have been carried out at Kaupang every summer since 1956. The burial places were examined first, then the area of the town and port. All the rich discoveries brought to light confirm and expand what was already known of the place from the sole surviving written source, the account given personally to King Alfred of Wessex at some time in the ninth century by the Norwegian merchant, Ottar (see page 50).

The settlement area along the edge of the bay occupies about five acres of the same sort of dark and greasy soil, known as Black Earth, that is found at Birka. Kaupang excavations have so far uncovered two piers. In construction both are the same, having a slightly rounded front facing the sea, and narrowing towards the settlement area. Near one of them, a heavy anchor of granite and oak was found. The shore opposite the larger pier has been faced with stones, giving the impression of a continuous pier. Behind these stone piers, just under plough depth, foundations of houses were found. The larger houses have slightly curved walls, the rest have straight walls. It is difficult to be sure whether these were the dwellings of a permanent population or whether they were occupied for short periods only, when markets were being held. Excavations at Kaupang have produced many finds which lend some colour to the rather monotone picture presented by the remains of the houses. Masses of animal and fish bones provide evidence of a farming and fishing economy. Slag, fragments of iron and waste from the working of lead, bronze and silver — and occasionally of gold too — show that a metal industry flourished in the town. Fragments of spinning and weaving implements prove that textiles were produced. The great quantity of soapstone waste and half-finished objects suggests

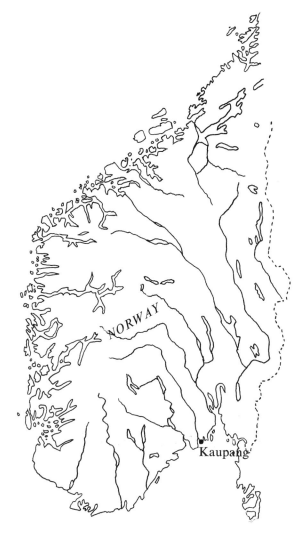

THE SAFE HARBOUR

The location of the Viking trading centre at Kaupang on the Norwegian coastline is shown on this map. The route of the merchant Ottar from the far north of Norway, so precisely described to King Alfred, hugged the coast. For some reason Ottar dared not make the short cut from the southernmost point of Norway (Lindesnes) to the top of Jutland, but preferred to follow the Norwegian coast as far as Kaupang. From Kaupang he must have crossed the Oslo Fjord to the Swedish (then Danish) coast, and sailed through Danish waters to Hedeby.

production of cooking-pots on a scale intended to meet more than purely local needs. Among imported objects, potsherds are the most numerous, mostly Rhenish ware. It is tempting to suppose that these big-bellied pots from the Rhineland were the wine casks of the day. If so, the wine must have been transferred subsequently to other containers, because shards of the Rhenish ware have not been found in any part of Norway except Kaupang. The great quantity of fragments of glass beakers that has turned up is something of a mystery to archaeologists. Most of the commerce at Kaupang was probably conducted on a barter basis, though a few fragments of coins have turned up there.

The relics emphasize a West European outlook, which even today is character-istic of the Vestfold area. Vestfold enjoys speedier sea routes to the Continent than any other part of Norway, and few Norwegians are as European in their attitude as the people hereabouts. Finds from the burial places also reflect an outlook directed seawards and westwards. In the twentieth century a thorough investigation of a burial ground was begun. One hundred and forty burial mounds or barrows were found, most of them in the marshy parts to the north of the settlement area. Most were cremation burials, and nothing notable was found other than shards of a very fine west European pottery. The burial ground situated beside the rocky hill known as Bikjholberg, which in Viking times projected like a ness or promontory into the sea opposite the settlement, was also excavated in the 1950s. The diggings revealed boats and coffins sunk into the sand, often not very deeply. They were covered not by mounds but by a heavy stone packing. Obviously these were the graves of rich people, for they contained objects showing workmanship of a high quality, probably of native and Anglo-Irish origin. The situation of these graves, their character and the quality of the grave-goods suggest that this burial ground was the last resting-place of big merchants and of their families. Perhaps it would be better to call them farmer-merchants, and assume that they worked their farms fur-ther inland in the fertile countryside, devoting themselves to trade as a season-al occupation, at market times only. The layer of Black Earth at Kaupang is between one and two feet deep. This corresponds well with the theory that Kaupang flourished for only about a hundred years: from the beginning of the ninth to the beginning of the tenth century. The place was probably aban-doned as a market town because the sea level dropped too much to permit larger vessels to enter the bay.

A NORWEGIAN MERCHANT GIVES SAILING DIREC-TIONS

In part of the translation, ordered by King Alfred of Wessex, of Orosius' *Universal History*, Ottar (Ohthere), a Norwegian merchant, men-tions Kaupang, which he calls Sciringesheal: "Ottar related that the district in which he lived is called Hålgoland. No one, he said, lived far-ther north than he. But there is a port in the southern end of the country. This port people called Sciringesheal, and to it, he said, one could not sail in less than a month if one camp-ed by night and had favourable winds by day. And one must ever sail along by the land. And Ireland will be on the starboard side, and then the islands which are between Ireland and this country [England]. Then it is this country till one comes to Sciringesheal. And all the way on the port side is Norway. South of Sciringe-sheal a large sea runs up into the country. The sea is wider there than any man can see across."

THE BAY OF KAUPANG

This pleasant countryside, where rich fields slope gently to the shores of a shallow bay, was the site of Kaupang, the only known Viking trading centre in Norway. It was first discovered and excavated in 1956 when archaeologists noticed that the soil lying on either side of the road (fore-ground) near the bay was especially dark and greasy — just like the "Black Earth" at Birka. A pilot trench was dug, and continuing work (pro-tected by the row of plastic tents) indicates that Viking traders worked and lived where farmers now grow potatoes. In Viking times, when the water level was six feet higher, the bay was larger and deeper — deep enough at best to re-ceive Viking ships and serve as a busy trading port.

WESTERN EUROPEAN ORNAMENTS FROM KAUPANG

The material found at Kaupang includes the largest collection of western European metal ornaments found on a Scandinavian site. The majority of the ornaments are ecclesiastical, original mountings for shrines and holy books in the churches and monasteries of Great Britain and Ireland, probably brought to Kaupang as Viking loot. Many were transformed into brooches, like the magnificent rectangular ornament no. 7 found in the neck region in a rich woman's grave. This is a first class piece of metal-work, as are also nos. 5 and 8, while no. 9 is of inferior quality. Numbers 3 and 4 are beautifully enamelled ornaments — perhaps for bronze cauldrons.

There are also pieces for secular use as, for example, a long pin, belonging to a pennanular brooch. (no. 6).

A unique object is the trefoil brooch (no. 2.) Its vegetable ornaments are completely alien to the nordic taste of the time. This brooch must have been imported from the continent.

GOTLAND THE TRADERS' ISLAND

During the whole of the Iron Age, before and during Viking times, the island of Gotland, situated in the middle of the Baltic, was a centre for trade from both east and west. Its world-wide commerce began early. A great many objects imported from Rome during the height of the Empire have been found there. By the late Viking Age, in the tenth century, Gotland enjoyed market conditions that must have made it, within a short while, a dangerous rival of Birka. In addition to richly-furnished burials of the tenth century discovered there, excavations in Gotland show a sharp increase in the quantities of silver coins from treasure hoards. Unlike Birka, Gotland seems to have enjoyed undiminishing richness of silver coins, Anglo-Saxon and German, until well into the eleventh century; so much so, in fact, that it must have been the true centre of Baltic commerce during this period. Out of the total number of 200,000 silver coins from the Viking Age found in Scandinavia, no less than half, that is 40,000 Arabic, 38,000 German and 21,000 Anglo-Saxon coins, were found on the little island of Gotland.

It is obvious that these coins, only recently unearthed, are only a fraction of what was, for one reason or another, buried on the island in the tenth or eleventh centuries. Moreover, buried coins do not, of course, represent anything like the entire amount of the silver that came to the island as the proceeds of trade. A total figure is hard even to guess at. But if one coin out of every thousand that constituted the proceeds of trade has been preserved — probably an optimistic estimate — the Gotlanders must have had an income of more than a hundred million silver coins during their century and a half of heaviest trade, possibly as much as a million a year. In spite of being called a penny, every Anglo-Saxon silver coin had a purchasing power of at least ten to twenty shillings (up to three dollars) in current values, so the proceeds of Gotlandic trade during the later part of the Viking Age were worth about one million pounds sterling (or nearly three million dollars) a year.

Judged even by the standards of Europe as a whole, this suggests trade on remarkably grand scale. This huge income may be explained in the same way as that of England's Honourable East India Company during the seventeenth and eighteenth centuries: the greater the risk from pirates and other enemies, the greater profits to be reaped on such goods as actually reached port. Perhaps the Gotlanders, because of exceptional sailing skill, possessed the fastest ships on the Baltic, enabling them to evade the Jomsvikings and other sea-going predators. Thus they would have been able to save their cargoes of furs from the north-east for the new-rich mine-owners of central Germany, and load

KORPKLINT

VÄSTERGARN

GOTLAND

MÄSTERMYR

THE TRADING CENTRE WITHOUT A TOWN

The island of Gotland, shown on the map above, seems to have been an active trading centre both before and throughout the Viking era, but archaeologists have never found any town-like settlement. Gotland's rich farmers must have doubled as merchants. They had a turnover of the most amazing proportions, as the many finds of foreign money on the island show.

THE CLIFFS AND SHOALS OF GOTLAND

The harsh granite cliffs at Korpklint, on the west coast of Gotland, shown on the facing page, would have repelled the deep-draught trading ships of most nations, for the island has few natural harbours to accomodate them. But it does have shelving beaches, which were ideal landing-places for the shallow-draught Viking vessels. As a result Gotland became one of the richest of the Scandinavian trading centres.

their ships with ever-profitable woollen cloth on the return voyage. Despite certain archaeological evidence of Gotland's prosperity, contemporary records are strangely silent about her wealth. The historian Adam of Bremen, who did much of his reporting towards the end of the eleventh century, has not one word to say about Gotland. On the other hand, it was obviously this large-scale trading that provided the foundation for the prominent place which Gotland held, at the outset, among the new Hanseatic trading towns of the twelfth century. This position is particularly remarkable because the island has, and had, very few good harbours. The only exception was Visby (after the Viking Age), which was populated almost entirely by foreigners. But the rest of Gotland, too, continued to prosper up to the middle of the fourteenth century, in spite of having nothing but shelving shores. These, however, were easily negotiable for shallow-draught ships of the Viking type, which also could easily, without rehandling of cargo, penetrate long distances up all the rivers of the eastern Baltic, even as far as Novgorod in Russia. They possibly also reached the Slav lands on the southern coasts of the Baltic. From here the journey to the rich new silver mines of Harz in Germany was short. If the Gotlandic trade with Germany did go via the pagan, illiterate Slavs, that would explain the silence of the Christian commentators at least until the new town of Lübeck succeeded Slav cities as Gotland's trading partner.

The island of Gotland is also of particular interest for its wealth of monumental stones. These stones, which date from the 5th to the 11th century, may be simple limestone or sandstone slabs, rune stones or picture stones. Especial interest attaches to the last, which are adorned with pictures carved in low relief on the relatively soft stone. Their most characteristic shape is in the form of a keyhole with a slightly widened base and they may be as much as twice the height of a man. They are most frequently found in the vicinity of cemeteries and churchyards, although the latest of them date from earlier than the first known churches on the island. Their origin and purpose is not always clear, but many were probably tombstones, while others appear to have been wayside memorials and some have been found on the sites of ancient farmhouses. They most frequently depict boats and ships, men and women, the former frequently with weapons, particularly swords and axes, while other stones represent mythical subjects. The picture stone shown in the illustration comes from the parish of Lärbro in the north of the island. In the semicircular part at the top it depicts a battle scene, below which are two scenes probably representing a burial and the entry of a warrior into Valhalla. The use of the wider part near the base to depict a ship is typical.

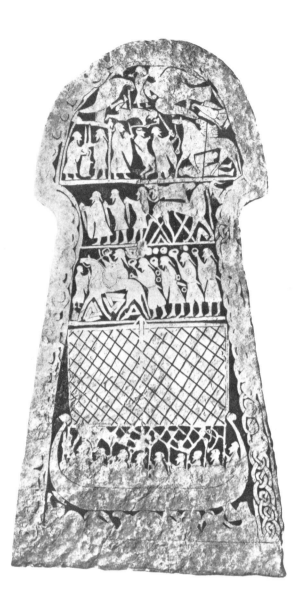

A TYPICAL PICTURE STONE

This bas-relief was found in the northern part of Gotland. It is carved in limestone, now nearly nine feet high but originally about eleven feet, before the root stone was cut away.

In the Frankish Royal Annals for 804 A.D. a place called Sliesthorp, situated on a shallow bay at the head of a creek called the Schlei, on the site of the present town of Schleswig, is mentioned for the first time. It is often mentioned later in other written sources. Icelandic sagas, and the contemporary account of an Arab traveller, Ibrahim Al-Tartushi, testify that the town was known from Iceland to Baghdad. The names by which it is known, however, differ widely: Sliesthorp (the settlement on the Schlei), Slieswich, *aet haethum* (on the heath, at the heaths), Haithabu. All these names refer to the one place, Hedeby, which during the eighth century became of very great importance as a centre of trade between western Europe and the Orient, and as a junction for traffic between the Baltic and the North Sea.

The Norwegian merchant, Ottar, talking to king Alfred of England, described the voyage from Kaupang (Sciringesheal) southwards to Hedeby in these words:

"And from Sciringesheal he said that he sailed for five days to *æt hæthum*: mark [the Danish parts of Sweden] lay to port, while to starboard for three days was the open sea; and after that there was a further two days' sail to Hedeby during which Jutland, Sillende [south Jutland], and many islands lay to starboard; here the Angles had lived before they came to this country [England]. During those two days the islands belonging to Denmark lay to port."

The route eastwards from Hedeby into the Baltic is described to King Alfred by an Anglo-Saxon, Wulfstan: "Wulfstan said that he left Hedeby and came to Truso after seven days and nights and that the ship was under sail all the time. Vendland lay to starboard, while to port were Langeland, Loland, Falster, and Skåne, all of which belonged to Denmark. After that Burgundaland [Bornholm], which has its own king, was seen to port, and, after that, first the land called Blekinge, then Möre, Öland, and Gotland, all belonging to the Swedes. Right up to the mouth of the river Vistula, Vendland lay to starboard all the way."

Archaeological excavations have shown that the place must have been inhabited for about two generations before the earliest written reference to it. At first, there were three small villages situated close together, beside streams near the bay. Two of these villages, the northern and the southern, were abandoned towards the end of the eighth century. Their inhabitants may have joined forces with the people in the middle village to form a bigger community. In that way the place known as Sliesthorp in the year 804 and later as Hedeby came

THE STRATEGIC POSITION OF HEDEBY

At the southern extremity of the Jutland peninsula, now German territory, lies the narrowest neck of land between the water systems of the Baltic and the North Sea. Just here Hedeby was situated. It was easy to sail to the east through the long fjord of the Schlei. Today, just south of, and almost parallel to, the main Viking trade route which once ran from Hedeby to Hollingstedt on the North Sea is a modern trade route of great importance — the Kiel Canal.

into existence. In those early days the town was restricted to an area in the immediate vicinity of the shore.

A semicircular earthwork still remains as a prominent feature of the landscape. It is up to forty feet high, and encloses an area of sixty acres. The town could be entered only through two gates in the wall, on the south and north, or from the harbour. The side of the harbour that faced the inlet of the Schlei was protected by a strong palisade. The date of the Hedeby earthworks is not known. It includes two burial-grounds within its area. By the end of the tenth century, buildings covered the whole of the area enclosed by the earthwork. A third burial-ground lies outside the earthwork to the south, and a fourth, smaller one outside the northern gate. The most impressive of the burials is a chambered tomb, covered by a boat of which only the rivets remain. It is situated on the edge of the southern burial-ground, and dates from about 900. Hedeby's position, on the borders of Denmark and the Frankish kingdom, offered the best of prospects for the growth of trade. Because for two and a half centuries Hedeby controlled the traffic between the Frankish kingdom and Scandinavia, it was a place of great significance politically, too. Its strategic situation helped in this, because the town lay at the eastern end of a system of defensive earthworks called the Danevirke, which stretched right across the narrowest part of the Jutland peninsula. The Danevirke was begun by the Danish king Godfred early in the ninth century as a defence against attacks from the south. Its western end reached the marshy coastlands of the North Sea. Towards the east it branched off into what is known as the "Margareta-wall", which joined up with the semicircular earthwork of Hedeby. The Danevirke thus formed an effective barrier across the whole neck of the Jutland peninsula. In addition to the semicircular wall and the Danevirke, there is yet another defensive earthwork at Hedeby. It is immediately to the north of the settlement area on a stretch of steep hillside. The flat hilltop is surrounded by an embankment, and looks like a stronghold which may have served as a place of refuge for the inhabitants of Hedeby before they had built the larger semicircular wall. Small burial mounds have also been found here. As the town lay at the head of the very long and narrow Schlei creek, it was protected from sudden sea attack from the Baltic. The length of the Schlei made it possible for merchant ships to penetrate so far inland that the distance goods had to be transported overland to the North Sea was only ten miles (see map page 55). The corresponding port on the North Sea was Hollingstedt. In the harbour of Hedeby, it looks as if long rows of rammed-down piles formed piers which sheltered the ships tied up or at anchor. Larger ships must have been made fast at the pier, while smaller boats which could

THE HEDEBY AREA FROM THE AIR

In the aerial view of the Hedeby district on the facing page, the line of the great semicircular wall that protected the landward side of the town, now overgrown by trees, is visible in the centre middle distance. This formidable forty-foot barrier was probably built by the Swedes, who captured the town from the Danes in the middle of the Viking Age. The wide extent of the town area, which lay between the wall and the Schlei fjord (left), is clearly seen. The buildings erected at the archaeological diggings are just visible between the wall and the river, to the left of the lateral white road.

easily have been pulled up on land transported goods to and from them. The nature of the soil near the stream which flows eastwards through the town favoured the preservation of objects buried in it. This is also true of the area down by the shore, and from these two parts of the town one can gain a good idea of the ground plan and the constructional details of the wooden buildings, though their upper sections have long since decayed. Houses and storehouses, workshops, yards, washing places, wells, and roads have been all revealed. These give an accurate impression of how a commercial town of the Viking Age was built. The roofs of the houses nearly met across the narrow, wood-paved lanes. Some large buildings were set back behind fences, and had their own wells. Elsewhere, small workshops were packed closely together.

Although hardly any traces of trade goods made of organic materials like cloth have been found, those of imperishable material point to extensive commercial contacts: pottery from the Rhineland; basalt for grindstones from the Eifel area; soapstone from Norway; Frankish, Byzantine and Arabic coins; and ornaments from the Baltic and from Ireland. On the sites of the workshops raw materials and tools for making implements of various types were found, and also the actual implements, some finished, some half-finished. Workshops for many different products were situated side by side in the "craftsmen's quarter" of the town. In addition to pottery, iron, bronze, and gold were worked. The largest group among the craftsmen seems to have been the comb-makers. In addition to combs they carved spoons, needles, and spindle-whorls of antler. As glass slag has been found, it is even possible that glass was worked at Hedeby. It is conceivable that the so-called Haithabu half-bracteates (coins made from very thin plates) were struck there — which would make them the first money minted in Scandinavia.

Hedeby was the gateway through which Christianity was introduced into Scandinavia. The big commercial centres, Birka and Hedeby, which already had many Christian inhabitants, most of them foreign merchants of Frisian origin, were looked upon with eager eyes by the German Church as ripe for missionary endeavour. The first missionaries to come to Hedeby, in 823 A.D., had no success at all. In 826, the next, Anskar, who was at that time a monk and became a bishop, arrived. He made better progress, and it is known that he held services for foreign merchants. However, a few years after his arrival he proceeded to Birka, where he was well received by King Björn (see page 34) and by many of the inhabitants. He succeeded so well that when he returned to Hamburg, he was made a bishop. But he did not forget his failure in Hedeby. He returned, and by clever negotiation, obtained permission to build a church. This was in 832 A.D.; though it was not for some years that Anskar was

THE EARLIEST SCANDINAVIAN COINS?

These silver pieces, found at Hedeby and called " Hedeby half-bracteates", date from the beginning of the tenth century, and may be the first coins actually minted in Scandinavia. Until then, all coins were imported.

allowed to ring the church bell: it was thought that doing so would frighten the pagan gods.

Evidently everything went well as long as Anskar was still alive, but after his death in 867 A.D. no more is heard about a Christian mission in Scandinavia until 934, when the German king Henry I compelled the Danish king Gnupa, who may have been of Swedish origin, to accept the new religion. This event put new life into the missions. Unni, bishop of Bremen, went to Scandinavia, but in Birka he fell ill, and died there in 936. His trunk was buried at Birka, but his head was carried to the cathedral of Bremen and interred there.

A carved antler figurine of a child, with hands raised as if in adoration, may be the earliest representation of the Christ-child in Scandinavia. The discovery of moulds for the casting of such pagan objects as hammers of Thor as well as Christian crosses, shows that the pagan gods as well as Christ were worshipped at Hedeby. The co-existence of Christianity and paganism is unequivocally shown by other finds — among them several hammers of Thor, and a bronze representation, in relief, of a hero being greeted in Valhalla by a Valkyrie, one of the handmaids of the god Odin. Side by side with these were Christian objects such as a symbol of the Evangelist Luke dating from the tenth or eleventh century, a bronze crucifix, and a disc-shaped brooch with enamel bearing the representation of a saint. That two radically opposed religions should have overlapped in this way is not so surprising, when one recalls that merchants from the four corners of the then-known world came to Hedeby to do business. In fact the missionaries did not succeed in Christianizing the Scandinavians. If they wanted to do business with Christian merchants, some Scandinavian traders had to let themselves be signed with the Cross and declare themselves Christians, but they were not baptized, thereby avoiding offence to their own gods. Ibrahim Al-Tartushi, who visited Hedeby about 950 A.D., tells us that the people of the town "worship Sirius, except for a few who are Christians and have a church there. They hold a feast where all meet to honour their deity and to eat and drink. Each man who slaughters a sacrifical animal — an ox, ram, goat, or pig — fastens it up on poles outside the door of his house to show that he has made his sacrifice in honour of the god. The town is poorly provided with property or treasure. The inhabitants' principal food is fish, which is very plentiful. The people often throw a newborn child into the sea rather than maintain it. Furthermore women have the right to claim a divorce; they do this themselves whenever they wish. There is also an artificial make-up for the eyes: when they use it beauty never fades; on the contrary, it increases in men and women as well."

The evidence shows, therefore, that life in Hedeby at the turn of the millennium

THE THRONGING WATERFRONT AT HEDEBY

Life in Hedeby, reconstructed in the drawing on pages 60-61, must have presented a lively, cosmopolitan and noisy scene. Women pound and rinse their laundry at the edge of the water (where the hairpins they dropped have been found by archaeologists). A cart-basket — the multi-purpose container of those days — filled with goods is being lifted from a boat onto its cart to be transported further along the Danevirke to Hollingstedt, for re-shipping there. Unmindful of the noise, two good neighbours play backgammon on the quay in the sunshine. A troop of horsemen in rig of Magyar cut, borrowed from the Hungarians via the Germans, come riding through the crowd. A pig has got loose and runs squealing among the cart-wheels and horses' hooves. According to the Arabian merchant Ibrahim Al-Tartushi, who visited Hedeby, the inhabitants made offerings of domestic animals to the gods by placing them on projections above the doors of houses. An offering of this kind has been made on one of the houses to the right. The permanent inhabitants all knew one another's names and trades, and the foreign merchants were easily recognized from their dress and behaviour. Many languages were bandied back and forth among the crowds milling in the narrow streets where they spent much of their daily life, but the peoples of the North Sea coasts probably understood one other easily enough at this time, before national boundaries grew up.

was diverse and colourful, characterized by intensive commerce and industry, opposing religious beliefs, and political antagonism. The political history of the town is obscure in places. Hedeby lay on Danish territory and its rulers are described as Danish kings, but Adam of Bremen says that, earlier in the tenth century, a certain Olaf, coming from Sweden, conquered Denmark. He also tells us that Olaf's sons, Gurd and the Gnupa already mentioned, inherited the kingdom after their father's death. He mentions, too, a king named Sigerich, and still another called Hardegon. Adam himself was rather at sea. He adds: "It is very uncertain whether some of these kings (or rather tyrants) ruled the Danes at one and the same time, or whether one survived another for a short time." The inscriptions on two rune-stones found near Hedeby might help to solve the puzzle. One runs: "Asfrid created this memorial to Sigtrygg, her son and Gnupa's." The other stone says that "Asfrid, the daughter of Odinkar, set up this memorial to King Sigtrygg, her son and Gnupa's." Of these two written sources, the rune-stones, being contemporary with the events, should be the more reliable. At the same time, it can be assumed that the king called Sigerich by Adam is the same as the Sigtrygg of the rune-stones. But this merely gives us one of the names of the kings. We still do not know whether Denmark was divided into several parts, or whether Olaf conquered the whole of the country, or Hedeby alone. The archaeological finds at Hedeby do not help, for they are of a common Scandinavian type, without special Danish or Swedish character.

At all events, by the early decades of the eleventh century, the town was falling into decay, for reasons as yet unknown. In 1050 the Norwegian king Harald burnt Hedeby in the course of a battle against the Danish king Svein Estrithson. In 1066, the same year as the Battle of Hastings in England, a destructive attack was made on the town by the Slavs. This probably led to its abandonment. Its trading role was taken over by Schleswig, on the northern shore of the Schlei. Schleswig, in its turn, came to be superseded by the Hansa town of Lûbeck.

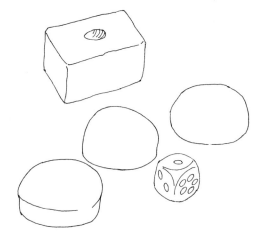

THE VIKINGS AT PLAY

Life for the Vikings was not always the serious business of fighting, trading, or wresting a living from the land and the sea. They threw dice, and played games with counters, as these finds from Hedeby show.

The drawing at the head of this page is a recon-struction, from archaeological finds, of how a military camp might have looked as carved on a picture-stone. In fact, no known illustration of such a camp exists on a picture-stone.

MILITARY BASES IN DENMARK

This map shows the distribution of the military camps of the Danish kings at Trelleborg in Zea-land, Nonnebakken at Odense in Funen, Fyrkat near Hobro, and Aggersborg near Limfjorden. All were so situated as to command important waterways or other lines of communication.

The Vikings established many military bases in the countries they invaded, but at least in Denmark, it appears that they also built up complex armed camps at home. So far the remains of such camps have only been found in Denmark — which may be explained by the fact that royal power in Denmark was stronger at that time than in the other Scandinavian countries, and so able to command such works. Moreover, around the beginning of the eleventh century, when the camps were built, Denmark was on more than one occasion preparing to conquer England. The camps could accommodate far more men than were in the king's bodyguard — his only permanent force — so they must have been intended for a special, limited purpose.

Four camps have so far been found, at Trelleborg in Zealand, at Nonnebak-ken on Funen (in the town of Odense), at Fyrkat near Hobro, and at Aggers-borg at Limfjorden. Of those, Trelleborg is the only one completely excavat-ed. It lies on a small foreland where two small rivers meet. The main forti-fication consisted of a circular rampart with four gateways, one facing each of the four points of the compass. They were situated at the ends of two streets, which crossed each other and divided the area inside the walls into four equal segments. Four houses with elliptical ground-plans arranged in a square whose diagonals intersected in the centre were built in each segment. Additionally some smaller guard-houses at the gateways broke up the symmetry of the geo-metric ground-plan. A ring road, paved with wooden strips, ran around the rampart's inner side. The rampart itself was palisaded outside and inside. Iron rings and keys for the heavy gates have been found at the excavations at Trelleborg. The main rampart was further protected on three sides by streams and a marsh. On the exposed fourth side beyond the main rampart, an outer rampart with double the radius of the inner one had been built. Its northern end described a right-angle to enclose the camp graveyard, and thirteen houses lay inside it. These were of the same construction as the houses within the main fort. The unit used was the Roman foot (11.8 in.). The houses in the main fort are each exactly a hundred feet long, those in the outer fort exactly ninety feet long. The radius from the fort's centre to the main rampart is 234 feet, and it is exactly 234 feet from the main rampart to the outer rampart. Where did the Danes learn such exactness? At present, no historian or archaeologist can say, although the scrupulous military precision of all this fits in very well with the strong discipline which is known to have ruled the king's personal bodyguard.

Trelleborg was so strongly isolated from the outside world that even the graveyard was situated inside the ramparts. Of the 160 or so graves, most, of course, were for men. But one or two were for women and children. Communal graves were found as well, as might be expected in a military camp, the largest containing ten men, who must all have met their deaths at the same time. The right leg of one was cut off a little above the knee. Smith's tools were found, naturally enough, but so, surprisingly, were ploughshares, corn sickles and scythe-blades. It seems that the garrison was to some extent self-sufficient, and tilled fields around the camp. The presence of spinning and weaving tools also suggests that women lived in the camp. The fort at Nonnebakken has the same strong geometrical construction as Trelleborg. Fyrkat too, is generally constructed like Trelleborg, but with no outer rampart, so its little graveyard lies unprotected. It was situated strategically on a cape in the river Onsild, which gave access to the sea. Aggersborg is nearly double the size of Trelleborg: its diameter is no less than 960 Roman feet. Indeed, a sizeable village had to be destroyed to make room for it. Because of its location, whoever controlled Aggersborg could control all traffic on the Limfjord. From here many of the expeditions against England probably started. The last to be organized was that of Cnut the Saint, who in 1085 planned to recapture the island kingdom after it had been lost for Denmark under the sons of Cnut the Great. Before it could be launched, however, a revolt broke out against the king in Denmark, during the course of which, in 1086, Aggersborg was destroyed.

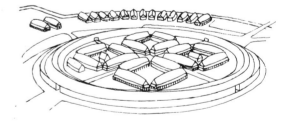

RECONSTRUCTION OF A VIKING MILITARY CAMP

This drawing shows Trelleborg in Denmark as it must have appeared at the time it was constructed, around the year 1000 A.D. Its military origins are obvious from the extreme geometric regularity of its layout. Inside the outer rampart can be seen the outer row of houses, while in the foreground is the main, circular rampart, enclosing the central groups of houses.

At top right, a Viking ship from a Gotlandic "picture-stone" sails out to sea filled with warriors. The emigrants going to the Atlantic islands were well-armed and prepared to win their new homes in battle.

In the course of two centuries, Scandinavian seamen discovered and colonized almost all the habitable islands that lie between Scandinavia and the mainland of North America. Already before 800 A.D. they had established themselves in the islands of Orkney and Shetland, and in the early part of the ninth century they were in Ireland. Later in that century Iceland was first discovered, and its colonization, partly from the British Isles, had begun. Before 1000 A.D. Erik the Red had led the first settlers into the fjords of south-west Greenland. It was from this treeless land that the settlers crossed to Labrador and Newfoundland. They called part of their new discovery, appropriately enough, Markland: the land of forest. To the north of this lay Helluland, the land of rock, and to the south lay Vinland.

According to Icelandic tradition many of the early discoveries, including Iceland itself, Greenland and the mainland of America, were accidentally made by men who were driven off course. This kind of mishap must often have occurred and no doubt important discoveries were made in this way, but the Norse discoveries and colonization were not entirely fortuitous. Britain was certainly known in Scandinavia, and the existence of Iceland was known to the Irish, among whom some Norsemen settled. For some weeks at midsummer, through a mirage effect, the mountains of Greenland can be seen from the hills of north-west Iceland — where Erik the Red lived — and the possible existence of Labrador may have been suggested to the Greenlanders by the sight of clouds forming over the land, which could have been seen from the hills behind the Greenland settlements.

Even so, the North Atlantic retained its terrors, which were the more frightening when they were unfamiliar. The following description of an encounter with a whirlpool in Greenland waters is given by Adam of Bremen, writing about 1076 A.D., and concerns a voyage undertaken by North Sea sailors in the eighth century: "Archbishop Adalbert, of blessed memory, told us that in the days of his predecessor, certain noble men of Frisia spread sail to the north for the purpose of ranging through the sea, because the inhabitants claimed that by a direct course toward the north from the mouth of the Weser river, one meets with no land. The partners pledged themselves under oath to look into this novel claim and, with a joyful call to the oarsmen, set out from the Frisian coast. Then, leaving on the one side Denmark, on the other Britain, they came to the Orkneys. And when they had left these islands to their left, while they had Norway on their right, the navigators landed after a long passage on icy Iceland. And as they furrowed the seas from that place towards the farthest northern pole, after they saw behind them all the islands spoken about above, they commended their way and adventure to Almighty God and the holy confessor Willehad. Of a sudden they fell into that numbing ocean's dark mist which could hardly be penetrated with the eyes. And, behold, the current of the fluctuating ocean whirled back to its mysterious fountainhead and with most furious impetuosity drew the unhappy sailors, who in their despair now thought only of death, on to chaos; this they say is the abysmal chasm — that deep in which, reports has it, all the back flow of the sea, which appears to decrease, is absorbed and in turn revomited, as the mounting fluctuation is usually described. As the partners were imploring the mercy of God to receive their souls, the backward thrust of the sea carried away some of their ships, but its forward ejection threw the rest far behind the others. Freed thus by the timely help of God from the instant peril they had before their eyes, they seconded the flood by rowing with all their might."

THE VINLAND MAP - THE SCHOLARS ARGUE

Since its discovery and acquisition by Yale University, the famous map on the facing page has revived bitter controversy on both sides of the Atlantic as to who first discovered America, the Vikings or Columbus. The argument has become emotional, and spread from the scholars to ordinary people of Norse or Latin descent, thus obscuring the rational arguments for and against the map's validity. The map is said to be an authentic attempt, made half a century before Columbus sailed, to depict the North Atlantic, and shows Vinland, with the words: "Island of Vinland, discovered by Bjarni and Leif in company." However, the authenticity of the dating of the Vinland map has been challenged on several grounds. It is suspicious that Greenland should be shown with so much accurate detail at so early a date (unless this is coincidence), while the British Isles and Scandinavia are so ill depicted. It is also strange that the map does not mention either Helluland or Markland — the latter, in particular, must have been important as a source of timber to the Greenlanders who first came to America. Despite these discrepancies the map is based on well-known traditions of the Vinland voyages. Whether it was really created before Columbus or afterwards, however, is very difficult to determine. In any case, it does not prove or disprove the prior Norse discovery; it shows only the map-maker's familiarity with this Norse tradition, the validity of which some scholars question.

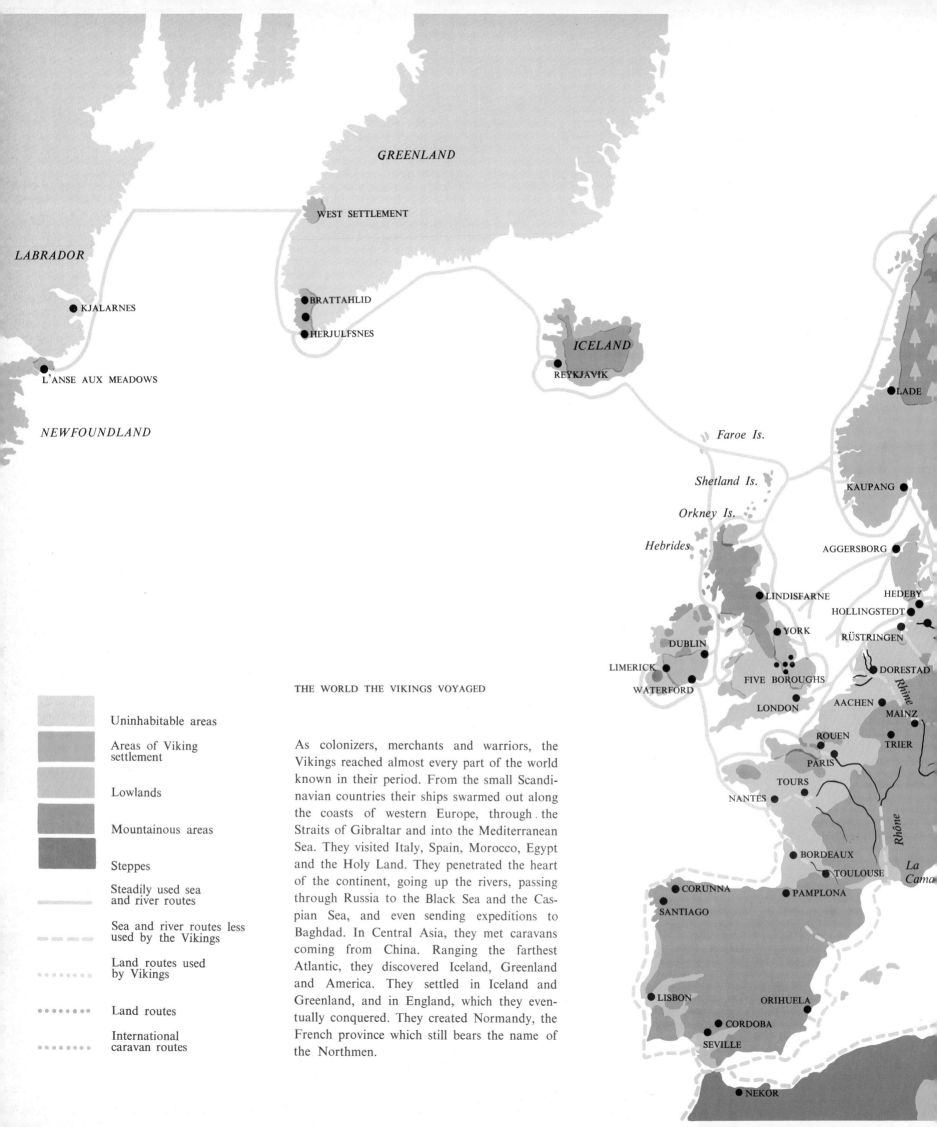

GREENLAND

LABRADOR

WEST SETTLEMENT

● KJALARNES

● BRATTAHLID

● HERJULFSNES

● L'ANSE AUX MEADOWS

NEWFOUNDLAND

ICELAND

REYKJAVIK

● LADE

Faroe Is.

Shetland Is.

KAUPANG

Orkney Is.

AGGERSBORG ●

Hebrides

HEDEBY
LINDISFARNE
HOLLINGSTEDT

DUBLIN   YORK   RÜSTRINGEN

LIMERICK   DORESTAD

FIVE BOROUGHS   *Rhine*

WATERFORD

LONDON   AACHEN

MAINZ

ROUEN   TRIER

PARIS

TOURS

NANTES   *Rhône*

BORDEAUX

TOULOUSE   *La Cama*

CORUNNA   PAMPLONA

SANTIAGO

LISBON   ORIHUELA

CORDOBA

SEVILLE

● NEKOR

THE WORLD THE VIKINGS VOYAGED

As colonizers, merchants and warriors, the Vikings reached almost every part of the world known in their period. From the small Scandinavian countries their ships swarmed out along the coasts of western Europe, through the Straits of Gibraltar and into the Mediterranean Sea. They visited Italy, Spain, Morocco, Egypt and the Holy Land. They penetrated the heart of the continent, going up the rivers, passing through Russia to the Black Sea and the Caspian Sea, and even sending expeditions to Baghdad. In Central Asia, they met caravans coming from China. Ranging the farthest Atlantic, they discovered Iceland, Greenland and America. They settled in Iceland and Greenland, and in England, which they eventually conquered. They created Normandy, the French province which still bears the name of the Northmen.

Uninhabitable areas

Areas of Viking settlement

Lowlands

Mountainous areas

Steppes

Steadily used sea and river routes

Sea and river routes less used by the Vikings

Land routes used by Vikings

Land routes

International caravan routes

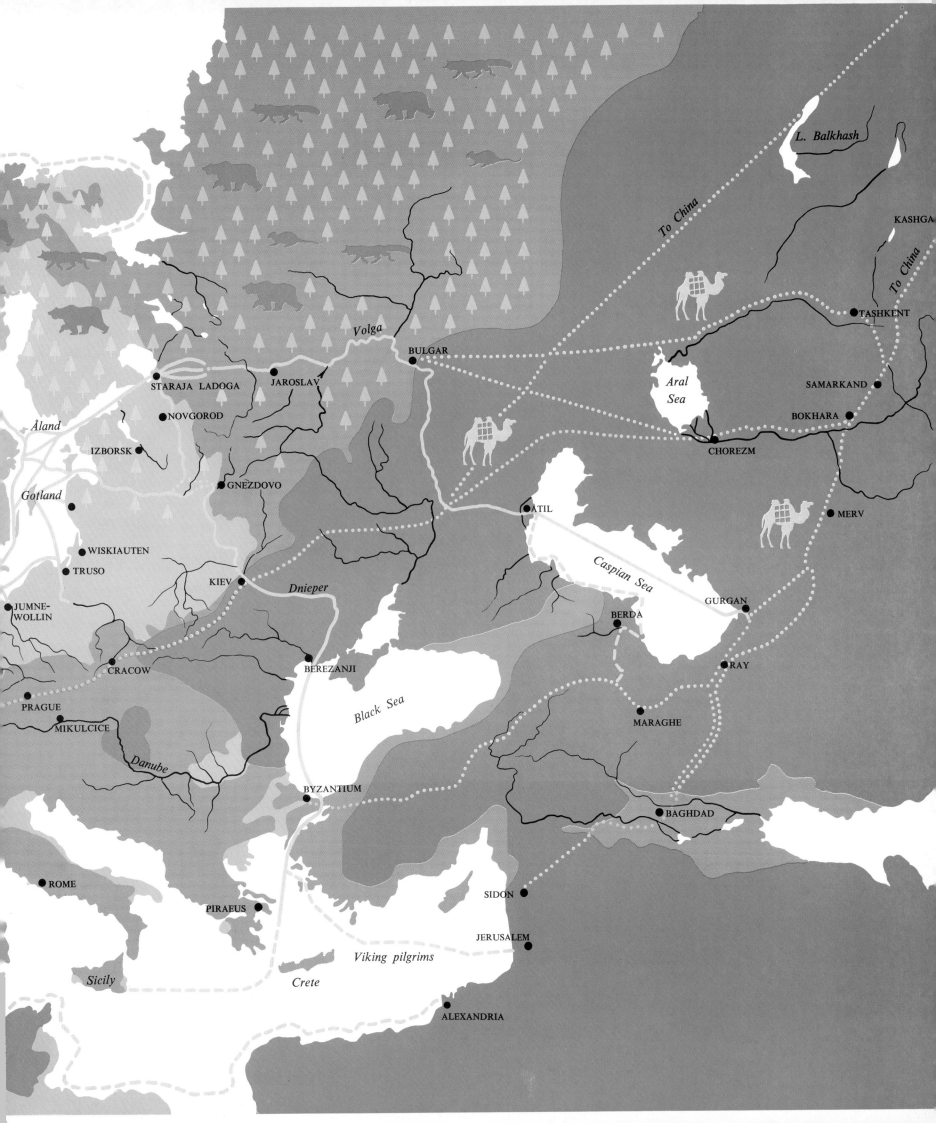

L. Balkhash

To China

KASHGA

TASHKENT

Aral
Sea

SAMARKAND

BOKHARA

CHOREZM

MERV

Volga

BULGAR

STARAJA LADOGA   JAROSLAV

NOVGOROD

Åland

IZBORSK

Gotland

GNEZDOVO

ATIL

Caspian Sea

GURGAN

WISKIAUTEN

TRUSO

KIEV

Dnieper

BERDA

RAY

JUMNE-
WOLLIN

CRACOW

BEREZANJI

Black Sea

MARAGHE

PRAGUE

MIKULCICE

Danube

BYZANTIUM

BAGHDAD

ROME

PIRAEUS

SIDON

JERUSALEM

Viking pilgrims

Sicily

Crete

ALEXANDRIA

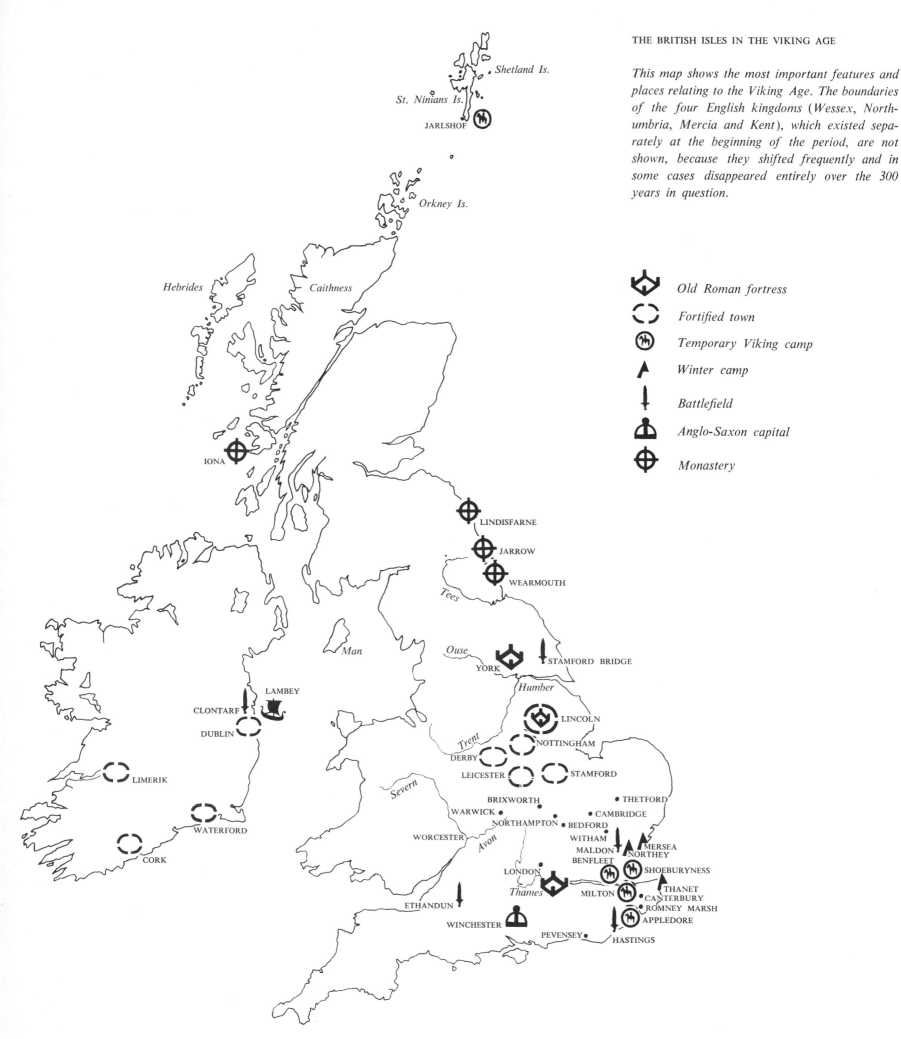

THE BRITISH ISLES IN THE VIKING AGE

This map shows the most important features and places relating to the Viking Age. The boundaries of the four English kingdoms (Wessex, Northumbria, Mercia and Kent), which existed separately at the beginning of the period, are not shown, because they shifted frequently and in some cases disappeared entirely over the 300 years in question.

Old Roman fortress

Fortified town

Temporary Viking camp

Winter camp

Battlefield

Anglo-Saxon capital

Monastery

Shetland Is.

St. Ninians Is.

JARLSHOF

Orkney Is.

Hebrides

Caithness

IONA

LINDISFARNE

JARROW

WEARMOUTH

Tees

Ouse

YORK — STAMFORD BRIDGE

Man

Humber

CLONTARF — LAMBEY

DUBLIN

Trent

DERBY — LINCOLN

NOTTINGHAM

LEICESTER — STAMFORD

LIMERIK

WATERFORD

Severn

BRIXWORTH — THETFORD

WARWICK — CAMBRIDGE

NORTHAMPTON — BEDFORD

CORK

WORCESTER

Avon

WITHAM

MALDON — MERSEA

BENFLEET — NORTHEY

LONDON — SHOEBURYNESS

Thames

MILTON — THANET

CANTERBURY

ROMNEY MARSH

ETHANDUN

APPLEDORE

WINCHESTER

PEVENSEY — HASTINGS

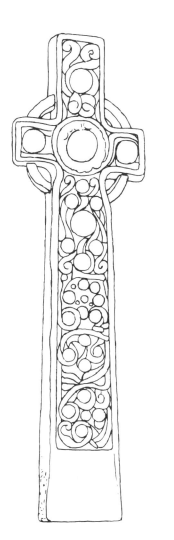

THE IONA CROSS

This great Celtic cross still stands close by the church of Iona in the Hebrides, founded by the Irishman, Saint Columba, in the middle of the sixth century. Carved during the ninth century, it is one of the very few surviving monuments which date back to the Viking Age. Iona was one of the great spiritual centres of the Celtic world, and suffered many Viking raids, notably in 806 A.D. when, according to a contemporary Irish chronicle, sixty-eight monks were killed.

The islands of Orkney and Shetland, to the north of Britain, were probably the first to be colonized by Scandinavians, and their settlement may have begun before the end of the eighth century. The Icelandic tradition was that the migration to these islands was caused by the growth of the autocratic power of the Norwegian king Harald Fairhair. According to the greatest of the Icelandic historical sagas, *Heimskringla*, "During the times of warfare when King Harald brought Norway under his domination, foreign lands such as the Faroes and Iceland were settled. There was a great exodus to the Shetlands, and many of the nobility fled King Harald as outlaws and went on Viking expeditions to the west, staying in the Orkneys and the Hebrides in winter, but in summer harrying in Norway where they inflicted great damage." It also tells how King Harald himself launched an expedition to subdue the Vikings in these islands, and how he gave them new rulers: "King Harald gave Earl Rognvald dominion over the Orkneys and Shetlands, but Rognvald promptly gave both lands to his brother Sigurth." Sigurth and some friends harried in Scotland, "taking possesion of Caithness and of the Hebrides as far as Ekkjalsbakki [the river Oykell, between present-day Sutherland and Ross]. Sigurth slew Melbrighti Tooth, a Scottish earl, and fastened his head to his saddle straps. The calf of his leg struck the tusk protruding from the skull, mortification set in, and he died from it."

Harald Fairhair did not rule in Norway until the end of the ninth century, so this explanation of the original Norse emigration is certainly wrong. Irish sources, some of which are contemporary, speak of the plundering of Irish monasteries by Viking raiders early in the ninth century, and it is likely that the early attacks on the island monasteries of Lindisfarne and Iona were a by-product of Norwegian colonization of the northern isles. The Norwegian character of the settlement is clearly shown by the placenames. The Old Norse word *bolstaör* meaning "farm" is common in such names as Bimbister, Braebister, and Grimbister. Old Norse *vagr*, meaning a creek or bay, is found in Kirkwall, Ronaldsvoe, Snarravoe, and, naturally enough, the Old Norse word for an island, *ey*, is very common, as in such names as Egilsay and Ronaldsay. It is clear from the text of *Heimskringla* that there was some settlement on the mainland of Scotland, particularly in Caithness, and many Scandinavian placenames exist in the Hebrides, but most of them are names of mountains or headlands, like Vaternish in Skye or Treshnish in Mull, in which the Scandinavian *ness*, meaning "headland", has been modified. Such names seem to represent seamarks, and this is not surprising, since islands like Skye and Mull

A NORSE FARM IN THE SHETLANDS

The farm of Jarlshof lies near the southern tip of Shetland in the natural harbour of Sumburgh Voe, close by the ruin of the Broch of Mousa (opposite page). The site had been occupied since the Stone Age, but migrant Vikings built their own new long houses of stone and turf, illustrated in the reconstruction above, and the farm flourished, for additional buildings were added by later generations. Life seems to have been very simple. The remains of oxen, sheep, pigs, deer, whales, fishes and birds have been found to give some idea of their diet. Viking homesteaders kept domestic animals like dogs and ponies, but despite their great skill as seamen they seem to have acquired very few foreign imports. Though Shetland may have been an important staging post on the journey between Scandinavia and the west, this role is not borne out by any evidence located on farms like this. The objects found on it suggest that this was a peaceful farming community, not a base for raiders. Very few weapons, in fact, have been discovered. The graves, however, have not yet been found and studied. When they are, they may bear witness to a more warlike (and more commercial) way of life.

lay athwart the seaway leading from Scandinavia or Iceland to Ireland and west Britain. The use of this route by the Scandinavians is testimony to the superb seamanship which made settlement among the islands possible in the first place. To the stranger, these bare, forbidding islands with their treacherous currents, tides and winds are inhospitable and dangerous. But to men accustomed to western Norway they would have seemed familiar and even inviting, offering the heartening prospect of a home away from home like the one shown above. Some placenames that the Vikings gave to their new homes indicated the direction from which they came. For instance, the Hebrides were called "the Southern Isles", showing that the newcomers arrived from the north; that is to say from Norway, or from an earlier settlement in the Orkneys or Shetlands. The persistence of placenames that seem contradictory to the present inhabitants is demonstrated by the fact that a part of northern Scotland is still called Sutherland, a name revealing a Norwegian orientation.

AN ANCIENT ISLAND LANDMARK

A great prehistoric tower, the Broch of Mousa in the Shetlands, not far from Jarlshof, stands by the sea now much as it did when the first Viking ship sailed into the bay in search of shelter 1100 years ago.

The Vikings who raided Northumbria, the northernmost kingdom of Saxon England, at the end of the eighth century came from Norway. They were colonists whose main concern was to find new homes in the familiar environment of the islands of the north and west — Orkney, Shetland, the Hebrides and Ireland. The attacks on the Northumbrian holy places of Lindisfarne and Jarrow, which shocked contemporary churchmen, do not seem to have been the major reason for their voyages, and probably occurred during reconnaissance raids, when several shiploads of Viking settlers were exploring. In 794, a year after their discovery of and attack on Lindisfarne, the Vikings returned and plundered the monastery of Jarrow, but this time they lost one of their leaders, and a storm wrecked several of their ships. Thereafter, the Norwegians do not seem to have attacked Northumbria for many years. It may be that the raids had proved too costly, and that the loot gained was just not worth the trouble. At about the same time, a band of Danes or Norwegians raided the south coast of England, but this turned out to be an isolated attack.

The main Viking attacks on England were the work of Danes. After their first authenticated raid in 835, there were few years in the ninth century when a Danish assault was not reported. In 850, Danish raiders wintered in England for the first time, in Kent, and in 866 a large force of Danes came, apparently determined to find new homes. This " Danish army ", as it was called, campaigned in many parts of England for ten years before it broke up into three main sections. One group settled in Northumbria, another in the north-east midlands, and the third, after an abortive attempt to establish itself in the heart of Wessex, found new homes in East Anglia. The English defence against these Danish raiders and colonists and their successors was led by the kings of Wessex, the most famous of whom is Alfred. The story of the English resistance is best told in the Anglo-Saxon Chronicle, which was first put together at the end of the ninth century by someone eager to praise the Wessex dynasty. By about 880 the English may well have thought that the great danger had passed. Two years earlier the Danes had been decisively defeated at Ethandun in Wessex and the last part of the army that had been threatening that kingdom had begun to settle down. In the following years Alfred set out to reduce the area under Danish control. In 886 he retook London. A treaty was agreed between Alfred and the Danish leader Guthrum, in which the boundary between them was defined. Thus began the painful adjustment to a new situation, in which the kings of Wessex shared England with Scandinavian kings. Suddenly a new threat appeared. A second Viking army began operating along

VIKING ATTACKS, FIRST PHASE — THE END OF THE EIGHTH CENTURY

Isolated raids only, on Lindisfarne and Jarrow in Northumbria, and on the Channel coast of Wessex.

VIKING ATTACKS, SECOND PHASE —- 835 - 896 A.D.

Danish attacks occurred nearly every year during this period, and ended in settlement in the Midlands, East Anglia and Northumbria.

VIKING ATTACKS, THIRD PHASE — 980 - 1016 A.D.

Repeated large-scale Danish raids led to the conquest of the Anglo-Saxon kingdom of England and the temporary establishment of a Scandinavian dynasty there.

A COIN OF ALFRED

This silver penny was struck at London in about 886, soon after Alfred's reconquest of the city from the Vikings. His profile is shown on it.

THE HOLY ISLAND

The colour illustration on the following pages shows the lonely landscape of Lindisfarne, known as the Holy Island, off the Northumbrian coast; the island monastery which had been founded in the middle of the seventh century by a company of missionaries from Iona, and which suffered one of the very first reported Viking attacks in western Europe. Led by a monk named Aidan, they originally chose this tidal island for security, and were safe until the advent of the sea raiders from the north.

the Channel coasts between England and France. In 885 it briefly penetrated the Thames estuary, departing only to return seven years later in 892. King Alfred recognized that the sea was the first line of defence against Viking attacks, and he had ships specially constructed. The Anglo-Saxon Chronicle describes them as "twice as long as the Danish ships. Some had sixty oars, some more. They were both swifter and steadier and also higher than the others. They were built neither on the Frisian nor on the Danish pattern, but as it seemed to him [the king] himself that they could be most useful." Their size was obviously an advantage in fighting, but it meant that they did not have such a shallow draught as the attacking boats, and this put them at a tactical disadvantage, as was shown very clearly in the Chronicle's account of the naval battle fought off southern Wessex in the year 896 (See illustration pages 84-85).

A large part of the Danish invasion army of 896 settled in the north and east of England, powerfully reinforcing the original conquerors. They continued to attack the southern parts of England by sea and land. The campaigns were largely fought on land. The local levies who made up the bulk of the king's forces were assembled to meet particular threats and could not be kept in the field indefinitely. Given time an army could be gathered, and the English inflicted many crushing defeats upon the enemy, but the initial advantage always lay with the attackers. The best defence against such attacks was the construction of a series of strongpoints, in which the local people could, if necessary, shelter, and from which counter-attacks could be launched. The value of strongholds of this kind was dramatically demonstrated across the Channel. In the winter of 885-886 the island city of Paris was able to withstand a prolonged Viking siege. The lesson does not seem to have been lost on the Vikings themselves. When the raiders who had failed to take Paris moved on to England in 892, they built a series of camps to serve as their own bases, and the English used similar camps to oppose them. At the same time as the Danish army arrived from France, 140 ships came from the Danish-occupied part of England, the Danelaw, and attacked at many points on the southern coast of Wessex. These two assaults, made at the same time, look like a co-ordinated attempt to conquer Wessex, but the Danes did not succeed against Alfred's growing skill in counter-attack. He won a major victory when he took Appledore in southern Kent, one of the Danes' strongholds, and recaptured the booty stored there. He sent this up to London in ships captured from the invaders. At this time the attacks on Wessex stopped for a short period, but the Danes still hoped to conquer all England.

WOLVES FROM THE SEA

The attack on Lindisfarne sent a shock through the Christian world. The scholar Alcuin, himself a Northumbrian, though he was then living on the continent of Europe as an adviser to Charlemagne, wrote a letter to Ethelred, king of Northumbria, when he heard of the attack, and said: " Lo, it is nearly 350 years that we and our fathers have inhabited this most lovely land, and never before has such a terror appeared in Britain as we have now suffered from a pagan race, nor was it thought that such an inroad from the sea could be made. Behold, the church of St. Cuthbert spattered with the blood of the priests of God, despoiled of all its ornaments, a place more venerable than all in Britain is given as a prey to pagan peoples. "

The Anglo-Saxon Chronicle, written about a century later, reported the raid in the following words: " In this year, dire portents appeared over Northumbria and sorely frightened the people. They consisted of immense whirlwinds and flashes of lightning, and fiery dragons were seen flying in the air. A great famine immediately followed these signs, and a little after that, in the same year on the eighth of June, the ravages of heathen men miserably destroyed God's church on Lindisfarne with plunder and slaughter. "

A twelfth-century writer gives the following vigorous account of the raid: " In the same year the pagans from the northern regions came with a naval force to Britain like stinging hornets and spread on all sides like fearful wolves, robbed, tore and slaughtered not only beasts of burden, sheep and oxen, but even priests and deacons, and companies of monks and nuns. And they came to the church of Lindisfarne, laid everything waste with grievous plundering, trampled the holy places with polluted steps, dug up the altars and seized all the treasures of the holy church. They killed some of the brothers, took some away with them in fetters, many they drove out, naked and loaded with insults, some they drowned in the sea. "

Throughout the early years of the tenth century, Alfred's son Edward the Elder strove mightily to contain the Viking threat from the north and east, and to reassert the authority of his dynasty over Danish-occupied territories. The English began to build fortifications in a determined way, and with great success. The south of England was straddled by a series of at least thirty boroughs, as these fortresses were called, and from 910 onwards they were used as bases for the reconquest of Danish-occupied England. Such camps were certainly on a much larger scale than those of the ninth century. For example, the borough of Witham in Essex, built by King Edward in 912, consisted of an elaborate maze of embankments and ditches covering a total area of twenty-seven acres. Witham is an exception, not in the scale of its defences, but in the fact that it was never developed into anything more than a camp. Some of these fortifications were constructed around existing towns, like those at Worcester and Winchester. In other cases the fortification quickly became a local centre of economic and administrative importance, and many, like Warwick, grew into the chief town of the shire. These boroughs were constructed, maintained and manned by local forces drawn from the countryside around. The arrangements for this are well known because of a tenth century text known as the Burghal Hidage, in which many boroughs are named and the assessed area to support them is given. At Winchester, arrangements were made to defend 3,300 yards of wall, which is so close to the 3,280-yard length of the old Roman walls that it is clear the defences were based on those of the Roman town. Before Edward's death, he was accepted as king by all men living south of the river Humber, English and Danes alike. North of the Humber, the Scandinavian settlers seemed more secure. The native Northumbrians had little love for their southern neighbours, and may even have welcomed the Vikings for the help they could provide in resisting the pretensions of the kings of Wessex. The original Danish settlers in the north were soon joined by Vikings from the west, men of Norwegian descent who had at first settled in Ireland, and then been driven out. Early in the tenth century, in any case, Norwegian adventurers from Ireland established themselves as kings of York. But the Northumbrian attempt to assert independence finally failed in 954 when the last Scandinavian king of York, Eric Bloodaxe, was expelled and killed. England was then, at last, united. But it was not for long to be left in peace.

In 978 King Edward the Martyr was murdered and his place was taken by his half-brother Ethelred. Within two years a fresh series of Viking attacks

A HOLY BOOK RANSOMED

The picture on the facing page is taken from the Codex Aureus in Stockholm, a gospel book made in England in the eighth century. At some time in the ninth century, it was taken as loot by Viking raiders, and bought back by one Earl Alfred, whose recovery of the book is recorded in the English text written at the top and bottom of the page. This begins: "In nomine domini nostri Jesu Christi. *I, Earl Alfred, and Werberg my wife, have acquired this book from a heathen army with our true money, that is, with pure gold, and this we have done for the love of God and for the good of our souls, and because we were not willing that this holy book should remain any longer in heathen hands. And we now desire to give it to Christ Church [Canterbury] for the praise and glory and worship of God and as a thank-offering for His Passion and for the use of the religious community which daily celebrates God's praise in Christ Church.*"

A KING'S REEVE DIES

At almost the same time as the attack on Lindisfarne, another raid (reconstructed at left) was reported from the south coast of England. For the West Saxon chronicler who told of it, "those were the first ships of the Danish men which came to the land of the English." The chronicler calls them Danes, but he also says that they came from Horthaland, that is, from Norway. The account preserved in another version of the Chronicle is precise and extraordinarily effective: "When the very pious king Brihtric was ruling over the domains of the West Saxons, the people spread over their fields were then making furrows in the grimy earth in serene tranquillity, and the burden-bearing frames (i.e. sides) of the oxen placed their necks under the yoke in nearest love. Suddenly a not very large fleet of the Danes arrived, speedy vessels to the number of three; that was their first arrival. At the report, the king's reeve (a royal official with duties like a steward) who was then in the town called Dorchester, leapt on his horse, sped to the harbour with a few men (for he thought they were merchants rather than marauders) and admonishing them in an authoritative manner gave orders that they should be driven to the royal town. And he and his companions were killed by them on the spot. The name of the reeve was Beaduheard."

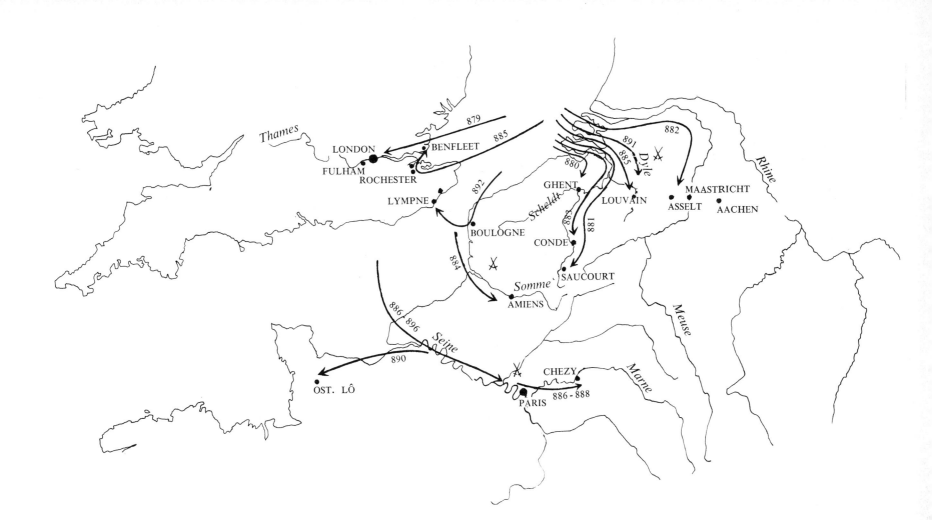

Thames
LONDON
FULHAM
BENFLEET 879
ROCHESTER 885
LYMPNE 892
BOULOGNE
884
Somme
AMIENS
886-896
890
OST. LÔ
Seine
PARIS
CHEZY
886-888
Marne
GHENT
Scheldt
LOUVAIN
CONDE
SAUCOURT
883
188
880
885
891
882
Dyle
ASSELT
MAASTRICHT
AACHEN
Rhine
Meuse

MOBILITY: THE MAIN VIKING WEAPON

For four years, beginning in 892, King Alfred was engaged in a bitter struggle against the second great Danish army to land in England. The chronicler who told of his efforts was careful to describe the movements of this army before it attacked England, and the map above tracing their progress back and forth across the Channel is based on his account. It shows the extreme mobility of the raiders, and the difficulty of maintaining an effective defence against them in an age when regular standing armies and navies were rare.

began, soon developing into large-scale raids. This new generation of Vikings came not for land, like their predecessors in the ninth century, but for booty, which they found in huge quantities, for England was then rich.

Among the leaders of these renewed attacks were such men as Olaf Tryggvason of Norway, who in 991 won a famous victory (celebrated in one of the greatest Anglo-Saxon poems) over the English forces at Maldon in Essex. Leaders like Olaf, or the Dane Svein Forkbeard, soon overcame the defensive system that had been so effective against the earlier settlers. In 1009, for example, a Viking army, in the words of a contemporary, "journeyed as it pleased" and burned the borough of Oxford; an act of destruction that is confirmed by numismatic evidence, for the Oxford mint ceased to produce coins from that year until the end of Ethelred's reign. In the following year the boroughs of Thetford, Cambridge and Northampton were burned. The essence of the English problem was that they were facing a mobile enemy interested not in land, but in tribute. The English could have coped with a settled enemy with the boroughs — they had shown how to do that a century before — but the latter were less successful against the raiders of Ethelred's reign, not just because many of the defences had by then fallen into disrepair, but because the raiders bypassed them if they were well-held. The popular idea of Ethelred as being "Unready" is not therefore, entirely deserved; and in any case this adjective is a

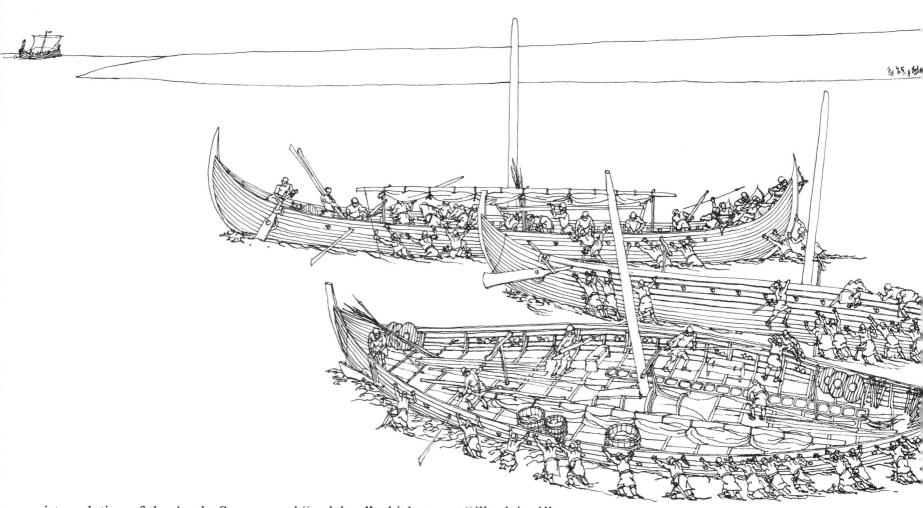

mistranslation of the Anglo-Saxon word "redeless" which meant "ill-advised".
The continued usefulness of defences at key points was shown by Olaf of
Norway's unsuccessful attack on London, also in 1009.

The renewed onslaught from the Northmen reawakened interest in sea defences. Early in the eleventh century King Ethelred "ordered that ships should
be built unremittingly over all England." Towards the end of his reign, he
began to employ Scandinavian mercenaries, and in 1012 some forty-two longships "came over to the king and they promised to defend this country." The
problem of naval defence was to maintain a fleet in a constant state of readi-
ness, and there was the additional difficulty that a wind favouring an attacking
fleet would tend to blow the defenders away. The advantage always lay heavily with the invaders.

In the end the Danes conquered England, and in 1016 A.D. Cnut the Great,
Svein Forkbeard's son, was accepted by the English as their king. The pagan
warrior became a Christian, a benefactor of churches and a pilgrim to Rome.
He, or one of his advisers, wrote: "I humbly render thanks to Almighty God
who has permitted me in my lifetime to visit his holy apostles, Peter and Paul,
and all the sacred places of which I could learn, either within or without the
city of Rome, and to worship and adore them in person there in accordance

ALFRED'S NEW SHIPS IN ACTION

*The best description of a naval battle against the
Vikings is found in the Anglo-Saxon Chronicle
under the year 896 A.D. An episode is reconstructed in the drawing above. "Six ships came to
the Isle of Wight and did great harm there, both
in Devon and everywhere along the coast. Then
the king ordered [a force] to go thither with nine
of the new ships, and they blocked the estuary
from the seaward end. Then the Danes went out
against them with three ships, and three were on
dry land further up the estuary; the men from
them had gone up on land. Then the English captured two of those three ships at the entrance to
the estuary, and killed the men, and the one ship
escaped. On it also the men were killed except
five. These got away because the ships of their
opponents ran aground. Moreover, they had run
aground very awkwardly: three were aground on
that side of the channel on which the Danish
ships were aground, and all [the others] on the*

other side, so that none of them could get to the others. But when the water had ebbed many fur-longs from the ships, the Danes from the remain-ing three ships went to the other three which were stranded on their side, and they then fought there. And there were killed the king's reeve Lucuman, Wulfheard the Frisian, Aebba the Frisian, Aethelhere the Frisian, Aethelfrith the king's geneat*, and in all sixty-two Frisians and English and 120 of the Danes. Then, however, the tide reached the Danish ships before the Chris-tian could launch theirs, and therefore they rowed away out. They were then so wounded that they could not row past Sussex, but the sea cast two of them onto the land, and the men were brought to Winchester to the king, and he ordered them to be hanged. And the men who were on the one ship reached East Anglia greatly wounded.''

* *Companion*

with my desire.'' Cnut may have been transformed, but England was not. There was no great wave of land-grabbing such as followed the Norman Conquest fifty years later, and Cnut ruled in all respects just like an English king, except that he maintained a force of Scandinavian mercenaries who were paid by a tax levied on the English. His sons who succeeded him continued the practice, and one of them, Harthacnut, was well-hated for his extortion. Eventually the kingship passed back to Alfred's heirs, to Ethelred's son, Edward, known as the Confessor. The threats from Scandinavia continued. Magnus of Nor-way and Svein Estrithson of Denmark both thought they had claims on the English throne, and the threat of Scandinavian invasion was only eli-minated by the defeat of King Harold Hardrada of Norway by Harold of England at Stamford Bridge in 1066, about two weeks before the battle of Hastings, and, later, by the failure of a plan by the Danish king Cnut the Saint to invade England in 1085. The Norman Conquest meant that for centuries England was to be ruled by men with important and extensive inte-rests in France. Except for the fact that William the Conqueror had in his veins the blood of the Viking conquerors of Normandy, the links between England and Scandinavia in this period were economic and religious, not political or dynastic.

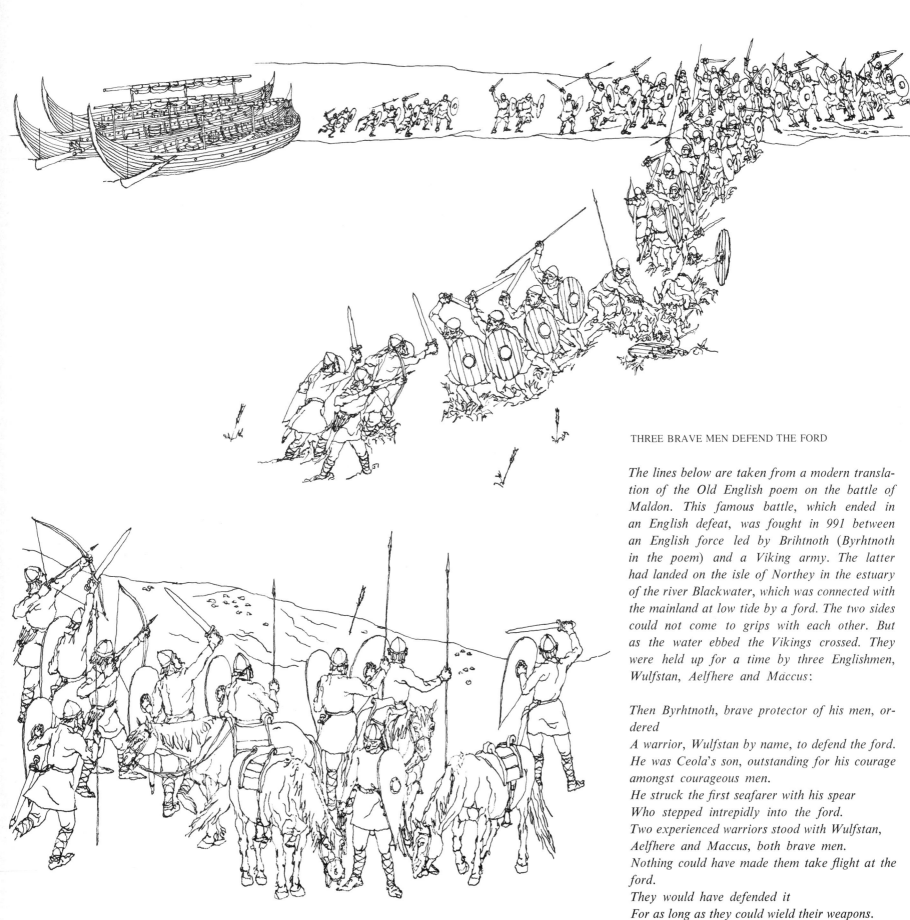

THREE BRAVE MEN DEFEND THE FORD

The lines below are taken from a modern translation of the Old English poem on the battle of Maldon. This famous battle, which ended in an English defeat, was fought in 991 between an English force led by Brihtnoth (Byrhtnoth in the poem) and a Viking army. The latter had landed on the isle of Northey in the estuary of the river Blackwater, which was connected with the mainland at low tide by a ford. The two sides could not come to grips with each other. But as the water ebbed the Vikings crossed. They were held up for a time by three Englishmen, Wulfstan, Aelfhere and Maccus:

Then Byrhtnoth, brave protector of his men, ordered
A warrior, Wulfstan by name, to defend the ford.
He was Ceola's son, outstanding for his courage amongst courageous men.
He struck the first seafarer with his spear
Who stepped intrepidly into the ford.
Two experienced warriors stood with Wulfstan,
Aelfhere and Maccus, both brave men.
Nothing could have made them take flight at the ford.
They would have defended it
For as long as they could wield their weapons.
But as it was, the Danes found the dauntless guardians
Of the ford too fierce for their liking . . .

KING CNUT AS A CHRISTIAN CONVERT

This pen drawing was made early in the reign of Cnut, and comes from the Liber Vitæ *of New Minster, Winchester. It shows Cnut, now a Christian king, with his wife Aelfgifu, placing a cross on the altar of New Minster.*

A CHURCH 1300 YEARS OLD

Brixworth Church (right), near Northampton, built in Roman brick and tile in the late seventh century, is one of the most remarkable monuments from the Europe of the Dark Ages. The tower was enlarged in the tenth century by the addition of a spiral straircase, and originally the central body of the church was surrounded by small chapels. But even in its present altered state it provides an idea of the kind of building encountered by the Vikings when they plundered the Christian west. It is shown without its later spire.

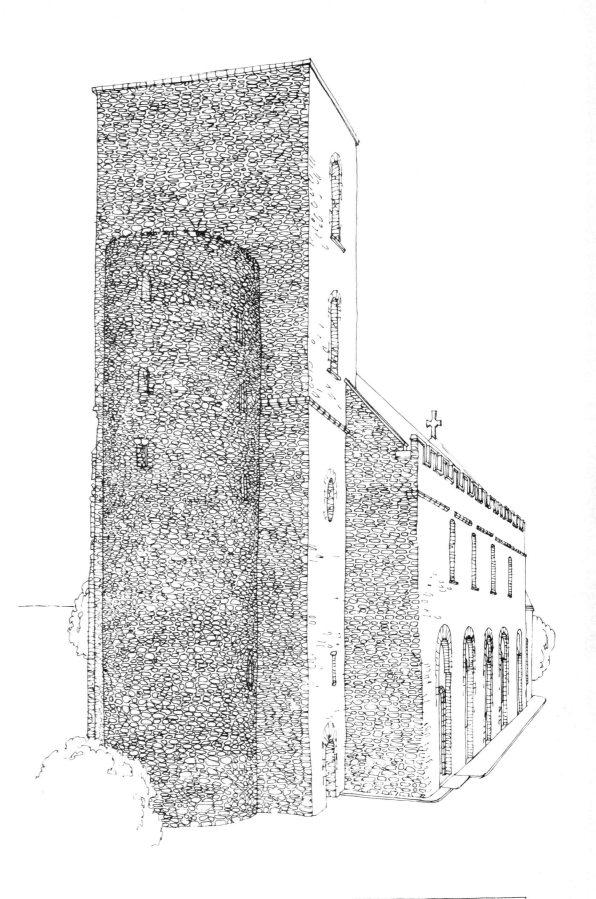

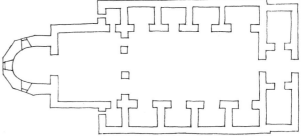

No one knows how many Scandinavians settled in England in the ninth and early tenth centuries. Contemporary writers, all of them Christian churchmen, naturally dwelt more on Vikings as raiders and plunderers than as settlers. The Anglo-Saxon Chronicle's account of the settlement in England is consequently very slight. In fact the only useful sources of information are linguistic evidence, and names. The language spoken by the Norse newcomers was closely related to the language of the English. But there were many differences of vocabulary and pronunciation, and the dialect of the areas in which the Scandinavians settled was greatly affected by them. Some important and useful English words, such as "them", "they", and "take" are of Scandinavian origin. The Scandinavian influence on placenames is even more obvious. The Vikings brought with them a fairly distinctive stock of personal names and words, which they used to describe farms and villages, hills, streams, woods and fields. Where the English would call a farm or a village a *tun*, from which we get the modern "town", the Scandinavians used their own word *by*, which means the same thing and is commonly used nowadays in the word by-law, meaning, literally, the law of the village. The English placenames Stanton and Stainby mean the same thing, but one is English and the other Scandinavian. When the Scandinavians used their own personal names, the contrast is sometimes even more marked: Aismunderby in Yorkshire and Osmondeston in Norfolk are basically the same name, but one, "Aismund's by", is Scandinavian, while the other, "Osmond's tun", is English. In the north and east of England a large number of such names are still in use; over 700, for example, end in *by*, and many others have the element *thorp*, meaning a lesser settlement. The study of these names can reveal a great deal about the extent of Viking settlements, about the main areas of colonization, and about the intermixture of the English and Scandinavian populations. It is also possible to distinguish Norwegians from Danes. If there is still disagreement about the number of colonists, there is no doubt that in most parts of the country the Scandinavian settlers and conquerors did not so much displace the English homesteaders as establish new homes on land that was as yet unoccupied. This was clearly the case in the north-west of England, where men of Norwegian descent settled in the late ninth century on land that was very thinly populated, or may, indeed, have been entirely free of human settlements. The areas of intense Scandinavian settlement were probably very limited in extent, and many of them were outside the main centres of population and wealth.

The Scandinavians were, however, conquerors as well as settlers, and in

VIKING ENGLAND

The map above shows English parishes which still have Scandinavian names. It also shows the line of the boundary agreed between King Alfred and the Danish leader Guthrum, probably soon after Alfred's capture of London in 886. According to their treaty the border was said to run "up the Thames, and then up the Lea, and along the Lea to its source, then in a straight line to Bedford, then up the Ouse to the Watling Street."

many parts of England, Scandinavian warriors replaced English lords. One such place was probably Middleton in the Vale of Pickering in Yorkshire, a village with an unmistakably English name but where, in the church, there are a number of crosses with distinctive Scandinavian ornament, two of them bearing representations of an easily recognizable Scandinavian burial. These must have been erected by the descendants of some Scandinavian chieftain who made his home in the village. Even so, the newcomers, particularly the relatively wealthy ones who settled in such villages as Middleton, soon became indistinguishable from the English, and acknowledged an English king. The Scandinavian conquests of English settlements were short-lived and had little effect on the main development of English history. Scandinavian settlements on new land, however, were far more significant, because their efforts at making a living in the north and east contributed greatly to the economic improvement that, in the eleventh century, made England such a rich and tempting prize to later Viking raiders.

THE VIKINGS CONVERTED

One of the remarkable Scandinavian-Christian crosses from the church at Middleton in Yorkshire. The panel shown here depicts a typical pagan Viking burial.

THE NEIGHBOURS

The map on the right shows part of the East Riding of Yorkshire with the large number of Scandinavian placenames that are found there. The best sites, with convenient access to the hills above and to the low-lying ground, generally have English names. There is a concentration of Scandinavian names, shown as dots, on the waterless Wolds (shaded areas). Others are less important settlements below the line of English settlements (the crosses).

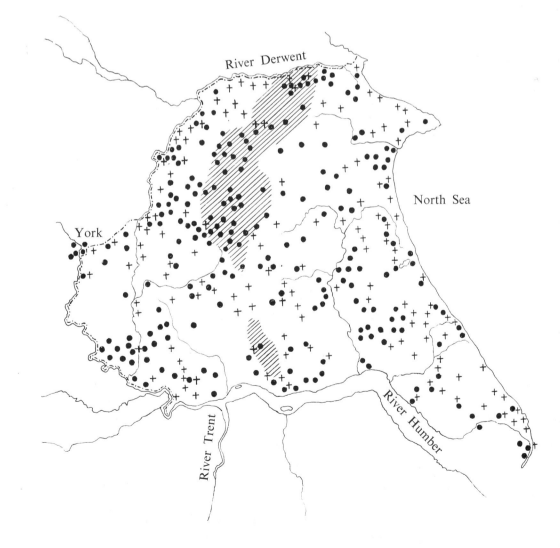

On September 26th, 1066, Harold, king of England, won one of the most significant victories in the history of medieval warfare. At Stamford Bridge the English showed that they had the answer to precisely the kind of mobile threat that had been posed by recent generations of Viking raiders. These marauders depended for their success on the speedy movement of relatively large bodies of well-armed men, and the psychological effect of their sudden appearance where they were least expected was as important an element in their success as their military skill. The real answer lay in being able quickly to mobilize a force adequate to counter the invaders wherever they popped up. That is exactly what the English Harold did at Stamford Bridge. His predecessor as king, Edward the Confessor, had left no heirs with strong direct claims. Harold, as Earl of Wessex, was the most powerful man in England, and being on the spot, was able to get himself crowned as soon as Edward was buried. However, in 1038 or 1039 Magnus king of Norway and Harthacnut, the last Danish king of England, had agreed that if either died without an heir, his kingdom should pass to the survivor. Harthacnut died without an heir, and Harald Hardrada, who succeeded Magnus as king of Norway, considered that the latter's rights had passed on to him. Allied to Harold of England's disaffected brother Tostig, he landed in the north of England, and on Thursday, September 20th, 1066 fought and won a battle against the local forces. When he then began proceeding the traditional way, demanding hostages and preparing to move south, he found himself forestalled by the unexpected arrival of the English king. The latter had made a forced march, probably from the south of England, and with the minimum of delay the Norwegians were brought to battle and defeated. Meanwhile, a second threat was developing to the south. William, Duke of Normandy, also considered that he had a strong claim to the English throne. It seems likely that Edward the Confessor had recognized William as his heir, probably during William's visit to England in 1051-52. Furthermore, when Harold had fallen into William's hands after being shipwrecked on the French coast in about 1064, he had solemnly acknowledged William as his lord and promised to help him to the English throne, or so William claimed. Harold can only have done this in order to escape from William's clutches, and regarded the oath as an empty one extracted under duress. When Harold gained the English crown, William proclaimed him an oath-breaker and prepared to make good his claim by force. Three days after Harold's victory in the north, William of Normandy made his long-awaited landing at Pevensey Bay, near Hastings. He knew what was

A CONFRONTATION OF COINS

The silver penny on top, showing King Ethelred, was struck about 1009. Below it is a coin of King Cnut, his Danish rival, with a portrait of the king in profile. Many coins like these found their way to Scandinavia in the purses of mercenaries employed by Cnut.

From *Heimskringla*:

Now the battle began. The Englishmen made a hot assault upon the Northmen, who sustained it bravely. And the fight at first was but loose and light, as long as the Northmen kept their order of battle; the English could do nothing against them. But when the Northmen thought they perceived that the enemy were making but weak assaults, they set after them, meaning to drive them into flight; but, when they had broken their shield-rampart, the Englishmen rode up from all sides, and threw arrows and spears on them. Now when King Harald Sigurdsson saw this, he went into the fray where the greatest clash of weapons was. There was a sharp conflict, and many people fell on both sides. King Harald then was in such a rage that he ran out in front of his men, and hewed down with both hands; neither helmet nor armour could withstand him, and all who were nearest gave way before him. It was then very near with the English that they had taken to flight.

King Harald Sigurdsson was hit by an arrow in the throat, and that was his death-wound; he fell, and all who had advanced with him, except those who retired with the banner. There was afterwards the warmest conflict, and Earl Tosti had taken over the king's banner. They began on both sides to form their array again, and for a long time there was a pause in the fighting. But before the battle began again, Harold Godwinesson offered his brother Earl Tosti peace, and also quarter to the Northmen who were still alive; but the Northmen called out all of them together that they would rather fall, one across the other, than accept of quarter from the Englishmen. They set up a war-shout, and the battle began again. Eystein Orri came up at this moment from the ships, with the men who followed him, and all were clad in armour. Then Eystein got King Harald's banner Land-Ravager. And now was, for the third time, one of the sharpest of conflicts; many of the Englishmen fell, and they were near to taking flight. This conflict is called Orri's storm. Eystein and his men had hastened so fast from the ships that they were quite exhausted, and scarcely fit to fight before they came into the battle; but afterwards they became so furious, that they did not guard themselves with their shields as long as they could stand upright. At last they threw off their coats of ring-mail, and then the Englishmen could easily lay their blows at them; and many fell from weariness, and died without a wound. Almost all the leaders of the Northmen fell.

needed, and had carefully prepared his fleet for the invasion. These preparations are well depicted in the Bayeux Tapestry, which also shows the landing itself with the horses stepping out of William's low, shallow-draught Viking ships. Harold was almost certainly still at York when he heard of the landing. He made a dramatic march south, covering the 250 miles in thirteen days. This achievement was the more remarkable when it is remembered that he had only shortly before made a similar rapid march north. He clearly recognized the need for speed, and his main mistake may well have been his over-confidence, which he paid for with his life at the battle of Hastings on October 14th.

William's landing proved the last successful operation of its kind to be mounted on a large scale in English history. The changes in the techniques of ship construction, which the needs of developing European commerce demanded, would in any case have made it difficult to stage an amphibious operation of this kind in the twelfth or thirteenth centuries. The traditional type of Viking ship continued to be used in Scandinavia, but generally for fighting in home waters, not for crossing the open sea. And even in Scandinavia there were changes leading to the development of larger fighting ships. The new need there was not so much for landing craft as for fighting platforms, and the advantage naturally lay with the larger ship that could command a battle. This was recognized and demonstrated by the Norwegian king Sverrir with his great *Mariasuden*, which, although unseaworthy, won its critical fight.

William himself was threatened by Scandinavian invasions. The most serious attack was that planned by Cnut of Denmark for the year 1085. The contemporary English chronicler describes how, when William found out about this, "he went to England with a larger force of mounted men and infantry from France and Brittany than had ever come to this country, so that people wondered how this country could maintain all that army. And the king had all the army dispersed all over the country among his vassals, and they provisioned the army each in proportion to his land." The real key in such operations lay, once again, in rapid mobilization and maintenance of an effective force. William found the answer in mercenaries, whose services could only be commanded by cash, which would also be needed to equip and keep them. The fact that England was rich had made it a prize worth attacking. But eventually, once the nature of the attacks and how to counteract them had been recognized, it was the richness of England that enabled her to insure herself militarily against invasion.

Ireland was much set upon by Vikings in the ninth and tenth centuries. The first attackers were Norwegians, whose landings seem to have been extensions of their settlement of Orkney, Shetland and the Hebrides. Already before the end of the eighth century the Annals of Ulster report: "Patrick's Island was burned by the Gentiles; and they took away tribute from the provinces, and Dochonna's shrine was broken by them, and other great incursions were made by them, both in Ireland and in Scotland." In the following years such attacks were common, and the Irish chronicles are full of tales of destruction and pillage by these pagan strangers from the north. Many such tales were exaggerated. One chronicler wrote: "The entire town of Munster, without distinction, was plundered by them, on all sides, and devastated. And they spread themselves over Munster; and they build duns,* camps and fortresses, and landing-ports all over Erinn, so that there was no place in Erinn without numerous fleets of Danes and pirates; so that they made spoil-land and sword-land and conquered-land of her, throughout her breadth and generally; and they ravaged her chieftainries and her privileged churches and her sanctuaries and they rent her shrines and her reliquaries and her books. They demolished her beautiful ornamented temples; for neither veneration, nor honour, nor mercy for Termonn [sanctuaries] nor protection for Church or for sanctuary, for God or for man was felt by this furious, ferocious, pagan, ruthless, wrathful people. In short, until the sand of the sea or the grass of the field or the stars of heaven are counted, it will not be easy to recount or to enumerate or to relate what the Irish all, without distinction, suffered from them; whether men or women, boys or girls, lay or clerks, free men or serfs, old or young; indignity, outrage, injury and oppression." The purpose of the raiders seems to have been the search for plunder rather than land; neither archaeology nor place-names suggest that the Scandinavian settlements in Ireland were dense or extensive. Their main holdings were along the coast where, in such centres as Dublin and Waterford, they established trading towns that later grew in importance. The monasteries of Ireland may well have attracted raiders because of their riches of gold and silver, and the hoard of silver objects recently found in the Shetlands on St. Ninian's Isle may well be the profits of such raids. The plundering expeditions of the Vikings were made easier by the complex and accessible system of rivers that reach far into the island. None of the holy places of Ireland was far from the coast or such inland waterways,

* hilltop camps

THE ISLE OF MAN

For the Scandinavian chieftains and traders who sailed the Irish Sea, the Isle of Man must have been a prominent landmark. The Scandinavians did not, however, simply use the islands as a landmark, they settled there. Scandinavian influence is revealed in such placenames as Ramsey or Laxey and in the Viking graves and ornate memorial stones that are found there, often in Christian burial grounds. It is significant that the unity once created by these Scandinavian seamen who pillaged Iona and other churches should be commemorated in a Christian diocese. The see of Sodor and Man unites the Isle of Man with the Sudreys, the Southern Isles, the name the Scandinavians gave to the Hebrides.

ODIN IS EATEN, CHRIST IS VICTORIOUS

The Thorwald cross at Andreas, in the northern part of the Isle of Man, is on a stone slab. Beside it is depicted a scene from the legendary Norse poem Ragnarök, *"Doomsday of the Gods", in which the great god Odin is eaten by the wolf Fenris. Another side of the same slab depicts the coming of Christianity, represented by a figure bearing a cross and a Bible.*

GALLOWAY

BANGOR

ARMAGH

CARLINGFORD

DUNDALK

SLIGO

ISLE
OF MAN

L. Ree

CLONMACNOISE

GALWAY

DUBLIN

CLONTARF

CLONFERT

LORRHA

R. Liffey

L. Derg

TIRRGLASS

CHESTER

R. Shannon

R. Slaney

LIMERICK

CASHEL

ARKLOW

IRISH SEA

WATERFORD

WEXFORD

WALES

CORK

R. Bride

BRISTOL

BRISTOL CHANNEL

IRELAND AND THE IRISH SEA IN THE VIKING AGE

*This map shows the principal places and main
rivers, and towns in Britain that had trade connections with Ireland. The Irish kingdoms and
their boundaries are not included, as they did not
remain permanent throughout the Viking Age.*

and they all suffered in consequence. The raiders were also aided by the bitter internal rivalry between warring Irish clans and chiefs and by the fact that some Irish hoped to use the Vikings as useful allies.

A number of Irish went into exile to escape the ravages of the heathens, some of them finding refuge in the Carolingian lands, in places like Liège, Laon and Rheims. These men brought books and drawings which had some influence on the thought and art of the time. The most famous of all these Irish emigrés was John Scottus, the great philosopher who was one of the few men in his time to master Greek. In the margins of a book brought from Ireland at this period is a little verse which reflects the fear of the Vikings that drove some men from their native land:

> Bitter is the wind tonight
>
> In tosses the ocean's white hair.
>
> Tonight I fear not the fierce warriors of Norway
>
> Coursing the Irish Sea.

The Irish were not the only emigrants from Ireland in the ninth century. Within a century of their first attacks, men of Norwegian descent were leaving Ireland to search for new homes westward toward Iceland or eastwards in England. The reasons for this are not clear. The Scandinavians who stayed on in Ireland were those interested in war or in trade, but for both, the key area was the Irish Sea. There were several attempts in the first half of the tenth century to join Dublin and York together under the rule of one chieftain, and after these had failed, the men of Dublin, the Ost men, so called because of their Scandinavian or eastern origin, were active in a trade that joined the west of France, Bristol, Chester and the Scandinavian north. The commercial importance of the towns, and of Dublin in particular, survived the great military defeat of the Scandinavian intruders at the famous battle of Clontarf, outside Dublin, in 1014. In this battle, the great men on both sides, Brian, king of the Irish, and Sigurth from Orkney, both fell. But the king of Dublin, Sigtrygg Silkbeard, took no part, and watched the battle from the security of Dublin, which he continued to rule profitably for another twenty years.

BURIED TREASURE, PERHAPS FROM IRELAND

For ten centuries, a treasure which may be loot from a Viking raid on Ireland lay buried in the remains of a tiny, pre-Viking church on St. Ninian's Isle, a lonely dot of land in the southern Shetlands not far north of Jarlshof. Some of the articles are bowls, brooches and sword furniture, but others are of ecclesiastical origin.

1. *Communion spoon, with dog's head lapping from the bowl, and a one-pronged edged implement possibly used for cutting and picking up the Host.*
2. *Bowl with design of four pairs of animals.*
3. *Sword-pommel, once gilded. It has a silver pin inside, possibly for using the pommel as a brooch.*
4. *Inscribed hooped mounting with animal heads. It may have been a protective tip for a sword scabbard, or else a weight for a stole.*
5. *Silver bowl with loop attachments for hanging up.*
6. *Detail of underside of the hanging bowl, showing a spreadeagled dog or boar.*

Among the most northward Atlantic islands are the Faroes, or "islands of sheep." They are difficult to approach, with steep jagged cliffs rising from rough seas. But above are green fields, and a climate so mild that the sheep which have given the islands their name can stay out all the year round. For some reason, however, there have never been any trees on the Faroes. There were no true "aboriginal" people there. But when the first Norwegians came to the Faroe Islands they nevertheless found some inhabitants. About 825 A.D. the Irish monk Dicuil said in his book *De Mensura Orbis Terra* (Concerning the Distances of the Earth) that: "For a century the hermit's life has brought large numbers of Irish monks to the many islands in the northern part of the British Sea, which one could reach from the north British islands in two days and nights when the wind was favourable. Those islands, uninhabited and unnamed since the world began, have now been abandoned by the hermits in consequence of the arrival of Scandinavian pirates. There are countless sheep and a lot of different seabirds to be found..." The islands alluded to may include Iceland, but at any rate they certainly include the Faroes, because the rest of the Atlantic island groups, even the most distant of the Shetlands, could be reached in half of the stated sailing time. The reasons for the Viking settlement appear to have been the search for new land to cultivate, due to a shortage of land in the homeland, and emigration in protest against King Harald Fairhair's régime, which also characterized the emigration to Iceland. The Faroes have their own saga, *Färoeinga Saga*, which was written down in Iceland about 1200 A.D.: "There was a man called Grim Kamban," runs the saga, "He was the first one who settled in the Faroe Islands in Harald Fairhair's time. At the time many left the country because of the king's lust for power. Some settled down on the Faroe Islands and cultivated new land there." The Icelandic historian Snorre Sturluson says that in the summer the colonists cruised back to their former homes in Norway to ravage there.

At Tjörnuvik on the island of Streymöy, a small graveyard from the tenth century has been found. The only object which could be dated is a ring-headed pin of bronze, of Scottish type. At Kvivik, also on Streymöy, two house-sites have been excavated, both of a well-known oval shape with a "long-fire" in the middle of the floor, which have these and other features in common with the Lindholm Höje site in Denmark. However, they cannot be dated more accurately than around the year 1000. A similar house-site is known in Fuglafjördur on the island of Eysturoy.

THE FAROES

These bleak islands are situated in the North Atlantic, about midway between Scotland and Iceland, and 415 miles from Norway. Traces of Viking settlement have been found at Tjörnuvik and Kvívík on Streymöy, and at Fuglafjordur on Eysturöy.
The total area of the twenty-one islands is approximately 540 square miles. Narrow waters and dangerous currents separate them.

THE ISLANDS OF SHEEP

The Faroese landscape, seen at right at the village of Kirkeby, is bleak and windswept, consisting of bare rock and grass lashed by the wind and the sea. It must have reminded the Viking settlers of the islands off the Atlantic coast of Norway.

Iceland is the third largest island in the North Atlantic, after Greenland and England, Scotland and Wales. Lying across the Arctic Circle, it is made habitable for human beings only by the warm currents of the Gulf Stream. The history of Iceland shows how the Vikings took a previously uninhabited country and made it their own, and how they set up an organized community after their own tastes without any external pressures. Iceland was destined to become a chosen sanctuary for Norse culture, a place where the memories and history of the North Germanic race were more diligently preserved than anywhere else, and recorded in books which are today the richest source of knowledge of the Viking Age.

Who were the people who colonized Iceland? Imagine that we are in one of the deep, winding fjords of Western Norway, some time in the last decades of the ninth century A.D. Along the shoreline, drawn up on the beach, are some long, narrow boats, set with shields from stem to stern, easily recognizable as the war galleys or longships of the Viking voyages. Beside them are other ships, shorter, wider and with a higher gunwale; not so lithe and deadly-looking as the warships, but solid, sea-going vessels. A small one is being loaded. People are carrying all kinds of baggage and stores aboard — household articles of every sort, and livestock: sheep, cattle, horses, pigs, even squawking chickens. Finally the people themselves embark — rugged, bearded men, young and old, girt with swords, carrying spears, axes and shields; women in full-length gowns of homespun, youngsters and babies. They say goodbye to a group of friends; then the boat is pushed off and rowed out into the fjord. When a fair wind begins to blow, a square sail is hoisted and the vessel moves slowly out of the fjord to sea. The course is northwest. Gradually the sail grows smaller and smaller to the lingering watchers left behind, and it finally disappears. Such scenes were common. The captain and owner of the boat was on his way to colonize Iceland with his family and attendants.

The story of the "Landtaking" or Time of Settlements and of the earliest history of Iceland is recorded mainly in the priest Ari Thorgilsson's *Book of the Icelanders*, written about 1100 A.D. But other elements also appear in the various versions of the *Book of the Settlements*, a large work by many writers, as well as in the great Family Sagas, like *Egil's Saga*, dealing with events in the tenth century.

The basic elements of the ancient records are undoubtedly based on sound tradition. Although the discovery and the earliest settlement of Iceland were not reported in any written sources, it can be inferred from archaeological

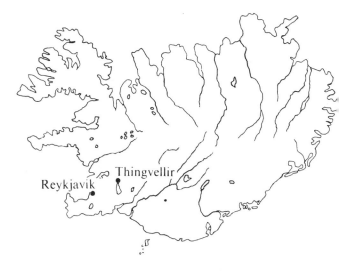

A NEW LAND GETS A COLD NAME

The Book of the Settlements *relates how an early Viking voyager, Floki, and his followers reached the east coast of an island in the North Atlantic:* "*They sailed then to the south of the land. But when they sailed west of Reykjanes, and the fjord opened so that they saw Snaefellsnes, Faxi said: 'It must be a big land which we have found; here are large rivers.' That is since called Faxaós. Floki and his men sailed westward over Breida-fjord. The fjord was full of fish, and because of the fishing they neglected to provide themselves with hay, and their cattle all died in the winter. The spring was rather cold. Floki went north on the mountain and saw a fjord full of ice; and they called the land Iceland, as it has since been called. In the summer they returned to Norway.*" *The latitude of the southernmost point of the island is 63° 24' North, and that of the northernmost, 66° 32' North. The coastline is indented with firths and inlets, and the interior of the country is mountainous, with glaciers, stretches of sand and lava fields.*

THE FIRST SETTLER'S PILLARS ARE FOUND

From the Book of the Settlements
*As soon as Ingolf sighted Iceland, he cast his
high-seat pillars* overboard for an omen, vowing
he would settle where the pillars came ashore.
Vifil and Karli found his high-seat pillars by
Arnarhval, west of the heath. In the spring Ingolf
came down over the heath, to site his home where
his pillars had come ashore, and lived at Reykjavik. Ingolf was the most celebrated of all the
settlers, for he came here to an unlived-in country
and was the first to settle down in it: the other
settlers did so by his example.*

* *part of his house furniture*

THE ISLANDS OF MURDER

*The Westman Islands, seen on the next page, rise
majestically out of turbulent seas off the south
coast of Iceland. Grim and forbidding, they are
an appropriate setting for the story told in the
Book of the Settlements, which says that the
islands got their name from some Irish slaves
(Westmen) killed there by Ingolf the settler.*

finds that Iceland was first populated very near the middle of the Viking Age.
And yet, according to Ari Thorgilsson, the settlers found a few Irish hermits,
whom the Norsemen called *papar*, *i.e.* priests. These people must have managed to get to Iceland from Ireland in their frail currachs; tiny oared boats of
skin and wicker. They are reported to have fled when the Norsemen came because they hated the heathen ways of the new arrivals.

Iceland was separated from the nearest inhabited land, Scotland and Norway,
respectively by 431 and 529 miles of open sea. The North Atlantic is not a
gentle ocean, so such distances as these presented an almost insurmountable
barrier prior to the remarkable advances made in ship-building and navigation

in Norway in the Viking Age. The Norwegians had their eyes turned to the west, looking for land no less than for fame and booty. Once discovered, Iceland was bound to become populated, since in many ways it offered farming conditions similar to, and in some respects better than, those in Norway. Norway was almost certainly an overpopulated country in the Viking Age, exhausted from long exploitation of its agricultural resources — a fact which in part explains the Viking voyages in general.

From the *Book of the Settlements* we know the names and families of all the leaders among the settlers, and where they came from, back home. The great majority were of Norwegian descent, and a few were probably Swedish or Danish. Some settlers were of mixed stock, and did not come to Iceland direct from Norway. They belonged to families who had lived for some time in the

INGOLF OF ICELAND

From the *Book of the Settlements*
Iceland was first settled from Norway in the days of Harald Fairhair, son of Halfdan the Black, at the time (according to the belief and account of Teit my tutor, son of Bishop Isleif, and the wisest man I have known) when Ivar, Ragnar Lodbrok's son, had the English king Saint Edmund put to death, and that was 870 years after the birth of Christ, according to what is written in his, Edmund's saga. A Norwegian named Ingolf is the man of whom it is reliably reported that he was the first to leave there for Iceland, when Harald Fairhair was sixteen years old, and a second time a few years later. He settled south in Reykjavik.

NORSE EMIGRANTS LEAVING FOR ICELAND

Though Iceland was a Viking settlement, a great many of the settlers had never taken part in the famous and infamous Viking raids. They were simply people looking for land, more interested in cattle and sheep and good pastureland than in warfare, loot and glory. The drawing above is an attempt at reconstructing a scene in a Norwegian fjord towards the end of the ninth century, based on archaeological finds and contemporary chronicles. An emigrant family are taking leave of their friends, bringing their livestock and household articles on board ship for a three-week trip which will take them to their new home on the distant island in the ocean.

Viking colonies in the British Isles. Not a few of the settlers had Celtic blood in their veins, other had Celtic wives, and they certainly brought with them many followers of Celtic stock. Even so, the prevailing culture — material, spiritual and social — was Viking.

In Iceland Viking settlers established themselves as farmers. Although great tracts of this land of glaciers and volcanoes are uninhabitable, especially in the interior, everywhere near the coast there are plains and valleys with wide sweeps of grassland, excellent for raising sheep and cattle. Among the cereals, only barley could be grown successfully in these cold northern latitudes. Fish abounded in the seas, lakes and rivers, and from the very beginning formed an important part of the people's livelihood. The island harboured many kinds of birds. In many parts of the country there were extensive birch-woods, which

IRISH HERMITS IN ICELAND

From the *Book of the Icelanders*:
There were Christian men here then whom the Norsemen call "papar". But later they went away because they were not prepared to live here in company with heathen men. They left behind Irish books, bells and croziers, from which it could be seen that they were Irishmen.

From the writings of Dicuil, an Irish monk, about A.D. 825:
It is now thirty years since priests who lived in that island from the first day of February to the first day of August told me that not only at the summer solstice, but in the days on either side of it, the setting sun hides itself at the evening hour as if behind a little hill, so that no darkness occurs during that very brief period of time, but whatever task a man wishes to perform, even to picking the lice out of his shirt, he can manage it precisely as if in broad daylight. And had they been on a high mountain, the sun would at no time have been hidden from them.

RUNIC INFLUENCE IN ICELANDIC ART

The carved panel on the opposite page was discovered on Flatatunga farm in the north of Iceland. No rune-stones have been found in Iceland, but this panel shows foliage of rune-stone type in full bloom, as well as haloed human figures which show how Christian saints were represented in Northern art.

provided fuel for heating the houses and making charcoal. Great quantities of bog ore allowed the settlers to pursue the ancient art of iron-working. The ocean protected the islanders against external enemies, yet it was not too wide to prevent Icelandic and foreign merchants from keeping up a lively trade between Iceland and several other countries. Above all, there was plenty of room for everybody — at least in the beginning.

Then, there were about 400 *landsnámsmenn* or leading colonizers. The total number of the people who migrated to Iceland is, of course, much higher. Some scholars think that the population totalled about 30,000 by 930. Until that time there was no universal system of law and justice in Iceland. Naturally the settlers brought their own codes from their homelands. The main characteristics of the Viking were individualism and personal pride, and these found fertile soil in the new country. As time passed, however, the need for a more organized political system was more and more keenly felt. It was an ancient custom of the Teutonic peoples to settle their disputes at meetings called *things*, where every free man could come and defend his rights. In the year 930 the first great event in the history of Iceland occurred — the establishment of the general assembly or parliament of the whole nation (Althing). This was the first step in the foundation of the old Icelandic republic. "*Apud illos non est rex, nisi tantum lex*", wrote the historian Adam of Bremen, discussing the Icelanders about 1076 A.D. "They have no king; only law." The republic was a democracy, or, as it is sometimes called, an aristo-democracy, in which the chiefs divided the power between them and formed the Althing. As a meeting-place they chose the magnificent lava plain of Thingvellir in the south-west of Iceland.

What appeared to be a republic was a kind of interlocked family dynasty. Most of the chiefs who were given the greatest power at the foundation of the Althing are thought to have been either members of the same family or connected with it through marriage, descendants of a certain Björn buna, a chief of Sogn in Norway. According to this theory, the members of the family joined hands and divided the power between them throughout the country. This explains how a tricky operation such as the foundation of the Althing and the republic could take place peacefully. The country was divided into twelve, later thirteen, lesser *things* (a word which also meant jurisdictions), and there were three chiefs in each *thing*. These thirty-six (later thirty-nine) chiefs formed the legislative body of the Althing, where the laws were made, and so shared the supreme power between them.

In the course of time the Icelanders compiled extensive codes of law, which in later times were known as the Grágás, the laws of the ancient republic. During the first couple of centuries, these laws were not written down. The Law-speaker or *lögsögumaör* presided over the legislature (*logrétta*) and in a way was the president of the Althing. He had to know all the laws by heart and proclaim them at the Althing during his three years in office, reciting one-third of them each year. Eventually the ancient laws were put into writing in the year 1118.

The parliament was also a judicial assembly with four courts, one for each quarter of the country, and later a fifth court was set up, the supreme court or court of appeal. But strangely enough, the Icelandic parliament had no executive power. When sentence had been passed, it lay in the hands of individuals to enforce it. In the long run this primitive feature proved dangerous to the stability of society. During the fourteen days every midsummer that it lasted, the Althing was a national meeting-place, a festival in which everybody was entitled to take part. Chieftains from all parts of the country brought large groups of followers with them. Young people liked to go to the Althing, men and women, craftsmen of many kinds, traders, tramps and adventurers. At Thingvellir people met in friendship and in hostility, sentences were passed and fates were sealed.

More than anything else, the Althing helped to form a nation from the more or less unorganized masses of people who kept pouring into the new country for various directions during the last years of the ninth century.

The free republic of ancient Iceland survived in its original form until 1262, when the king of Norway succeeded in his long-cherished plan of bringing the Icelanders under his rule. The old governmental system of the Viking Age had had its day. But the memory of it lived on, and for the Icelanders of to-day, the descendants of the Viking settlers, Thingvellir symbolizes the golden age of freedom. For them, it is a challenge to preserve an inheritance that can be traced back over a thousand years.

Half way through the eleventh century, the population of Iceland had probably almost doubled, to about 60,000. That, roughly speaking, was the greatest number of people Iceland could support at this stage of agricultural development (although the *Book of the Icelanders* says that all land had been " occupied " — " possessed " is more likely — a century earlier). Farms had been built wherever it was possible to live, from the outermost coastal headlands to the deepest valleys that reached inland towards the barren and uninhabitable parts of the highlands. Many farms built hopefully in the no-man's-land between habitable and uninhabitable country quickly fell into disuse. Some of them have not been rebuilt or lived in since.

Places of this kind offer a fine opportunity for investigating the kind of house

THE LAWSPEAKERS

From the *Book of the Icelanders*:
Wise men have said that in the space of fifty years Iceland was fully occupied, so that after that there was no further taking of land. About then Hrafn, son of Haeng the Settler, took the lawspeakership next after Ulfljot and held it for twenty summers [A.D. 930-49]. He was from Rangarhverfi. This was sixty years after the slaughter of King Edmund, and a winter or two before King Harald Fairhair died, according to the reckoning of well-informed men. Thorarin, brother of Ragi and son of Oleif Hjalti, took the lawspeakership next after Hrafn and held it a further twenty summers [950-69]. He was a Borgarfjord man.

FAIR SHARES FOR ALL

From the *Book of the Settlements*:
Some of those who came out earliest lived close up to the mountains, remarking the quality of the land there, and how the livestock was keen to get away from the sea up to the high ground. Those who came out later thought that these first-comers had made over-extensive settlements; but King Harald Fairhair made peace between them on these terms, that no one should settle land more widely than he and his crew could carry fire round in one day. They must light further smoke-fires, so that each might be observed from the other, and those fires which were lighted when the sun showed in the east must burn till nightfall. Afterwards they must walk until the sun was in the west, and at that point light other fires.
. . . It was the law that a woman should not take land in settlement more widely than a two-year-old heifer, a half-stalled beast in good condition, might be led round on a spring day between the rising and setting of the sun.

From the *Book of the Icelanders*:
And when Iceland had become settled far and wide a Norwegian named Ulfljot first brought law out here from Norway (so Teit told us); this was called Ulfljot's law. He was the father of that Gunnar from whom the Djupadalers are descended in Eyjafjord. For the most part these laws were modelled upon the then Gulathing Law, on the advice of Thorleif the Wise, Horda-Kari's son, as to what should be added, taken away or be differently set out. Ulfljot lived east in Lon. It is said that Grim Geitskor was his fosterbrother, he who at Ulfljot's direction explored the whole of Iceland before the Althing was established. For this every man in the land gave him a penny, which he later donated to the temples.

A STRANGE SITE FOR A PARLIAMENT

The lava plain of Thingvellir (shown on the following page), where the Icelandic parliament met each summer is not merely a landmark in Scandinavian history; it is also famous for its strange and bright-hued geological formations.

the Vikings built in their new-found country. Ari the historian, in the *Book of the Icelanders*, states that at the time of the settlements the country was covered with forest between mountains and seashore. This must not be taken too literally. The " forest " must have been the same kind of birch-wood that is still found in Iceland. It does not yield timber suitable for building. Probably an abundance of driftwood made up for this lack. The Viking settlers built their houses with thick walls of turf and rough stones. The houses were basically oblong, but slightly oval in shape, and consisted of a large hall with a *langeldr* or long fire burning in the middle of the floor, and sleeping-benches along the walls. These houses were quite impressive, and followed more or less perfectly the building customs that the settlers had known in their own countries. This type of house proved ill-suited, however, to the cold and wet climate of Iceland. Before long came the development of the feature that particularly characterizes Icelandic house design: the large hall was divided into a number of smaller apartments, which did not need such large timbers for their construction, and were far easier to heat.

The other major group of archaeological finds in Iceland, the grave finds, yield much information on the religion of the Vikings. The settlers of Iceland were for the most part heathen, though some of them knew a little of the Christian faith, and others were actually Christian. Some were mixed in their beliefs. Helgi the Lean, for instance, believed in Christ, and called his farm Kristnes in His honour. But he made vows to Thor before sea voyages, when in a tight corner, or in fact whenever circumstances of real importance arose. All over Iceland there are farms with the name *hof*, *i.e.* temple, and it may be assumed that on all such sites heathen places of worship once stood. But it has proved as difficult in Iceland as elsewhere to decide what these edifices were like, and the same is true of many other details in the Icelanders' religion. The most important sources of information on this subject are the Poetic Edda, a collection of poems about gods and heroes of ancient times composed in Iceland, and the Prose Edda, the mythological treatise compiled in 1220 by the Icelandic chieftain, poet and historian Snorre Sturluson. This was two centuries after heathendom had come to an end in Iceland, and parts of the Edda may, therefore, be unreliable.

Graves from the Viking Age have been found in most parts of Iceland. It is surprising that cremation seems to have been quite unknown there, even though the settlers came from countries where cremation was as frequent as burial. The dead were buried in low mounds of earth and rough stones. They were fully dressed, the men with their weapons — which in some cases are of the finest quality — the women with their jewellery. Sometimes the deceased was buried

THE ALTHING IN SESSION

A reconstruction (left) of a part of the scene at Thingvellir during a session of the Althing, the Icelandic parliamentary session held once a year at about the end of June and the beginning of July. To the right is the so-called Law Rock, which was the centre of parliamentary activites and the place where the president of the Althing, the Lawspeaker, took his stand. A group of men are gathered at the Law Rock, and more are on their way to it. A lawsuit is about to be cited, or some public announcement made. The Law Rock is an excellent place from where to speak, for voices reverberate from the perpendicular wall behind, known as Almannagjá. On the plain below and in front of the Law Rock, the attendants of the chieftains are going about their everyday duties, cooking food and carrying water, and looking after the horses and the booths or huts, of which there were many hundreds. The walls were of turf and stones but the roofs were homespun woollen cloth, and put up for the occasion only.

From the *Book of the Icelanders*:
The Althing was established where it is now at the instance of Ulfljot and all the people of Iceland; but before this there had been a thing at Kalarnes, which Thorstein, son of Ingolf the Settler, and father of Thorkel Mani the Lawspeaker, held there together with those chieftains who allied themselves with it. But a man who owned the land at Blaskogar had been outlawed for the murder of a thrall or freedman. His name is given as Thorir Cropbeard, and his daughter's son was called Thorvald Cropbeard, the one who later went to the Eastfirths and there burnt his own brother Gunnar to death (so Hall Oraekjuson told us). The name of the murdered man was Kol, from whom the ravine gets its name, which has ever since been called Kolsgja, where the corpse was discovered. The land thereafter became public domain, and the Icelandic people set it apart for the use of the Althing, for which reason wood can be cut free for the Althing in the forests there, and on the heaths there are common pastures for the use of the horses. This Ulfhedin told us.

in a boat, as in Scandinavia, but the custom was rare. It was, on the other hand, usual — more so than elsewhere in Viking areas — to bury a horse with the body. Strong and hardy Icelandic ponies had become numerous early on. They had found excellent living conditions, and it cost little to provide the dead man with a mount for his last journey.

When, by the consent of the Althing, the Icelanders officially adopted Christianity in the year 1000, heathen burial customs ceased. Odin, Thor, Freyr and other heathen gods were gradually replaced by Christ and the saints. The Icelandic church was not, however, fully organized until the first Icelandic bishop, Isleif, was consecrated in 1056. The establishment of an episcopal see in Iceland marks the end of the real Viking Age there, since from that time onwards the country is just one of the many strongholds of the Church of Rome. But in spite of this, much of the spirit of the Viking Age lived on with remarkable tenacity in this remote island in the Atlantic. Even today, the Icelanders speak a language which is only slightly different from that spoken by their Viking ancestors who claimed the country for human habitation nearly 1100 years ago.

THE CONVERSION OF THE ICELANDERS

From the *Book of the Icelanders*:
The next day Gizur and Hjalti (who were trying to get Christianity adopted in Iceland) went to the Law Rock and made known their message, and report says that it was remarkable how well they spoke. And what followed from this was that one man after another, Christian and heathen, called witnesses, each swearing that he would not live under the same laws as the other, after which they left the Law Rock.
Then the Christians requested Hall of Sida that he should proclaim that law which was right and proper for Christians; but he got out of this in that he made payment to Thorgeir the Lawspeaker that he should proclaim the law — even though he was still a heathen. And later when men had returned to their booths, Thorgeir lay down and spread his cloak over him, and lay quiet all that day and the night following, and spoke never a word. But the next morning he sat up and announced that men should proceed to the Law Rock, and once men had made their way there he began his speech . . .
"I think it policy that we do not let those prevail who are most anxious to be at each other's throats, but reach such a compromise in these matters that each shall win part of his case, and let all have one law and one faith. It will prove true if we break the law in pieces, that we break the peace in pieces too." And he so concluded his speech that both sides agreed that all should have that one law which he would proclaim.
Then it was made law that all men should be Christians, and be baptized, those who so far were unbaptized here in Iceland. But as for the exposure of infants, the old laws should stand, and for the eating of horseflesh too. Men might sacrifice in secret if they so wished, but it would be a case for lesser outlawry should witnesses come forward. But a few years later this heathendom was abolished like the rest. This was the way, Teit told us, that Christianity came to Iceland.

THE FLATEYJARBOK, THE MOST MAGNIFICENT OF THE MEDIAEVAL ICELANDIC MANUSCRIPTS

A detail from a page in the Flateyjarbók, which contains among other things the lives of the kings of Norway. The miniature shows the Viking and missionary king, Olaf Haraldsson, being killed in the famous battle of Stiklarstad 1030 A.D.

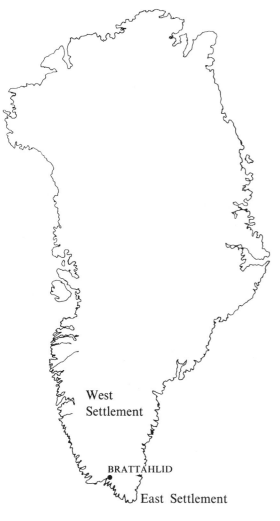

GREENLAND

Greenland is the largest island in the world, having an area of 840,000 square miles, a length of 1650 miles and a breadth of 760 miles, but nearly all of it lies inside the Arctic Circle, and about five-sixths is permanently under ice. From Viking times onwards, European settlers have been confined mainly to the south-west, where grass, bushes and a few small trees grow.

"GREENLAND": A STRANGE EXPLANATION

From the writings of Adam of Bremen, about 1076 A.D:
In the ocean there are very many islands, of which not the least is Greenland, situated far out in the ocean opposite the mountains of Sweden ... To this island, they say, it is from five to seven days' sail from the coast of Norway, the same as to Iceland. The people there are greenish from the salt water, whence, too, that region gets its name. The people live in the same manner as the Icelanders, except that they are fiercer and trouble seafarers by their piratical attacks. Report has it that Christianity of late has also winged its way to them.

GREENLAND: A STRUGGLE FOR LIFE

Around the year 960 a boy named Erik, later called Erik the Red, and his father Thorval were forced to leave their home in Jären in southern Norway, after Thorval had been concerned in a murder. Erik and Thorval found a new home in Iceland, like many others before them. Erik had inherited his father's quarrelsome temper. History repeated itself. After committing two murders, in about 985, he was outlawed for three years. Erik had heard about a man, Gunbjörn, whose ship, early in the same century, had been driven off course, far to the west. Here he had seen a hitherto unknown land. Erik decided to try to find " Gunbjörn's Rock ", as the land had been called. It was as good a way as any other of staying away from Iceland for a while. He eventually reached " Gunbjörn's Rock " at its most inhospitable point, the east coast, where nothing tempted him to go ashore. The drift-ice threatened his ship every hour of the day and night. Nevertheless he set course south, and worked down to Cape Farewell, then turned north again. Here he found fertile valleys with green grass suitable for cattle and sheep, rivers full of fish, and walrus and seal in the sea. After exploring for two more summers as far north as Disko Island, Erik went home to Iceland. He had sailed about 2800 miles, not counting detours into the fjords. On Iceland land was short, so it was easy for Erik to find people who were interested in moving with him to Greenland. Erik had named the new country thus because, he said, people like to go to a new land only if it has an attractive name. In the following summer Erik led a fleet of twenty-five ships, each fully loaded with eager emigrants and their goods. There must have been about 500 people in all. But only fourteen of the ships got through. Some were wrecked in the high seas, currents, fogs and ice off Greenland. Others drifted back to Iceland. In the succeeding years, several more ships went off to Greenland. The East Settlement, in its prime, included about 200 homesteads. The West Settlement, which lay about 300 miles further north, comprised about a hundred homesteads. In all, the Viking population of Greenland might have totalled about 3000 inhabitants. Erik seems to have chosen the place for his own home on his first voyages. It was called Brattahlid, and was situated at the inner end of Erik's Fjord, which today is called Tunigdliarfik. Its ruins have been excavated, together with those of other village farmhouses, monasteries and churches. Christianity inevitably reached Greenland. It was Leif, the son of Erik the Red, who first brought the Faith with him, after he had been christened by King Olaf Tryggvason of Norway in 999. He took a priest back with him to undertake missionary work in Greenland.

The saga has this to say about the homeward voyage, which became historic: "Now Leif went off on his homeward journey. He drifted around on the sea for a long time, and he found countries of which he had earlier known nothing. Here [Vinland] there were self-sown wheat fields, and trees so big that they could be used as timber for house-building. Leif also found some people who had been shipwrecked on a rock, and brought them back with him. Leif landed in Erik's Fjord, and later went home to Brattahlid, to a warm welcome. Soon he started to preach the Christian faith, and delivered King Olaf Tryggvason's message to the people, that explained how much holiness and glory there was in the new religion. His father Erik was slow to become a convert, but his wife Thjodhilde was soon persuaded, and she had a church built at some distance from the houses. There she and the others who had accepted Christianity said their prayers. From the time Thjodhilde adopted the faith, she refused to have intercourse with Erik, and this he disliked very much . . ."

So began the hard struggle for existence of a little society which stood fast for nearly 500 years before being extinguished. It was a poor life, ruled by the shortage of raw materials, among other things wood for building ships and houses. The settlers lacked iron too, but in most cases they understood how to make do with existing materials: driftwood, whalebone and stone.

They did not succeed in growing corn. Sheep and cattle, together with fishing and hunting, kept them alive. But these provided a bare existence, on the borderline of starvation. Just one hard winter could be disastrous. Cairns have been found on the island of Kingigtorssuag, 900 miles north of Cape Farewell, with a runic inscription commemorating the men who ventured thus far in the fourteenth century. It was the yield of such hunting trips that provided the Greenlanders with their main exports, the furs and skins, the walrus ivory, Greenland falcons and even Polar bears, which were in great demand in medieval Europe. The teeth of the narwhal should not be forgotten. In medieval Europe, they were thought of as the horns of unicorns. They were regarded as being full of potent magic, and therefore commanded enormous sums. By selling all these goods the Greenlanders were able to buy from Europe the goods, especially the tools, on which their life literally depended. By the fifteenth century these Norse settlements in Greenland had disappeared, possibly because the climate, already bad enough, got worse. After the union of Iceland with Norway in the middle of the thirteenth century, Greenlanders were forbidden to have ships of their own. They were in no position to defy such a ban, and total dependence on the ships of others to bring timber, iron and tools must have made their life still more precarious.

SIGNS OF LIFE AT THE EDGE OF THE ICE

The photograph above proves that now, as in Viking times, wheat crops can be raised along the sheltered edges of Greenland's south-western fjords and islands. On the shores of Erik's Fjord, shown on the left, now called Tunigdliarfik, stood Brattahlid, which was Erik the Red's home. The grass and moss is green, but the white of snow on the mountains and ice in the fjord dominate the scene.

It was inevitable that some traveller to Greenland sooner or later would be driven off course towards the west — and towards the North American coast. It was a much shorter distance from the villages of Greenland to Labrador than to Iceland. Some sagas mention a man called Bjarni as the first to have seen land to the westward, but whether it was he or Leif, the latter's narrative prompted many to seek out "Vinland", as he called it. The name Vinland had nothing to do with drinking. "Vin" is an old Norse word for "pastures" or "meadows". The saga certainly tells of vines, but this is a later addition intended to explain the name Vinland, whose original meaning had been forgotten by the time the saga was written down. Besides, the saga writer probably wanted to demonstrate his knowledge of the Bible, and of the story of Joshua who sent scouts into "the promised land", from where they came back with big clusters of grapes. His information about "corn sowing itself", and about timber so big that one could build houses of it, must have been particularly attractive. It was not long before a new expedition was equipped. This time, Leif's brother Torstein was the leader, and old Erik the Red also joined in. But they were not in luck. Storms and currents carried the ships to Iceland and to Ireland, and they had to return to Brattahlid without having reached their objective. The following autumn a couple of merchant ships came to Brattahlid, each with a crew of forty men. They stayed with Erik during the winter. As Christmas drew nearer, he gradually became more and more depressed. There was not enough corn to make the traditional Christmas beer. However, one of the skippers, Torfinn Karlsevne, provided Erik with the goods he had brought with him, so that, in the end, this became a Christmas so festive that "they had never seen such magnificence in such a poor country". Everyone being together during the long winter, Vinland was of course discussed again. They decided to risk another voyage of discovery, and even planned a new colony; a new emigration. In the spring of 1001, two Icelandic ships and a third from Greenland started on an expedition with Torfinn Karlsevne as leader. It included several women, and the Vikings' personal belongings and domestic animals. The little fleet first went north to the West Settlement, from where the distance to the coast of Vinland was shorter. Arriving in Vinland safely, they followed the coast southwards until they came to the neighbourhood of the places which Leif had described after his first visit. Here the expedition settled down for the winter. The Icelandic skippers, however, disagreed, and one of them returned northwards with nine men. After this, there were only two ships left to carry the Vikings and their cattle. These sailed further towards

"VINLAND" — NEWFOUNDLAND?

Recent research suggests that Vinland is to be found around L'Anse aux Meadows at the northern tip of the island of Newfoundland, which lies at the mouth of the Gulf of St. Lawrence, off the north-east coast of Canada. The rocky north-eastern shore of the island is cut up by fjords and studded with islands. "Markland" was probably located on the American mainland to the north-west, on the coast of Labrador. This, too, is deeply indented and fringed with islands.

the south until they reached a place which suited the settlers much better. Here they decided to stay. Then the unexpected happened — the expedition met other people. The natives rapidly turned hostile, after at first trading peacefully. The " Skraelinger ", as the Scandinavians called the natives, came back at the beginning of the winter, and began to attack in such great numbers that the emigrants did not dare to stay. They sailed back to the original Vinland, further to the north, where they spent a third winter. Though they had not suffered heavy losses in the fighting against the " Skraelinger ", they had been so frightened and depressed that they gradually became convinced of the hopelessness of the whole enterprise. Here are the words of the saga: " They now realized that even if the country was very rich, there would be danger of conflict with the original inhabitants of the country. They therefore made themselves ready to leave the country, and set out on the way to their home village. " On the northward voyage, they searched for the Icelandic captain and his men who had left them in the beginning, but without result. In another fight with the natives, Erik the Red's son, Torstein, was killed by an arrow. It can easily be seen how the Vikings became nervous and edgy, and when the men also started to fight over the few women, it was clearly time to go home. One of the ships was stranded on the coast of Ireland, but Torfinn Karlsevne's ship reached Brattahlid safely. A heroic enterprise had come to a sad end. This was an expedition which was doomed to failure from the beginning, if only for the reason that the distance from Greenland was so great that no help against the hostile natives could be counted upon.

Several sagas tell of the Vinland expedition, and even if they did not quite agree concerning events and their order, they still describe the same places, which were given names such as Vinland, Helluland (" flat-stone land "), Markland (" forest-land "), Furdustrandi and so forth.

How can these be identified? According to the saga texts, these localities are situated near to each other. Markland may be Labrador, and everything suggests that the original Vinland is Cape Bauld at the northern tip of Newfoundland. It is in this area, too, that there have been found what are said to be the remains of a Scandinavian settlement, at L'Anse aux Meadows. But it is still enormously difficult to date the ruins, which appear to be of an Iron Age site of Norse type. Excavations revealed traces of houses, the turf walls of which had all but disappeared. The hearths uncovered resemble those in the houses of Iceland and Greenland. In addition to the topographical justification for seeking Vinland and the other " lands " in this area, there are also ethnographical reasons — the descriptions in the sagas of the weapons of the natives. A kind of throwing weapon is mentioned, and suggests the harpoons

THE " ISLAND " TO THE WEST

From the writings of Adam of Bremen, about 1076 A.D:
Another island of the many found in that ocean is called Vinland because vines producing excellent wine grow wild there. That unsown crops also abound on that island we have ascertained not from fabulous reports, but from the trustworthy relation of the Danes. Beyond that island, no habitable land is found in that ocean, but every place beyond it is full of impenetrable ice and intense darkness.

THE "WONDERFUL BEACHES"

The thirty miles of sand beach at Cape Purcupine, south of Hamilton Inlet, Labrador, may have been the "Furdustrandi" ("wonderful beaches") of the sagas. For the Vikings on their voyage south to Vinland such beaches would have been a landmark visible far out to sea.

of the Dorset Eskimos. These Eskimos did not know anything about the bow and arrow, which, however, was the weapon preferred by the Indians. But in just these regions were found both the harpoon-throwing Eskimos and the archer-Indians mentioned in the sagas. During archaeological excavations near Sandnäs farm in the West Settlement of Greenland, an arrow-head of American origin was also discovered. It was made of a sort of quartz which is only found in Labrador. It seems likely, therefore, that it was an unpleasant souvenir of a journey to America made by one of the inhabitants of Sandnäs.

No more narratives about colonization experiments in Vinland are known, but nevertheless a later colony of Scandinavians may have existed. In 1121 a Greenlandic bishop, Erik Gnupsson, went to Vinland, and might have done so in order to visit a congregation in need of pastoral care. Anyhow, it is logical that the Greenlandic Scandinavians visited Vinland and Markland to find their vital timber, for the distance to Norway was much greater. Some investigators believe that the Vikings penetrated as far south as Cape Cod, in the neighbourhood of present-day Boston. This will not be proved until relics of their presence are found.

THE VIKINGS FIND HELLULAND AND MARKLAND

From the *Saga of Torfinn Karlsevne*
There they approached the coast, and when they had let fall the anchor they lowered a small boat, rowed to land and saw no grass there. Farther away there were only huge glaciers, and the nearest strip of land between the glaciers and the sea was like one enormous slab of stone and the land seemed deprived of anything that could be useful. Then Leif said, " We have not failed to land, as Brani did. Now I will give this land a name, and call it Helluland" [*Hellu* — a flat stone]. Then they re-entered the boats and took to the sea, and then they found the next land in order. Once more they went to the coast, put down a small boat and went to the land. This coast was flat and full of trees, and here they found long stretches of white sand, and the shore was not steep. Then said Leif: " This land should be named after what is in it, and be called Markland" [forestland]. Then they went back to the ships as fast as possible. Then they went out on the sea with a wind from the north-east and they sailed on the open sea for two days before seeing land.

SOUTH TO THE MEDITERRANEAN AND EAST TO ASIA —
THE VIKINGS CARRY WAR, COMMERCE,
AND NEW PEOPLE INTO OLD EMPIRES

Whatever the Vikings came for, trade, land, or plunder, the people on the continent of Europe first saw and fought them as they are shown in the symbol from a picture-stone at the head of the page.

From the very beginning of the Viking Age, lively contacts existed between Scandinavia and the Frankish Empire. They took four forms: political and military conflicts, trade, religious and cultural connections, and settlement, the last mainly confined to Normandy. At first, violence overshadowed all the rest, and remained as a bloody thread running through Viking history even after more peaceful relations had generally been established.

In 799 A.D. the first Vikings landed in Aquitaine. Around the year 800, the increasing threat of Viking raids forced Charlemagne, king of the Franks, to raise a number of forts, like Esesfelth near Neumünster, along the north-western borders of the Frankish Empire. In spite of this, the North Sea coast remained as wide open to Viking attacks as before, and later Frankish rulers relied more on diplomacy. In the year 826 the Danish king Harald — driven out of his own country — was given Rüstringen in Frisia. In 841 the island of Walcheren was presented to Harald by the German emperors, who in this way hoped to afford themselves and their empire some degree of protection. But even such notable concessions as these failed to produce permanent peace. On the contrary, only two years later new Danish hordes began forcing their way up the Frankish rivers, and in 845 Vikings sacked and burned the city of Hamburg. By 850 the Swedish Viking Rurik had no trouble in conquering the whole of Frisia on the North Sea coast, and in 882 bands of Vikings plundered all along the Rhine and burned a number of towns to the ground. The raiders, moving by ship and on horseback though fighting on foot, had the advantage of mobility. They could strike and escape. The traditional, slow methods of defence — assembly of local forces by the king's regional representatives — were useless against such a flexible enemy. Also, the local levies were mostly ill-armed, undisciplined peasants who could not stand against the

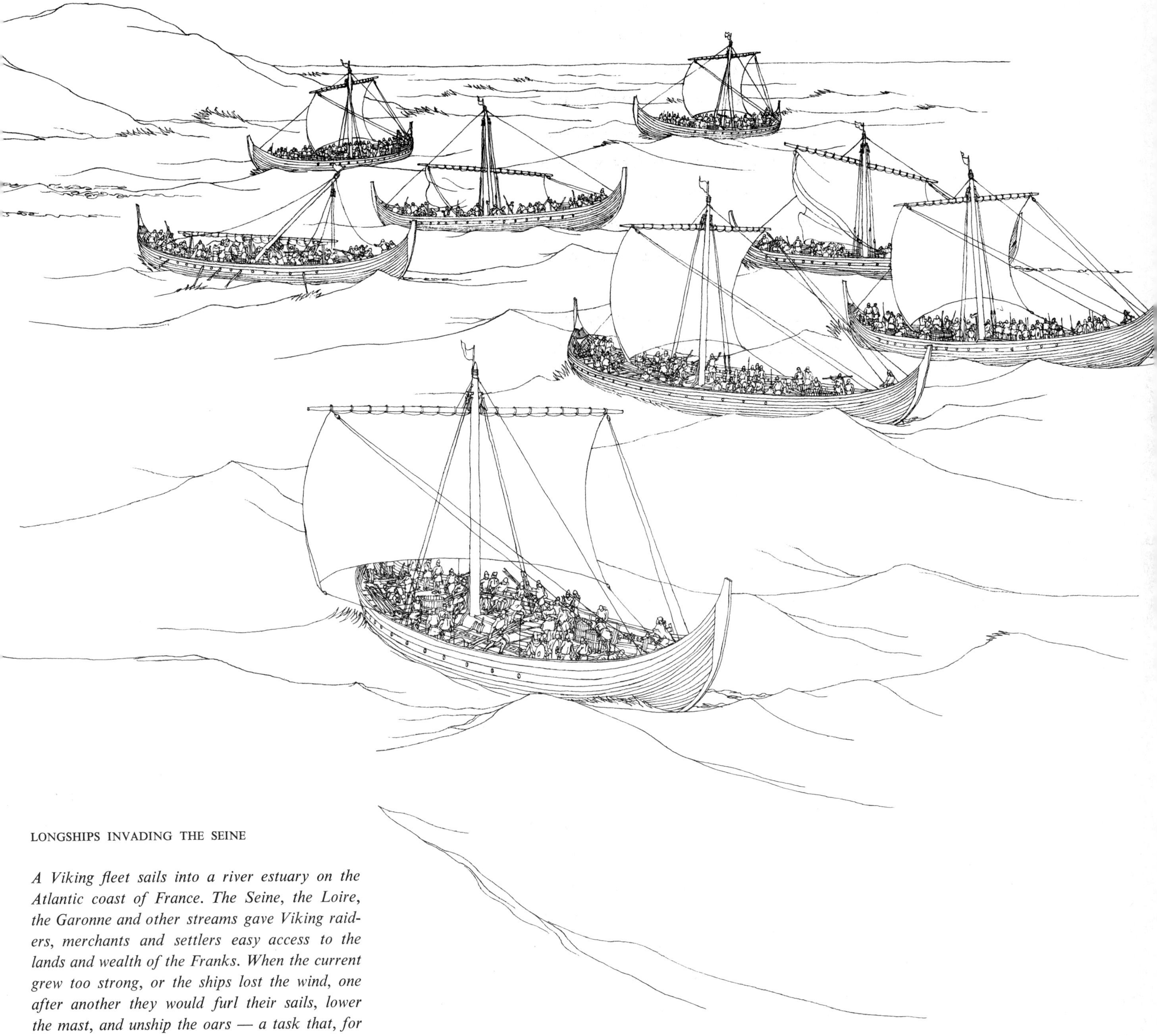

LONGSHIPS INVADING THE SEINE

A Viking fleet sails into a river estuary on the Atlantic coast of France. The Seine, the Loire, the Garonne and other streams gave Viking raiders, merchants and settlers easy access to the lands and wealth of the Franks. When the current grew too strong, or the ships lost the wind, one after another they would furl their sails, lower the mast, and unship the oars — a task that, for a trained crew, should not have taken more than a few minutes. With their combination of sails, oars, and shallow draught, Viking ships could adapt themselves to all waters.

formidable Viking warriors, even if they did bring them to battle. The failure of the Frankish kings to provide protection from Viking raiders both caused and reflected the decline of their power, and the rise of the power of local chieftains who could more successfully protect their own areas and peoples. The only effective defence against Viking attacks in France was the development of mobile, heavy cavalry to catch and break the Viking foot-soldiers, along with the construction of fortified centres: the beginnings of medieval castles. These strongpoints could resist attack, and in their turn could serve as the bases for counter-attack. The Franks were extraordinarily reluctant to recognize the inevitability of Viking raids, and it was only in the second half of the ninth century that they made efforts to create such strongpoints. When they did, and when heavy cavalry came into general use among the Franks, Viking raids quickly became much less profitable and more risky.

In the tenth century, Scandinavians were rarely found operating on the Continent. The success of these new techniques, and the beginning of the end of the Viking menace in France, was symbolized by the successful defence of Paris in the great siege of 885 - 886, when the defenders were led by Odo, count of Paris, who was shortly afterwards himself chosen as king. However, it was only after a peace treaty had been made in 927 between the Franks and the Vikings who had settled in Normandy, and after Gnupa, the Swedish ruler of Hedeby, had been defeated in 934 by the German king Henry the Fowler, that the way was prepared for more peaceful times. Even so, the tranquillity of the Frankish Empire continued to be disturbed for decades by bor der clashes and minor Viking plundering expeditions.

It is surprising that despite, and indeed during, these political troubles, commercial exchanges grew on a scale unheard-of earlier. A number of trading towns were established on Frankish and Scandinavian soil. They were necessary to the trade, and grew with it. The most important were Dorestad near the mouth of the Rhine, Hedeby on the southern boundary of Denmark, Kaupang in Norway and Birka in Sweden. The Scandinavian towns have already been described between pages 32 and 62. The commercial importance and wealth of Dorestad, which lay within the Frankish domains, is shown by texts like the ninth-century *Life of St. Anskar* (page 32), so it is not surprising that Viking raiders should have paid this town so much attention in the ninth century. The town's trade does not, however, seem to have been concerned with imports destined for the Franks so much as with goods that eventually found their way through Frankish territory to Islamic Spain. The relative importance of south-western France and therefore, probably, of Spain across the Pyrenees, is shown by coins from that area of France found at Dorestad.

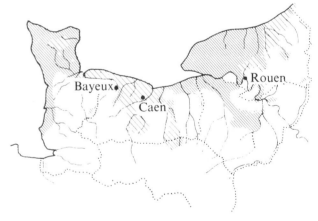

THE NORSE SETTLEMENT IN NORMANDY

On this map the darker shading shows where placenames of Scandinavian origin which still exist today are thickest, and the lighter shading where they are less thick, thus suggesting the extent of Viking settlement in Normandy. Some Norman placenames are of wholly Scandinavian type, like Yvetôt (compare with Ivetofta in southern Sweden), or contain a Scandinavian man's name.

When the Vikings came to France and settled down in Normandy, they put their stamp on the language. An notable example is the Scandinavian word *skipa* — pronounced with a short *i* — which meant to equip, especially a ship. This word is still used in French in the form *équiper*. (The Frankish tongue could not possibly manage the *sk* sound combination at the beginning of a word.) The English language has borrowed the word from the French in *equip* and *equipment*, and after seven or eight centuries the Swedish language has re-adopted the old word *skipa* in words like *ekipera* and *herr-* and *dam-ekipering*, now meaning "equipping" with clothes.

THE WATERWAY THAT LED TO PLUNDER

The Seine, shown on the following pages, was one of the rivers which Vikings used to penetrate the heart of France. This view is dominated by the ruins of the Château Gaillard, a post-Viking medieval castle at Les Andelys. Further upstream lay Paris, a rich prize which the Vikings besieged but never took.

Commercial relations did exist between Franks and Moslems, but what the Moslems really wanted, and could afford to buy, were furs and slaves, which came not from France but beyond.

Dorestad was also significant in another way. Not only was it the chief Frankish trading-port for Scandinavia, but it also furnished the main supply of coins for Frisia and the north. Silver pennies (or deniers) from Dorestad have been found in large numbers in Scandinavia. Finds at Dorestad also show trading connections with England. Dorestad did not survive into the tenth century. A disastrous change in the course of the Rhine took away its traffic. When Dorestad and similar towns like Domburg on the island of Walcheren declined, their trade was taken over by such places as Stavoren on the Zuider Zee and Tiel on the river Waal in present-day Holland.

The spread of Christianity promoted ecclesiastical contacts between the Frankish Empire and the North. In 834, the archiepiscopal see of Bremen was given responsibility for the whole of Scandinavia. Thirty years later the headquarters were moved to Bremen. About 950, thanks to the rising power of the German kings, who were Christian, it was possible to establish episcopal sees in Denmark, at Hedeby, Århus and Ribe. The majority of the missionaries working in Scandinavia were Frankish, although a number of Scandinavians were educated in Frankish monasteries, who later returned to their native land to spread the Gospel. There was also some Frankish influence on Scandinavian handicrafts. Highly-developed zoomorphic (animal) ornamentation had been part of the native Scandinavian tradition since pre-Viking times, but another style, plant ornamentation, ultimately derived from classical art, was imported from the Franks of Germany about the year 800, though it was not fully accepted by Scandinavian craftsmen for another 200 years.

As a result of all these contacts, the Scandinavian north gradually freed itself from its age-long isolation, and thereafter became part of Christendom. This development, however, marked the end of the Vikings' own, individual civilization, and of their characteristic political influence. Scandinavian heathendom was lacking in deep religious feeling. When, therefore, Christianity was established in Scandinavia about the year 1000 and western culture came with it, an independent culture capable of measuring up the rest of the world artistically was destroyed.

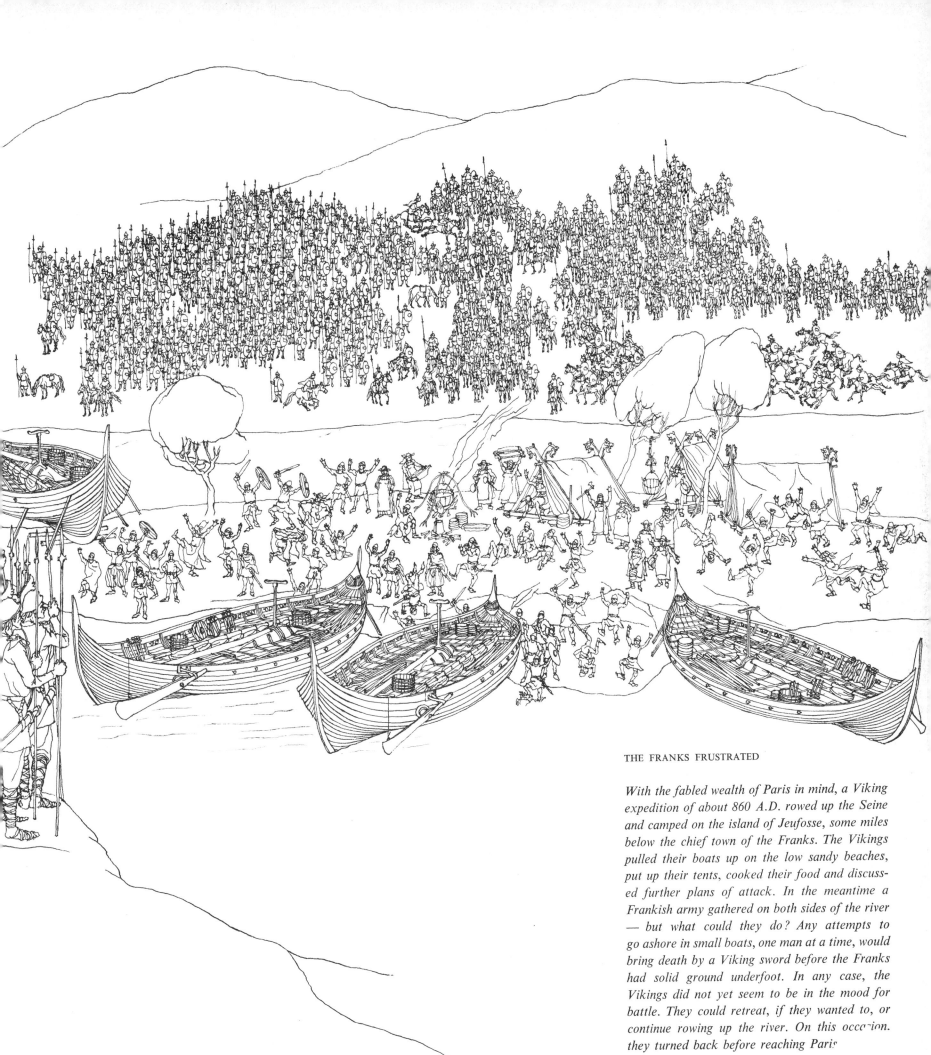

THE FRANKS FRUSTRATED

With the fabled wealth of Paris in mind, a Viking expedition of about 860 A.D. rowed up the Seine and camped on the island of Jeufosse, some miles below the chief town of the Franks. The Vikings pulled their boats up on the low sandy beaches, put up their tents, cooked their food and discussed further plans of attack. In the meantime a Frankish army gathered on both sides of the river — but what could they do? Any attempts to go ashore in small boats, one man at a time, would bring death by a Viking sword before the Franks had solid ground underfoot. In any case, the Vikings did not yet seem to be in the mood for battle. They could retreat, if they wanted to, or continue rowing up the river. On this occasion, they turned back before reaching Paris

The Scandinavians did not settle as extensively in France as they did in England. But they achieved a remarkable success in France, symbolized by the grant to their leader Rolf, or Rollo, in 911, of the area of north-western France that was the nucleus of the duchy of Normandy. Around the time when Rollo and his forces, consisting mostly of Danes, were established by King Charles the Simple in the region of the Lower Seine, other Vikings were also settling, on their own initiative, in western Normandy. In the course of the tenth century, a slow infiltration of Scandinavians reinforced these first arrivals. Studies of language have shown that many latecomers were Danes who had immigrated from England, or, less frequently, Norwegians from the western parts of the British Isles.

It is generally agreed that this colonization was mainly aristocratic in character. Above all, it provided reinforcements for a rural society which the native Frankish lords had, to all appearances, largely deserted. Most notably, the family of Rollo, the first duke, despite conversion to Christianity, preserved certain customs that were typically Scandinavian. The most celebrated example was a marriage custom called *more danico* by contemporaries, and plain polygamy by us. If the Scandinavian settlers brought women with them, they cannot have been many: an examination of texts dealing with Normandy in the period from 911 to 1066 shows only six women, as opposed to 300 men, having Scandinavian names. On various occasions during the tenth century, the dukes of Normandy, though technically Christians, appealed to the pagan Vikings for aid in opposing their Frankish adversaries.

The great changes seen in the placenames of Normandy between the end of the tenth century and the beginning of the eleventh show that many estates came into the hands of new rulers. These changes are particularly impressive in eastern Normandy, where, of the many placenames found in pre-Viking documents, only a very small number remain by the eleventh century. It is possible that in certain areas, particularly along the coasts, the Scandinavian immigration was still heavier. The fishing and boat-building terminology in the speech of coastal dwellers was very rich in Scandinavian elements in medieval times. Even today Norse terms are often used by fishermen and seamen on the northern coast of the Cotentin peninsula. On the other hand, the revolt of the Norman peasants (described by the chroniclers William of Jumièges and Wace), which disrupted the duchy in the closing years of the tenth century, has been offered as proof of a massive influx of Scandinavian peasants. These peasants, accustomed in their countries of origin to personal and

THE RIVER RAIDERS

The swords and black circles on the map opposite indicate places plundered or at least attacked by the Vikings. The map reveals how closely the Vikings stuck to their ships. They went up rivers such as the Garonne and the Rhône as far as Toulouse and Lyon, normally in search of booty or trade rather than land, ravaging monasteries and towns wherever resistance was weak.

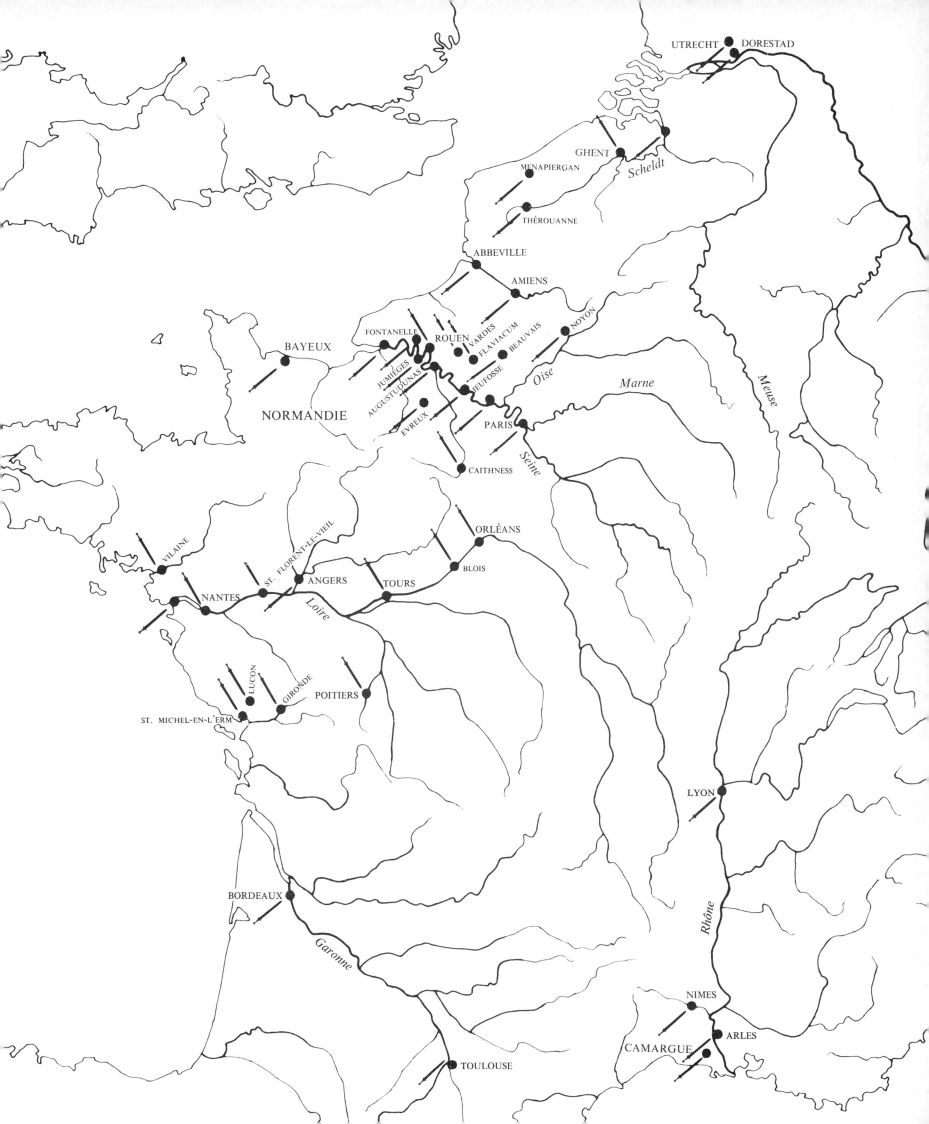

UTRECHT DORESTAD

GHENT *Scheldt*

MENAPIERGAN

THÉROUANNE

ABBEVILLE

AMIENS

FONTANELLE ROUEN VARDES NOYON
BAYEUX FLAVIACUM BEAUVAIS
JUMIÈGES JEUFOSSE *Oise* *Marne* *Meuse*
AUGUSTUDUNAS
NORMANDIE EVREUX
PARIS
Seine
CAITHNESS

ORLÉANS

VILAINE BLOIS
ST. FLORENT-LE-VIEIL
NANTES ANGERS TOURS
Loire

LUCON
GIRONDE POITIERS
ST. MICHEL-EN-L'ERM

LYON

BORDEAUX

Garonne

Rhône

NIMES
ARLES
CAMARGUE

TOULOUSE

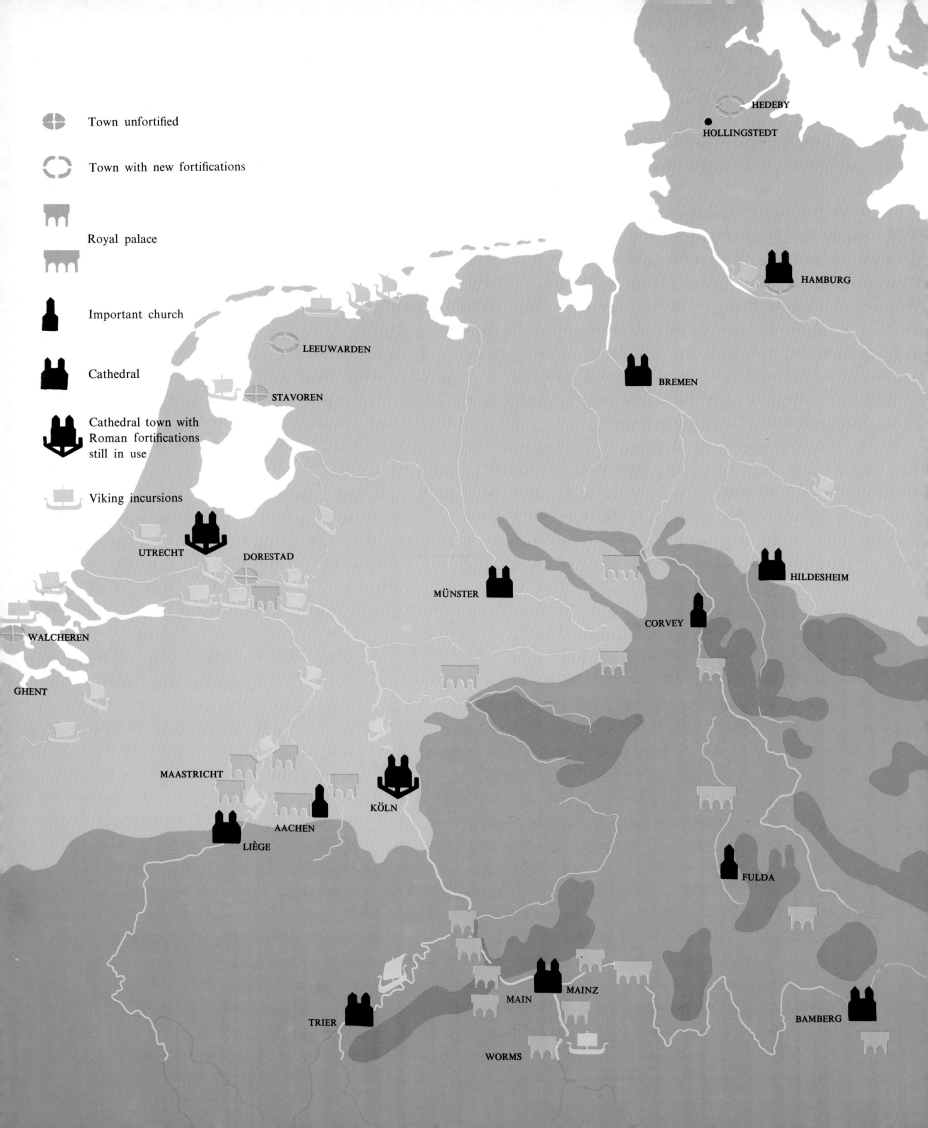

Town unfortified

Town with new fortifications

Royal palace

Important church

Cathedral

Cathedral town with
Roman fortifications
still in use

Viking incursions

HEDEBY
HOLLINGSTEDT

HAMBURG

LEEUWARDEN

BREMEN

STAVOREN

UTRECHT
DORESTAD

MÜNSTER

HILDESHEIM

CORVEY

WALCHEREN

GHENT

MAASTRICHT

AACHEN

KÖLN

LIÈGE

FULDA

TRIER

MAIN
MAINZ

BAMBERG

WORMS

economic liberty, would have been unwilling to accept the restraints imposed by the feudal customs of the north of France, which were adopted, or rather adapted, by their Norman lords.

Whatever the numerical strength and social characteristics of the Scandinavian immigration to Normandy, Duke Rollo's successors occupied a singular position in the France of the early Middle Ages. The best informed writers of the tenth, eleventh and sometimes even of the twelfth century, refer to the people of Normandy as foreigners. The very name "Normandy", given to the whole area fairly early, supports this point of view. During the whole of the eleventh century the Normans were remarkable for their dynamism. They were soldier-settlers who expanded the area and influence of the duchy at the expense of their Frankish neighbours, until Normandy was the most formidable power in western Europe, and was even able to conquer England, the richest of all. Normans also carved out new domains for themselves as far afield as southern Italy and Sicily, and eventually created the principality of Antioch in Syria after taking a major part in the First Crusade (1095 to 1099). While doing so, they struck fear and awe into Popes, Lombard dukes, Moslem Saracens, and Byzantine emperors alike. That the first achievement was due mainly to the skill and ruthless energy and determination of the dukes, no one will deny. But in the final analysis, were not both these movements of expansion the result of the infusion of Scandinavian blood that gave these people their extraordinary vigour, so that they became, in the eleventh century, what an historian has called "the masters of their world"?

INTO NORTH-WESTERN EUROPE

The map on the opposite page shows how ninth-century Viking raiders were able to make use of the rivers to penetrate into the heart of the German territories of the Carolingian rulers. These were rich lands, with numerous palaces, cathedrals and churches to offer profitable plunder.

Knowledge of what Russia was like in Viking times is slender at best, and room for speculation is great. Some Vikings — Swedes and other Scandinavians — certainly travelled, traded and died in the vast expanse of forest and steppe east and south-east of the Baltic. But the extent to which they traded, or settled, is very much open to question. The idea that the Vikings of Sweden ruled over large areas of Russia is based on the Old Russian Primary Nestor Chronicle, written in Kiev, which tells how the Slavs invited Swedish rulers, whom they called *Rus*, to govern their country, and says that this happened some time in the ninth century. However, the oldest manuscript of the Chronicle dates from the fourteenth century, and a 500-year-old tradition may not be reliable. A number of finds have been made in Russia which are of the same type as many Viking Age finds in Scandinavia. Most of these were in graves which in many ways resemble Scandinavian burials. So, superficially at least, extensive Scandinavian colonization in Russia seems reasonably certain.

But much of the detailed evidence is equivocal. The Russian grave finds, for example, include combs of a type which is common for the whole of north-western Europe, and the Swedes were not necessarily the most active traders along the routes through Finland to Russia in any case. Two runic inscriptions on wood have been found in the old fortified town of Staraja Ladoga, south of Lake Ladoga, and not far from present-day Leningrad, so at least the presence of Scandinavians here is proved. But some scholars have gone as far as to claim that the whole town was a Viking colony. According to their theory, Staraja Ladoga was a post where the Vikings rested before they began to pull their ships up the Russian rivers, over the watersheds and down to the Volga. There again, the evidence is inconclusive. It may have been that Staraja Ladoga was merely a staging station where goods were transferred from the Vikings' ships into smaller vessels, and it was in these that they were transported towards the south-east, up the numerous rivers of Russia. Some of the best-known Russian grave finds containing Scandinavian objects from this period have been discovered along these rivers. But while the actual graves are small mounds very similar to those of central Sweden, the mode of burial is often quite un-Swedish. For instance, a hearth with cooking utensils is often made the central point of the grave. Among the actual objects found, the oval brooches so typical of Scandinavia may have been imported. Many other ornaments found are typical of non-Viking areas.

Most of them, in fact, are Finnish, and right down into modern times, the

A GREEK LION DEFACED BY VIKINGS

This huge stone lion, which is now outside the gate of the Arsenal in Venice, originally stood at the Piraeus, the port of Athens. On its shoulder are traces of animal ornament, like those carved on eleventh-century Swedish rune-stones, filled with a runic inscription. Though the inscription is so worn that it cannot be read, it is evident that a Swedish Viking came to the Piraeus and, like many a modern tourist, could not help scribbling on the monuments he saw.

area around Lake Ladoga has been populated by people of exclusively Finnish origin. These facts seem to suggest that the Finns may have frequented the waterways which led from the Gulf of Finland to the Volga in greater numbers than the Swedes. The most convenient way of getting from Ladoga to the Volga was to travel not east along the Swir river with its rapids, but southeast to the sources of the Volga, along the small rivers, where, in fact, the majority of the graves have been found. What is important is that this route runs through an almost entirely Finnish-speaking area all the way to Bulgar, a trading post at the Volga Bend. A merchant who spoke Finnish could travel along this route without any language difficulties. Moreover the Primary Nestor Chronicle quotes a number of Finnish names in a supposed tenth-century trade agreement between Byzantium and the *Rus* dynasty of Kiev.

The question of the exact character of the *Rus* — a name reflected in the word *Russian* — has never been adequately solved. Over what period is it reasonable to talk of the *Rus* as Scandinavians? The oldest known use of the name is in 839 A.D. in the Frankish *Annales Bertiniani*, which tell how certain of the *Rus* people accompanied a Byzantine embassy to the Frankish Emperor on the Rhine. The latter, when he was told that these *Rus* were really Swedes, had them arrested as Viking spies. However, they also informed the Emperor that their king bore the title of *chakan*. This word is Turkish and means "over-king". It seems, therefore, that the *Rus*, although of Scandinavian origin, very quickly became assimilated, as did the Vikings of Normandy.

The most important other sources cited to demonstrate the Scandinavian character of the *Rus* are accounts given by Arab travellers and traders. It is true that these writers seem to distinguish between *Rus* and Slavs. But anyone reading their reports with an open mind, soon discovers that most of the *Rus* characteristics normally pointed to as being typically Scandinavian, could belong to any other people just as well. The only surviving *Rus* custom which could definitely be described as Scandinavian at the time the accounts were written is the funeral of a *Rus* chief, which involved burning the body in a ship. These Arab writers came into contact with the *Rus* near the trading post of Bulgar in the late ninth and early tenth centuries. Here goods were reloaded, and here the *Rus* bartered their wares with Turks, Bulgars and Khazars: peoples of the east. Bulgar was important as a trading post not merely because it was a convenient meeting place for a number of tribes. Its location had another great advantage: it lay on the edge of the vast expanse of Asiatic steppes. Like the sea, the steppes were a free area through which traders could pass at will without being subject to the heavy tolls which could otherwise swallow up the profits of long-range trading expeditions. From Bulgar the famous Silk

Road stretched out due east through almost entirely Turkish-speaking territory to China. Most of the silk that has been found in Viking graves in Birka must have been shipped by way of Bulgar. The town's importance as a centre for trade is further borne out by the many coin hoards which have been found in its neighbourhood. Most of these coins were minted in what is now Persia and Afghanistan, and in the area east of the Caspian where there were rich silver mines.

If we follow a succession of finds containing similar coins up along the Volga, we are led not only to Lake Ladoga along the route just described, but also along a more southerly route via the Oka River, south of present-day Moscow, to the area around Smolensk. Not far from Smolensk lies the vast burial field of Gnezdovo, with its 3,000 grave-mounds, many of them resembling Scandinavian mounds of the same period. It is clear that a number of these were made for Scandinavians, for they contain the remains of burnt ships. Other equipment, such as swords, has also been found which closely resembles that found in known Viking graves, but this, of course, is no proof of Swedish (or even Scandinavian) colonization. There is no type of sword which can be said to be entirely peculiar to Scandinavia at this time. The Arab writers already mentioned state expressly that Frankish swords were imported via Mainz, Prague, Cracow and Kiev, a trade route with which the Vikings had nothing to do. Graves containing such swords could have been made for Slavs, as well as Vikings. At Kiev, as at Bulgar, river meets steppe, and for this reason the town was important as a trading centre. That Scandinavians travelled the route between Kiev and the Black Sea can, however, be regarded as certain. In the first place, not far from the mouth of the Dnieper, on the island of Berezanji, a Norse runic stone has been found — the only known example from the area east of the Baltic. Additionally, the Byzantine Emperor, Constantine Porphyrogenitus, in his work *De Administrando Imperio*, mentions the names given by the *Rus* to a series of rapids on the southern part of the Dnieper, and these names are indisputably of Scandinavian origin.

That Kiev traded actively with Byzantium is clear, regardless of the accuracy or otherwise of the Primary Nestor Chronicle, but there is no real reason to assume that this trade was regularly extended further north into Scandinavia. Northern products like furs could have been more conveniently obtained from Finland and northern Russia, and shipped along a route leading from Ladoga and Novgorod up the Lovat and smaller rivers to the Dnieper. This route passes through Gnezdovo, where the transfer from the Dnieper to the northern river system could most easily be made. What is interesting is that Gnezdovo is also the starting-point for two further routes. The first of these, east along

TREASURE BURIED IN FOREST AND STEPPE

Viking-Age trade in eastern Europe can be traced on the map opposite by the location of Viking coin-hoards, most of them found in the lowlands along the coasts and rivers. Byzantine coins are scarce in Russia except in the south, in the areas closest to Byzantium. Arabic coins, on the other hand, are rare in the south, but are found concentrated on the rivers between the Baltic and the Volga Bend. Written sources as well as coin-hoards show that the trading centre of Bulgar on the Volga Bend attracted Arab merchants. In one direction the trail of coin finds leads along the Volga to the Ladoga area, and along the Oka valley in another. The central position of Gnezdovo, which lay between the Dnieper and the Duna at the junction of river routes to Bulgar, Ladoga and the Baltic, is clearly shown by the heavy concentration of treasure found nearby.

Baltic

Ladoga

Swir

St. Ladoga

Volchov

NOVGOROD

Lovat

Duna

Volga

Gnezdovo Smolensk

Volga

Kama

Bulgar

Oka

Don

Chernigov

Kiev

Don

Dnieper

rapids

Don

Sarkel

Dnieper

Don

Volga

Berezanji

Atil

Forest areas
Highlands
Steppe

River trade routes

Caravan routes

Finds of Byzantine coins

Grave-finds with
Scandinavian objects

Finds of West European coins
(Anglo-Saxon, German)

Finds of Arabic coins

Caspian Sea

Black Sea

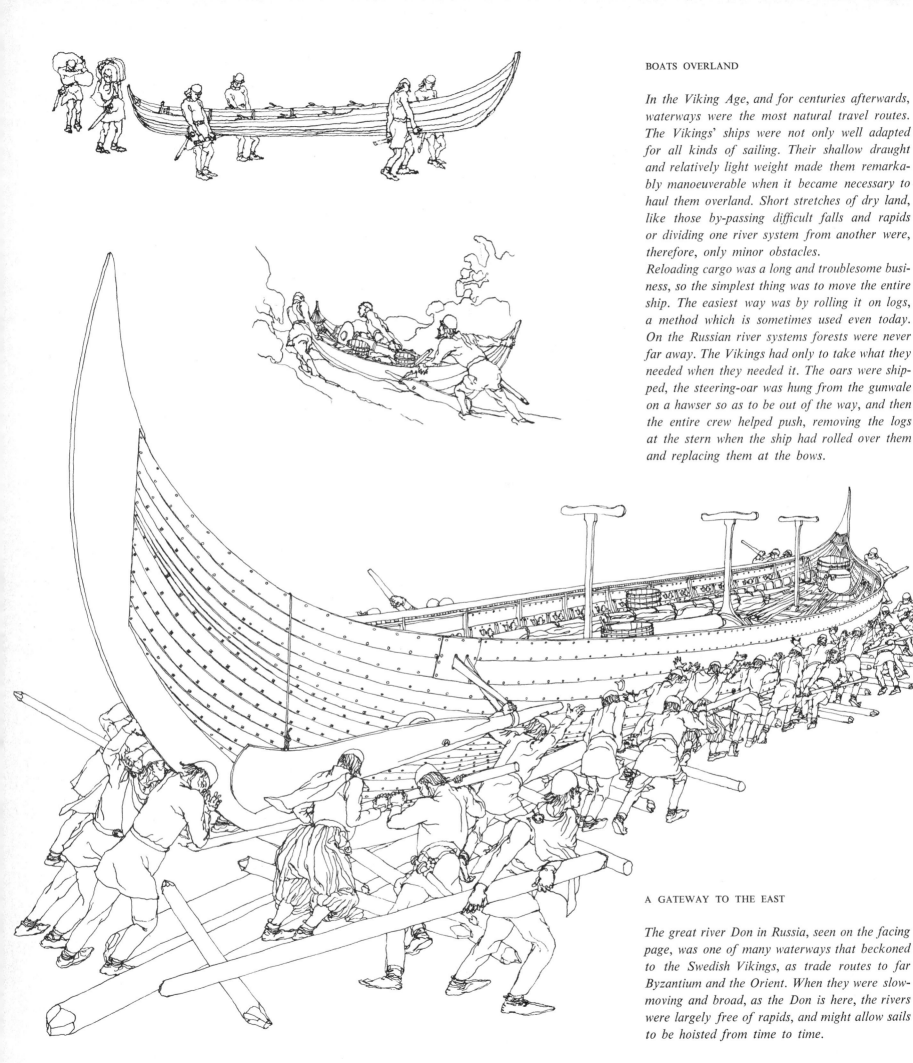

BOATS OVERLAND

In the Viking Age, and for centuries afterwards, waterways were the most natural travel routes. The Vikings' ships were not only well adapted for all kinds of sailing. Their shallow draught and relatively light weight made them remarkably manoeuverable when it became necessary to haul them overland. Short stretches of dry land, like those by-passing difficult falls and rapids or dividing one river system from another were, therefore, only minor obstacles.

Reloading cargo was a long and troublesome business, so the simplest thing was to move the entire ship. The easiest way was by rolling it on logs, a method which is sometimes used even today. On the Russian river systems forests were never far away. The Vikings had only to take what they needed when they needed it. The oars were shipped, the steering-oar was hung from the gunwale on a hawser so as to be out of the way, and then the entire crew helped push, removing the logs at the stern when the ship had rolled over them and replacing them at the bows.

A GATEWAY TO THE EAST

The great river Don in Russia, seen on the facing page, was one of many waterways that beckoned to the Swedish Vikings, as trade routes to far Byzantium and the Orient. When they were slow-moving and broad, as the Don is here, the rivers were largely free of rapids, and might allow sails to be hoisted from time to time.

the Oka and ultimately to Bulgar, has been mentioned already. The second runs along the Dvina and into the Baltic. These facts suggest that in Viking times Gnezdovo was not merely a burial place, but a central station for Russian trade.

In 969 A.D., an attack on the east-west route from Bulgar to the Baltic was made by Prince Swiatoslav of Kiev, who controlled the north-south route from Novgorod to the Dnieper. His aim may have been to destroy the silk trade along the Volga, for Kiev was also on the edge of the steppe commanding another east-west caravan route, and he might naturally wish to discourage rival trade. The rulers of Kiev might once have been Swedish, but the ruler here involved was by this time not even a Scandinavian. A Byzantine source describes his dress and his hair-style, which are obviously Slav or even Tartar. Moreover, the results of his attack on the Volga route were anything but advantageous for Scandinavia. Trade with Bulgar seems to have been given up,

The drawing above is a reconstruction of a scene described by an Arab trader, Ahmad ibn Fadhlan, who met Norse merchants on the Volga in the year 921. He wrote a description of the merchants' combination of business and religion, which was typical of Viking opportunism:
" When they [the merchants] came to this anchorage all of them left the boats with bread, meat, onions, milk and 'nabid' [a sort of alcohol]. They went to a high wooden pillar which had a human face. Round about it were small figures, and behind them tall posts were placed . . . He [the merchant] approaches the tall figure, prostrates himself before it, and says: 'Oh my Lord, I have come a long way with so many slave-girls and so many sable furs [and then he mentions all the goods he has with him]. Now I come to you with these offerings.' He places what he has with him before the tall figure, and says:

'*I want you to send me a merchant who has lots of dinars and dirhems* and will buy on my terms without being difficult.*' *If the bargaining slows down, he returns with an offering or two. If everything is going wrong, he will bring offerings to all of the small figures too, and asks for their intercession, saying:* '*These are the wife, the daughters and the sons of my Lord*'. *Sometimes business goes well, and he sells without difficulty. Then he returns to the tall figure and says:* '*My Lord has covered my needs. Now it is my duty to repay him.*' *Then he takes a certain number of sheep or cattle and kills them. Part of the meat is given away to the poor. The rest is thrown to the tall figure and the smaller figures standing around it. The heads of the cattle and the sheep are hung on the posts. When night falls the dogs will come and eat all the meat. He who has made the offering will say:* '*Assuredly, my Lord is pleased with me and has eaten my offerings.*'

* *Arabic currency*

and the flow of Arab silver into the north was stopped. It is possible that the sudden disappearance of Birka and the decline of Hedeby as trading centres were the direct result of Swiatoslav's attack.

There was quite a strong connection between the north and Byzantium, the capital of the East Roman empire, even though only a tiny proportion — about 500 — of the coins found in Scandinavia are Byzantine. Miklagárd —"the Great City", the Norsemen called Byzantium, and so it appears again and again in the sagas. These tell of how the Byzantine Emperor's bodyguard included a proportion of Scandinavians who had entered the imperial service. "Väringer", they were called, and they called themselves after their Greek nickname, which means "the hoarse ones". The best-known of all "Väringer" is the Norwegian Harald Hardrada, who became commander of the entire imperial bodyguard and also the Emperor's tax-collector in the Kiev district. A century at least before Harald, there were "Väringer" in the bodyguard. This appears in a book of Emperor Constantine Porphyrogenitus: *De Ceremoniis Aulae Byzantinae* — Concerning the Ceremonies of the Byzantine Household. On the ninth of the Twelve Days of Christmas, according to Constantine's account, people waited at both entrances of the Emperor's large dining-hall ready to perform the "Gothic game". At the left-hand door is the Admiral of the Fleet with a few men and flute-players from his ships. Behind him are two "Goths" (Väringer) dressed in fur coats with the hair-side turned outwards, and wearing masks. At the right-hand entrance, the commander of the body-guard is waiting with a detachment of his men. As soon as the Emperor arrives, he orders the Master of Ceremonies to lead in the performers, and "they then hurry into the room, and at the same time they hit the shields which they carry with their spears, and thereby produce a big noise, and they cry *jul, jul**: and they do not stop until they reach the holy table. There, the two units run together from both sides so that they form a double circle. After having run three times around the holy table in this way, both units withdraw to their places, the navy at the right and the army at the left, and those out of the two units who are called Goths then read out the so-called Gothic song". Then follows a long song in praise of the Emperor. It is perfectly true that the text says "Goths", but the real Goths or Germans had disappeared from the imperial mercenaries by about 500 A.D. In the tenth century it was the Scandinavians who formed the most important element in the bodyguard. This, incidentally, is the oldest known description of a Nordic Christmas celebration.

Byzantine monks or missionaries came to Scandinavia, but Byzantium was too far away to exert serious religious influence. The Roman Church prevailed in Scandinavia, because the bishopric of Hamburg was close by. However, very strong evidence of powerful Byzantine cultural influence can be seen in some of the coins which the eleventh-century Danish king, Svein Estrithson, struck. They are in a sharp contrast to the coins of his predecessors, which were of Anglo-Saxon design. One minted in Lund depicts Christ sitting enthroned with a Gospel book on one side, and on the other an angel presents a holy banner to the king, who appears dressed in Byzantine costume.

* Yuletide, the pagan Christmas.

HOW SWEDES CAME TO RULE RUSSIA
According to the Primary Nestor Chronicle

The tributaries of the Varangians* drove them back beyond the sea and, refusing them further tribute, set out to govern themselves. There was no law among them, but tribe rose against tribe . . . They said to themselves, " Let us seek a prince who may rule over us and judge us according to the law. " They accordingly went overseas to the Varangian Russes . . . [they] said to the people of Rus, " our land is great and rich, but there is no order in it. Come to rule and reign over us. " They thus selected three brothers, with their kinsfolk, who took with them all the Russes and migrated.

* A word applied to the inhabitants of all lands round the Baltic sea. According to the story, they had extorted tribute from the Slavs of Russia before the latter invited the Swedes, one of the Varangian peoples, to rule over them.

The picture-stones of Gotland include many abstract patterns, like the one at the top of this page. The meaning of the patterns, if any existed, has long since been lost. They may simply have been a form of artistic self-expression.

CLOTHES MAKE THE CHRISTIAN

Like many other people before and after them, the Vikings were perfectly prepared to be converted to Christianity if they found it useful. A contemporary narrative from the monastery of St. Gallen in Switzerland tells how: "Louis the Pious [king of the Franks] bade all the Northmen who came to him to let themselves be baptized, and very soon a great number came to him for that reason. But the real reason was that they wanted to get the white baptismal clothes which the Franks offered to the baptized. So once there arrived about half a hundred at one time who asked to be baptized. When there were not so many baptizing garments ready, they [the Franks] were forced in haste to cut each garment in two pieces and make do with these. A fragmentary garment of this sort was put on one of the oldest among them. Very surprised he looked at it, and then he said: 'Now I have been baptized more than twenty times, and I have always been given nice clothes, but this time I have been given a sack that fits a cowherd and not a warrior, and if I were not ashamed of being naked, you could immediately give it back to your Christ.'"

Much of what is known about the Vikings' pagan religion comes from a not entirely objective but always scrupulous work by the churchman Adam of Bremen. The following description of Uppsala in Sweden was written about the year 1076, when heathen practices still flourished there with official blessing. Adam wrote: "This nation maintains a particularly splendid temple called Ubsola; this is totally ornamented with gold. Here they worship the images of three gods: the mightiest of them, Thor, has his seat in the middle of the hall; on either side of him, Wodan [Odin] and Fricco [Freyr] have their places. To each of their gods, they have assigned priests, who make offerings for the people. If there is danger of plague or famine, offerings are made to Thor; if there is danger of war, then they are made to Wodan; if a marriage is to be celebrated, then they sacrifice to Fricco.

"Their sacrifice is performed in the following way: Nine of every living creature are sacrificed, and it is the custom to appease the gods with their blood. Their bodies are hung up in a grove which is near the temple. There the corpses of dogs and horses are to be found hanging alongside the bodies of human beings. One of the Christians has told me that he once saw seventy-two such corpses hanging together. The dirges which are sung when these sacrifices are carried out are many and obscene, and for this reason it is better to keep quiet about them."

Adam says that there was a large tree there which was always green. There was also a spring or well; a victim only had to be thrown into this to guarantee the effectiveness of any prayer made by the people who attended these rites. Adam sometimes misinterpreted what he was told, or else he was misinformed, particularly concerning the "priests" at Uppsala. Ceremonies such as the ritual first ploughing every year could just as well be performed by the head of the family or, in larger communities, by a chieftain or king. It was not necessary to organize such men into a special priesthood otherwise divorced from everyday life. It must also have been easy for Adam, as a man personally ignorant of Swedish customs, to regard any large heathen assembly at a place where a particular cult was practised as a purely religious occasion. In Sweden at this time, it was important to organize regular meetings to trade, and to carry on legal and administrative business, as well as for religious observance. The primitive nature of state organization and especially the scarcity of towns at the time made such assemblies necessary, so it is safe to assume that they served more mundane purposes than Adam's account suggests. This narrative can be compared with another written source. Shortly after 1000 A.D. the German bishop Thietmar of Mersebourg tells of a similar festival with sacrifices celebrated at Lejre in Denmark every nine years on January 1st. Here were sacrificed, he says, ninety-nine men, ninety-nine horses, ninety-nine dogs and ninety-nine cocks, in order to repel the spirits of darkness.

It was Thor, the thunder god, who occupied the place of honour in the middle of the hall. He was probably worshipped as early as the Stone Age by tribes who lived by fishing and hunting. Freyr, the god of fertility, is naturally to be connected with the agricultural peoples of the last part of the Stone Age and the Bronze Age. Odin, on the other hand, did not make his appearance until the Iron Age — the turbulent years of migration in the first centuries after Christ. He has a clear connection with the fierce and warlike Germanic hordes who, led by wilful and aggressive chieftains, forced their way into Europe at this time. It is not surprising to find the Icelanders representing him as the god of warriors and princes, nor to find that the early kings of Sweden, Denmark, Norway and even England all liked to trace their ancestry back to him. Odin (who was also the god of poetry and magic) was the god of aristocrats. At the other end of the social scale, Thor was often regarded as the god of the lowest members of the community, the thralls or slaves. Just as it was believed that kings and heroes assembled in Odin's hall, Valhalla, after their death, so it was thought that thralls found their last resting-place with Thor. Death was not considered as the end of everything familiar and pleasant. Even in the other world, the dead man would want to be surrounded by his property and gear. It is said in the *Ynglinga Saga* that all the things buried with the dead should be useful to them in the other world. That is why a great number of Viking graves contain grave goods. A man was, of course, buried with his swords, and if he was a rich man, even with his horse and his dog. The women had their ornaments. In a very few cases, a ship forms part of the grave furniture. One reason may be that the ship would be as necessary after death as

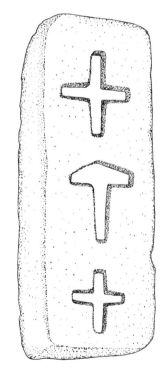

BUSINESS IS BUSINESS

A clever goldsmith could deal with pagans as well as with Christians. This mould of soapstone has been carved so it can produce two crosses and a Thor's hammer at the same time.

it was during the man's lifetime. Another is that the ship was given to him as a means of reaching Valhalla. The first theory is supported by the Oseberg ship, which was tied by a rope to a huge stone. Evidently the ship was supposed to remain in the burial mound. But in the case of the Danish ship burial at Ladby, the anchor lay inside the ship, which was therefore ready to sail with its burden to the world of the dead.

Naturally, only kings, queens or the greatest chieftains could have a real ship with them in the grave. The ordinary man's heirs could not afford such luxurious transportation either in life or death. He had to content himself with a smaller boat. A special sort of "ship burial" is sometimes found in connection with a cremation. Instead of a real ship or boat, the cremation grave was surrounded by a ship-shaped ring of stones, the deceased being supposed to possess sufficient magic power to change the stone ship into a real one that could carry him to his destination. These two different ways of burying people, cremation and inhumation, reflect two different beliefs: the cremated corpse took off immediately to Valhalla, while the buried corpse was sometimes miraculously believed capable of remaining in the grave at the same time as travelling to Valhalla. In one of the Eddic poems, for example, it is said that a man spent his days in Valhalla, but went back every night to his grave. Sagas also tell how some men's spirits did not rest easy in their graves, but rose to haunt the living, so that the latter were forced to dig up the corpse and cremate it.

Christianity came drifting in, little by little, with the merchants. When they met the new God of the Christians on their trading expeditions, the Vikings did not reject him, but gave him a place among the older gods. On the other hand, Christian merchants preferred to do business with other Christians. As a result an equivocal custom known as "primsigning" was worked out. That is to say, the Viking convert was not baptized, but was told about Christianity and then signed with the Cross. No water was poured over him. When this was done, he was considered a Christian by the Christian merchants, or at least Christian enough to engage in trade. But since no water was used, the Viking convert considered himself to be still faithful to his old gods. Thus he acquired a very favourable double position, acceptable to all parties. So in Denmark and Sweden Christianity sifted in quite peacefully, while in Norway the newly-converted kings used the sword to force the new religion on the people. Nevertheless, it was very difficult to exterminate many of the "old beliefs", most particularly the worship of ancestors. Some medieval laws mention that it is forbidden to worship ancestors, burial mounds, trees and *lunde* (tree clumps); a clear indication that the old practices survived the Viking Age.

A SCANDINAVIAN STAVE-CHURCH

No heathen temple from the Viking period has been found. But once Christianity had been accepted, the Scandinavians took to church-building on a big scale. In a very short time, many hundreds were erected. Naturally these were of wood, the raw material for all Scandinavian buildings until medieval times. In Denmark and Sweden such wooden churches are often found under existing ones. Some of the original churches, like the one illustrated here, have survived. It is at Borgund in Norway, and dates from 1150 A.D. A stave-church was so called because its walls were built of upright staves or planks with their ends sunk into the ground.

143

FREYR, THE GOD OF FRUITFULNESS

Freyr, Frö or Frej, to give him some of his names, was one of the three most important Norse gods. He presides over fruitfulness of humans, animals and crops, and is thus a power to be reckoned with. It is not known why the little statuette below was made. It is only about three inches high, but there is no doubt that it represents the phallic god. He is shown here with the characteristic gesture of twisting his beard — perhaps impatient because, according to legend, Gerd the giant's daughter made him wait nine long nights before she would meet him. The story, including the adventures of Freyr's servant Skirnis, who proposes to the girl on his master's behalf, is described in the Eddic poem For Skirnis *(opposite page).*

THE SERPENT'S SECRET

This little dried-up snake's skeleton in a copper box suggests magic, but whether black magic or white is hard to say. It could be a curse sent to an enemy to harm him, or some sort of charm intended to protect its owner's manhood.

Who exactly were the Vikings, these seafaring Scandinavians who suddenly appeared on the scene of history? Ethnically they were Teutons, and their language was Germanic. It was called "the Danish tongue", and it was common to all Scandinavians up to the end of the Viking period. The common language in the whole Scandinavian area created a feeling of solidarity, which should not be underestimated. Close contact with the sea, too, gave rise to a sense of shared experience between the three Scandinavian countries. There were no separate national states like those of today, so that it is perfectly justifiable to treat Scandinavia as a whole when speaking of the Viking Age. The differences in customs and trade routes were due mainly to the geographical position of the countries and to their physical make-up. Anyone will understand how it is that the Norwegians came to operate in the North Atlantic area, the Swedes in the Baltic Sea and via the Russian rivers towards the Orient, and that the Danes went in a south-eastern direction along the coasts to France, Spain and the Mediterranean. But these are only generalizations: none of the three countries ever had a monopoly of any of the routes mentioned. It is, moreover, obvious that people who lived in the rough skerries on the west coast of Norway would have a way of life different from that of the inhabitants of Denmark with its flat fields and cosy, sheltered fjords.

There were plenty of small wars inside Scandinavia during the Viking Age, but at least as far as the first half of the period is concerned, such wars were mostly attempts by rival local magnates to subjugate as many as possible of the neighbouring areas, rather than struggles between nations. It did not take much to call oneself king at that time, and it was not until towards the end of the Viking Age, that is about 1000 A.D., that the real national states arose. The peasants or carls formed the nucleus of society. They made up a large, broad "middle" class. They were free, and had the right to carry arms and to appear before the *thing* (local assembly) in their capacity as landowners. Thus far, there were no differences of rank, but it can be assumed that — as today — a man who owned a hundred acres of land was held in higher esteem than one who had only ten. Over the peasants was ranged a very small upper class, the earls or greatest chieftains, and the kings. They were leaders chosen by the people, and it was they who conducted the great campaigns of conquest. Their lofty descent and their wealth made them natural standard-bearers, but these attributes were not always enough. If a leader was unsuccessful, or if he was unjust, he was discarded, and his people joined someone else. The same was true of the king. He, incidentally, could not become the legitimate ruler unless the people

Although Viking marriages were usually arranged between heads of families, sagas and poetry sometimes suggest that the Vikings were far from strangers to romantic love. In the poem *För Skirnis* (Skirnir's Journey) the god Freyr describes to his servant Skirnir his passion for the giantess Gerd, daughter of the giant Gymir:
" From on high I beheld in the halls of Gymir
a maiden to my mind;
her arms did gleam, their glamour filled
all the sea and the air.
This maiden is to me more dear
than maiden to any man;
but aesir and alfs* all will have it
that strangers aye we stay. "
Skirnir journeys to Gerd's home, and persuades her to become Freyr's bride, but she insists on delaying the meeting for nine nights. When he hears this, Freyr is beside himself:
" Long is a night, longer are two,
how shall I thole† three?
Shorter to me a month oft seemed,
than half this hovering time. "

* gods and elves
† bear

145

(that is, those who were free) had sworn allegiance to him at the *thing* — in spite of the fact that, in principle, the son of a king was heir to the throne. The everyday life of the peasants has been copiously described in the sagas, and in general it does not seem to have differed much from the life of Scandinavian peasants as late as the beginning of the age of mechanization. All farms were self-sufficient. Only for rare, specialized tasks was a professional craftsman sent for. The latter made up a separate class, though they sometimes farmed as well as practised their craft. The most important was probably the village blacksmith, who was also often reputed to "know a thing or two" about darker arts. Other things which they could not produce themselves, especially luxury articles, the peasants had to buy from tradesmen. Merchants constituted another separate class, although they, too, might be landowners.

The greatest difference between the society of the Vikings and that of Scandinavia in more recent times is that they included still another class, the lowest of them all: the thralls. To the thralls was assigned all the hard, unspecified work, which required nothing but physical strength. They virtually belonged to their masters from birth. They had no legal rights and, of course, were not allowed to carry arms. A free woman who had a child by a thrall thereby degraded herself to the father's level. However, for a master to have children by his bondswomen was regarded as a useful increase in the manpower of the farm. It should be noticed, however, that in all other respects women were on an equal footing with men. It was significant that the insignia of the housewife was the bunch of the keys, which she carried at her belt. She was the ruler within the four walls of the home, and often she had to manage the whole farm when her husband and sons had gone out on a Viking or business expedition. All these things have been extablished by archaeological finds. There exist many examples of women having rune-stones raised to commemorate their husbands or sons. The arrangement of the graves also shows that women were regarded as the equals of men: there is no difference in the value of the grave-goods. Marriages were often contracted by agreement of the families, and love would have to come later as best it could. But this had always been a common practice among farming populations. In some cases, however, love might defy all economic considerations, as some of the sagas show.

Children, of course, were the pride and wealth of the family. The family as a whole was of greater significance than the individual, and without children the family could not go on. It is true that some ancient Scandinavian laws permitted the exposure of unwanted children in order that they might perish, but this was not a common practice: only deformed children might suffer this fate. Healthy babies were not exposed except in periods of severe famine.

THE UNFORGIVABLE CRIME

In King Olaf Tryggvason's saga we are told that Earl Hakon ruled over sixteen counties in Norway, and began using his power to possess not only the daughters of powerful men but also their wives. This, of course, made him a lot of enemies. When Olaf came back to Norway from an expedition to England, many put their trust in him, and the people rose against Hakon. Followed only by his bondsman Kark, Earl Hakon fled to one of his mistresses, Thora at Rimul, and asked her to hide him. Kark dug a trench in her pigsty, into which both men climbed. Thora then covered it up. Olaf and his army came to Rimul to look for Hakon: "Olaf summoned the people together out in the yard, and standing on the rock which was beside the swine-sty spoke unto them, and the words that he uttered were that he would reward with riches and honour the man who would work mischief to Earl Hakon. This speech was heard both by the Earl and Kark. Now by them in the sty had they a light there with them, and the Earl said: 'Why art thou so pale, yet withal as black as earth? Is it in thy heart, Kark, that thou shouldst betray me?' 'Nay,' said Kark, 'we two were born on the self-same night, and long space will there not be twixt the hour of our deaths.' Towards evening went King Olaf away, and when it was night Kark slept, and the Earl kept watch, but Kark was troubled in his sleep. Then the Earl awakened him and asked him whereof he dreamt, and he said: 'I was now even at Ladir*, and Olaf Tryggvason placed a gold ornament about my neck.' The Earl answered: 'A blood-red ring will it be that Olaf Tryggvason will lay about thy neck,

* Olaf's home

146

To have to let a child die, in any case, was regarded as a disgrace to the parents, and was an outright crime if the baby had once been given a name and the father had taken it on his knee and recognized it. Then it had become a member of the family, and to take its life was murder. In Viking society, old people were often regarded as a nuisance, and growing old was felt to be a misfortune, not only by the old men or women themselves, but also by their families, who had to take care of them. This seems cruel if we think of the respect of southern peoples for old people, but it should not be forgotten that the climate of the north was utterly dissimilar. There, it has always been more difficult to stay alive, and people who could not help do so were not considered worth keeping alive. In this connection, it is worth recalling something which has been quite usual almost up to our own time in Northern lands: if a doctor or a midwife had to be fetched to a remote place and the weather was rough, the old people would take the oars or the reins and go off. They did not matter so much for family survival — it would be far worse if one of the young people should die. At the same time, the moralistic Eddic poem *Hávamál* says that one should not laugh at the old and grey. They, too, may have something to say that is worth listening to.

Hávamál gives other directions on how to behave in everyday life, and they sound very modern and practical. You must have decent clothes. They need not be luxurious, but they must be clean and neat. If you have something to do, you must rise early in order not to waste time. Do not be the friend of your friend's enemy, and always tell the truth. Nevertheless, it is permitted to reward a lie with another lie. If you come as a guest, you can tell interesting news, but if you have none you must listen silently to whatever the host has to say. Do not be greedy. Drinking is allowed, but not getting drunk. There is no shame in going early to bed. If you are receiving guests, you must be polite to them. You must offer them water and towels so that they can wash themselves, and then offer them a place beside the fire so that they can get warm. Do not laugh at guests: it is too easy to sit at your ease and make the tired traveller feel ridiculous. First and last: be honest.

shouldst thou meet with him. Beware now, and betray me not, and thou shalt be treated well by me as heretofore.' Then stayed they both sleepless each watching the other, as it might be, but nigh daybreak fell the Earl asleep and was troubled at once, so troubled that he drew his heels up under him and his head likewise under him, and made as though he would rise up, calling aloud and in a fearsome way. Then grew Kark afeared and filled with horror, so it came to pass that he drew a large knife from his belt and plunged it into the throat of the Earl, cutting him from ear to ear. Thus was encompassed the death of Earl Hakon. Then cut Kark off the head of the Earl and hasted him away with it, and the day following came he with it to Ladir unto King Olaf, and there told he him all that had befallen them on their flight, as hath already been set forth. Afterwards King Olaf let Kark be taken away thence, and his head be sundered from his trunk."

This saga shows that for a low thrall like Kark to murder a noble earl was an unforgivable crime against the class structure, which outweighed any service he might have rendered to Olaf, and any promises Olaf had made.

THE POWER OF WORDS —
MAGIC RUNES, THE HEROIC SAGAS, POEMS OF
LOVE, HATE, TRIUMPH AND TRAGEDY

It was not until after the year 1000 that Christian missionaries succeeded in introducing the Latin alphabet into the Scandinavian countries. For a long time before this, however, the pagan Scandinavians had used an alphabet which was the common property of all the Germanic nations — the runes, or *futhark*, as the runic alphabet is often called because of its first six symbols. The origin of the runes is still disputed. The Vikings themselves believed that Òdin discovered, or rather stole them — though from whom is not reported. Some scholars believe that runes were developed by Germanic tribes in the Rhine-Danube area in the centuries immediately preceding the birth of Christ, and contained some symbols borrowed from the Latin alphabet. Whatever their origin, it is probable that runes were being used in Scandinavia by the third century after Christ. The majority of the inscriptions of the Viking Age were written in two sixteen-symbol *futharks*. The older of these two alphabets is known as the Danish *futhark*, which was originally used in southern Norway and south-west Sweden. Later on it spread to Denmark, and from about 1000 A.D. on, it began to used throughout Sweden. The less decorative Swedish-Norwegian runes are a development of the Danish runes. They were not only used in Norway and Sweden, but also in a slightly varied form in the Viking colonies in the west. Towards the end of the Viking period other local alphabets developed.

Runic inscriptions are found over an area almost as wide as that of the Viking expansion. Most are carved on stones: pen and ink did not come to Scandinavia until after the end of the tenth century. Although no genuine inscriptions have been found on the North American continent, there is a stone from Kingigtorssuag on the west coast of Greenland, at a latitude of 72°45′ N. In Iceland there are few early inscriptions. There are more in the British Isles,

The Vikings carved runic symbols like those above (left), from a Gotland picture-stone, wherever they went. They have been found incised in stones as far apart as Greenland and Greece.

ODIN TAKES THE KEYS OF KNOWLEDGE

From the Eddic poem called *Hávamál* (The Words of the High One) comes the god Odin's own description of how, after hanging himself in an ash-tree for nine nights, wounded with a spear as a sacrifice to himself, he discovers the runes:
I'm aware that I hung
on the windy tree,
Swung there nights all of nine;
gashed with a blade
bloodied for Odin
myself and offering to myself
knotted to that tree
no man knows
whither the root of it runs.

None gave me bread
none gave me drink
down to the depths I peered
to snatch up the runes
with a roaring scream
and fall in a dizzied faint.

Wellbeing I won
and Wisdom too,
I grew and joyed in my growth;
from a word to a word
I was led to a word
from a deed to another deed.

particularly in the Isle of Man (where about thirty runic crosses have been found) and in the Orkneys. Of all the Scandinavian countries, Sweden, with about 3,000 Viking-Age inscriptions, is richest in runes. On their expeditions to Russia and Byzantium, the Vikings left runes in localities as far afield as Berezanji on the Black Sea and Piraeus, the port of Athens.

Runic inscriptions generally tell of men who were unknown, and give their deaths as the most important event of their lives. This, however, is certainly not true of two stones at Jellinge in Jutland, which name some of the most important historical figures of tenth-century Denmark and in a few short sentences sum up their life's work. The first of these stones, dated about 935, reads: "King Gorm erected this memorial in honour of his wife, Thyri, restorer of Denmark." It is not certain from the runic Danish text whether "restorer of Denmark" (runic Danish: *tanmarkaR but*) refers to Gorm or his wife. Gorm did much to free Denmark from the encroachments of the Swedes and Germans. But Thyri seems to have an even greater claim to such a title. According to tradition it was she who recruited all able-bodied men in Denmark for work on the Danevirke, the barrier raised across the neck of Jutland against the southern enemies of the Danes. It was she who resisted the overtures of the German Emperor to lure her away from her husband, and it was she who, in addition to great beauty, reputedly combined "the sagacity of Nestor, the astuteness of Ulysses and the wisdom of Solomon". The son of Gorm and Thyri was Harald Bluetooth, who in turn commemorated his parents. Alongside the stone just mentioned, stands another more ornate. It reads: "King Harald had this monument made for his father Gorm and his mother Thyri; that same Harald who won all Denmark and Norway and who made the Danes Christian." Although Harald is, perhaps, simplifying the facts to his own advantage, what he says is true in its essentials. He drove the last of the Swedes from Denmark, for a time he controlled the ruler of Norway, and for reasons of diplomacy rather than faith he established the church in Denmark. Since only those who fell in battle went to Valhalla, and since the Vikings had the greatest contempt for a natural death, or "straw death" as they called it, death by the sword is often proudly recorded on runic stones from the Viking period. On Danish memorials, we hear of Ful "who died when the kings were at war", of Erik "who was killed when the champions besieged Hedeby", and of a third warrior who lies dead at Skia in England. A stone at Hällestad in Skåne, south-east Sweden (in Viking times a Danish province) commemorates a Danish chieftain who, according to tradition, had literally burnt his boats and so forced himself and his men to fight to the last at the battle of Fyrisvall near Uppsala. It reads: "Askil raised this stone in memory of Toki Gormsson,

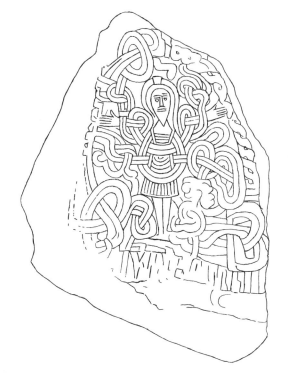

FOR TWO KINGS AND A QUEEN

This rune-stone from Jellinge in Denmark is a double monument to the deeds of the man who erected it, the tenth-century king of the Danes Harald Bluetooth, and to his parents, the Danish king Gorm and his wise queen Thyri.

his true lord, who fled not at Uppsala. In memory of their comrade, the champions set up this stone, standing firm with runes, the same men who fought closest to Toki". Swedish inscriptions record warriors' deaths in various far lands. For instance, a stone from Gripsholm tells of an ill-fated expedition to Serkland — "the land of the Saracens": "Tola had this stone set up in memory of her son, Harald, the brother of Ingvar. With manly prowess they travelled afar for gold. In the east they gave the eagle food. They died south in Serkland."

If these inscriptions mainly bear witness to the violence of the Viking Age, the Dynna stone from Hadeland, Norway, shows a gentler side reflecting the coming of Christianity. On one face of this monument appears, in verse: "Gunnvör, the daughter of Thrydrik, made a 'bridge' (*bru*) — for her daughter Astrid — the most accomplished maid in Hadeland." (see page 151). On another face of the rune-stone the Magi, the Manger and the Star of Bethlehem are represented. Just as Òdin is the god of magic, so the runes have always been intimately bound up with witchcraft. The word rune in Old English (*run*) and Gothic (*runa*) could also have the meaning "secret, mystery". In fact runes were widely used for magical purposes, particularly in charms and curses. An early thirteenth-century Icelandic saga, *Egil's Saga*, tells how a suitor, thwarted in love, cuts secret runes in the hope of seducing the girl by magic. He is not a master of his art, however, and the runes have the effect of making the girl delirious. In this condition Egil finds her. He searches in her bed, finds a piece of whale-bone on which the runes are inscribed, and destroys it. He then writes new runes, and puts them under the girl's pillow. These are immediately effective, and she is cured.

Runes might be used by the amorous to entice the opposite sex, but they could be used for more deadly ends. A copper box from Sigtuna in Sweden carries a curse directed against robbers, predicting a dreadful death for them: "The bird tore asunder the wan robber. I saw the carrion-cuckoo [a paraphrase for raven] growing fatter." Finally, runes could be used for protective purposes. On a brooch from the end of the eighth century found at Strand in Norway is an inscription which can be interpreted in two ways. Firstly: "This trinket is a relief from the pains of child-birth." Since the brooch was probably in the possession of a woman, this seems appropriate, although an alternative, more sinister interpretation is linguistically possible: "This trinket is a defence against walking corpses."

A RUNE-STONE "BRIDGE"

Here and there in the Swedish countryside, at the edges of streams and marshes, are markers in the form of standing stones. They are intended as landmarks or guiding-stones to help direct travellers in a snowstorm or fog. They marked the site of the only safe crossing-point — where a road had been built up to make a ford or causeway. When there is an inscription on one, it frequently states that the person who made the "bridge" did so "for the sake of the soul" of a deceased relative.

Fast-flowing streams and dangerous marshes served until recent times as clear boundaries between large farms. Only the farmer, his dependents and retainers knew the safe places to cross, and strangers could not safely pass without a guide. At the time when the king of the Svear was trying to extend his authority over the greater part of the country, he had to be able to cross farmland unhindered. Yet the Scandinavian peasant's right to be master on his own domain — which is rare in European history — was not easy even for a king to break. The Christian Church helped him to achieve his aim.

How did the Church persuade local farmers to go to the trouble of marking the way across their own property, and even build expensive, dead-straight roads, perhaps for more than a quarter of a mile across marshy ground? For the Christian, it was very important to be able to reach the church in all sorts of weather — to have his new-born child baptized, to be absolved from his sins. A time of even greater significance in the lives of Christian people in this missionary period — as it still is for Catholics — was the moment of death. It was of paramount importance to the fate of the Christian's eternal soul. Only if the priest could come to the dying person and administer Extreme Unction, would his soul be saved. And the most certain way of ensuring that the priest could come in that final emergency was to construct roads and fords that would help to keep the road open in all seasons. Even today, in certain areas, paths leading to churches have ancient precedence even when they have to cross cultivated land. The construction of paths and "bridges" also helped to break the autocracy of the wealthy landowners. Thus a king's desire for conquest and the peasantry's fear of eternal torment resulted in the construction of Sweden's first continuous, unbroken road network.

In contrast to the prose tales of the sagas, which came later, the poems of the Poetic Edda and the verses of the scalds, or bards, were essentially oral compositions. At first they were not written down when composed (this was only possible after Christianity had brought Latin letters to the north) but were memorized and passed along from singer to singer. Although the runic alphabet had existed for centuries, there is no conclusive evidence of its being used for literary purposes. The literary Viking hardly enters the picture before the twelfth century, when the real Viking Age had passed, and when everyday prose first began to be used for homilies and historical writings. The great flowering of saga literature, moreover, took place in the remote island of Iceland.

But the sagas nevertheless have their place in any serious account of the Viking Age. They are fascinating to read and are a prime source of general information about the Viking world. The value of the sagas as pure history, however, is questionable. Many historians reject them completely as sources for the early history of Scandinavia, arguing quite rightly that they are mainly products of the thirteenth century. No doubt the historians are right, though it is perhaps arbitrary to reject them all without making a separate estimate of the historical value of each individual saga. Although they must inevitably picture to some extent the Scandinavian scene of the twelfth and thirteenth centuries, they are at least the nearest thing to a contemporary account available to us that is written from the Viking, rather than the new Christian churchman's point of view. Furthermore, being written in Iceland, they mirror a society which must represent a natural development of a Viking community least affected by other civilizations. For Iceland (see page 98) was to all intents and purposes a virgin country when the Vikings first colonized it.

Two kinds of Icelandic saga are of particular interest for the Viking Age: the so-called Lives of the Norwegian Kings, and the Icelandic Family Sagas. The first claims to give an historical account of the reigns of the kings of Norway from the dawn of history down to 1177 A.D., and the second consists of biographies of men of note in Iceland in the tenth century, many of whom were the immediate descendants of the Vikings who first colonized the island. It is interesting to ask why, of all the Scandinavian nations, it was the Icelanders who recorded such stories for posterity. After all, oral historical traditions must have existed amongst them back home in Norway and Sweden, as it did among all other illiterate peoples. It is known, however, that stories from the past were particularly treasured by the Icelanders, possibly because their isolation and their remoteness from their motherland kept their memories keen, and prompted

From Njal's Saga:
In the autumn Mord Valgardsson sent word that Gunnar would be alone at home and that all his people would be down on the islands finishing off the hay-making. Gizur the White and Geir the Priest sent word to Starkad at Triangle; and all those who were to make the attack on Gunnar met there and discussed their plans. Mord said that they would never come on Gunnar unawares, unless they seized the farmer from the nearest farm (his name was Thorkel) and forced him to go with them to take the dog, Sám. Thorkel, the farmer, walked up to the buildings. The dog lay up on the roof. He enticed the dog along with him into the lane. As soon as the dog saw that there were men waiting there, he jumped up at Thorkel and fastened his teeth in his groin. Qnund from Witchwood struck at the dog's head with his axe so that it sank into the brain. The dog howled loudly in a way that none of them had ever heard before. Gunnar awoke in his hall and said: "Badly have you been treated, Sám, my friend, and who knows but it is meant that there should be but a short time between your death and mine." Now when they [the attackers] arrived there, they did not know whether Gunnar was at home, and so they decided that one of them should go up to the house to see what he could find out for certain. Thorgrim, the Norwegian, walked up to the hall; Gunnar saw a red cloak pass in front of the window and thrust out his halberd right into the middle of him . . . Thorgrim walked back to where Gizur and his men sat in the meadow. Gizur looked up at him and said: "Is Gunnar at home?"
Thorgrim answered: "It's up to you to find that out — one thing I do know, his halberd's at home." With that he fell down dead.
Gunnar shot out arrows at them, and defended himself so well that they could accomplish nothing. Some of them jumped up on to the roof, thinking to attack from there. But Gunnar was still able to reach them with his arrows, and they could get nothing done.
Gunnar said: "There is an arrow lying there on the wall, and it is one of theirs. I'll shoot it at them; it will bring shame upon them if they get injury from their own weapons."
His mother said: "Don't do that, you'll be rousing them again after they have fallen back."
Gunnar snatched the arrow and shot it at them. It struck Eilif Qnundarson and wounded him badly. But he was standing on one side by himself, and the others didn't know that he was wounded.

Mord said, " Let's burn him out. "

" That shall never be, " said Gizur, " even though I knew that my life were at stake. But [surely] it's easy enough for you to think up some sort of plan, such a cunning fellow as you are said to be. "

There were some ropes lying on the meadow which were always used to fasten down the house. Mord said, " Let's take these ropes and throw them over the ends of the roof-beam. We can fasten the other end round the rocks, twist a pole in them and so drag the whole roof off the hall. " They took up the ropes and did just as he said, and Gunnar noticed nothing until they had twisted the roof right off the hall ... At this point Thorbrand Thorleiksson jumped up on to the thatch and cut Gunnar's bow-string in two. Gunnar snatched up his halberd with both hands, turned quickly towards him, thrust it into him and threw him down to the meadow. Asbrand, his brother, jumped up — Gunnar thrust at him with the halberd, but he parried the blow with his shield ... Gunnar gave the halberd such a sudden twist that it split the shield and broke both the man's arms. He fell down from the wall.

So far Gunnar had wounded eight men and killed two. Then Gunnar received two wounds; and all agreed that he flinched neither at wounds nor death. He turned to Hallgerd [his wife] and said, " Give me two locks of your hair, and you and my mother twist them into a bow-string for me. "

" Does much depend on it for you, " she said.

" My life depends on it, " he answered, " for they'll never get at me whilst I can use my bow. "

" Then, " she said " I shall now remember against you that slap on the face you gave me, and I don't care whether it's for a longer or a shorter time you defend yourself. "

" Everyone does something to bring him fame, " said Gunnar, " and I'll not ask you again. " Gunnar defended himself well and boldly, and he wounded another eight men so seriously that many were near to death ... But the end of it was that they killed him.

Gizur said: " It is a great hero that we have now laid low, and we had a difficult time of it. This defence of his will be remembered whilst this land is inhabited ". He went up to Rannveig [Gunnar's mother] and asked, " Will you give us ground for our two men who are dead that we may bury them here? "

" All the more willingly for two, " she said, " because I should gladly give it for all of you. "

a stronger interest in the traditions of the past. This isolation and the comparative smallness of the population had another effect, too. It gave to the Icelanders a feeling of intimacy with and interest in their fellow-countrymen which, even at this early stage in their history, amounted almost to a feeling of nationalism. The outcome was a passion for genealogy, so that it was still possible in the twelfth century to record the names of some 400 of the principal colonizers of the island. These records still exist in the various versions of the *Book of the Settlements*, which includes many anecdotes from the early days of colonization. Out of such memories, works like the Lives of the Norwegian Kings and the Family Sagas could obviously grow.

But, just as oral stories told in the long winter evenings became mingled with folklore, so the sagas which succeeded them had entertainment value as well as an historical, informative purpose. The singers used old tales as sources, and added to them scaldic verses, and traditional lore — as well as flights of pure imagination. So the Icelandic poet and historian Snorre Sturluson, in his *Heimskringla* — one of the many versions of the Lives of the Norwegian Kings — is able to record not only the fact of the battle of Stiklastad, where St. Olaf fell, but also such things as the speech made by the king to exhort his men to battle, and the conversation between the emissaries of Harold, the king of England and his brother Tostig, ally of the king of Norway, before the armies of England and Norway clashed at Stamford Bridge in 1066 A.D. On the latter occasion, Tostig asks how much land Harold will give the king of Norway if he agrees to peace. The emissary replies: "The space of seven feet, or as much more as he is taller than other men." All such conversations are, of course, imaginative reconstruction, but they are marvellously done. Though *Heimskringla* may not record the true facts of history, it is recording the spirit of history as felt by someone seven centuries nearer to the event than the historian of today.

The picture of the typical Viking in the Family Sagas is more than a little idealized, for he is often presented as a young Icelander of good family who leaves home to gain fame and fortune at the court of the king of Norway, or to win wealth by plundering in foreign lands. Characteristic of the Viking is the heroic figure of Egil Skall-Grimsson in *Egil's Saga*, who undertakes many plundering expeditions, fights on behalf of King Athelstan of England at the battle of Brunanburh, and when captured, ransoms himself with a poem in praise of the Norwegian king, Eric Bloodaxe, at York.

The best of all the Family Sagas, however, is undoubtedly *Njal's Saga*, which portrays so magnificently the heroic if grim ideals of the North. It is the longest of all the Icelandic Family Sagas and surpasses them all in its sharpness of

characterization and the range of its action. Viking expeditions are by no means lacking, but it is the heroism of the Icelander at home, his steadfastness in adversity, and his courage which are mainly extolled. The two most famous scenes recount how Gunnar (pages 152-53) single-handedly defended his home against a host of enemies, and how the noble Njal was burned to death in his house with all his sons. The telling economy and strength of these descriptions is nowhere surpassed.

In these two sagas in particular, and in the Family Sagas generally, the realism of the portrayal of human relationships is far in advance of the general run of romantic medieval literature, and because of this, despite the great gulf between the Viking civilisation and ours, the sagas often seem modern.

Probably, however, the most surprising characteristic of the sagas for a modern reader is their variety. In addition to the two types of sagas already mentioned,

THE RAPE OF ASA

Ynglinga Saga by Snorre Sturluson tells the dramatic story of Queen Asa. Part of it is reconstructed imaginatively above, in the style used by Viking wood-carvers when decorating sledges, and the saga has this to say:

Gudrødr sent messengers west to Agder to Harald Redbeard, to ask for Asa, Harald's daughter, in marriage, but Harald refused to allow this match. And some time after this, King Gudrødr put to sea with a large troop of men and sailed to Agder. He landed there unobserved and attacked Harald at his home at night. Both Harald and his son Gyrr were killed and Gudrødr took a good deal of booty. He also carried off Asa and celebrated his wedding with her. Gudrødr went on a feasting tour and

on one occasion happened to be in Stiflusund. There was a good deal of drinking on board and the king himself was very drunk. In the evening when it was dark the king was leaving the ship, and when he came to the end of the gang-plank a man rushed at him and ran him through with a spear and killed him. This man was killed immediately, and the morning after, when it was light, he was recognized as Queen Asa's serving-man. Thus says the poet Thjódólfr:

Then was Gudrødr	Dastardly death
the greatest king	deceitful servant
in days gone by	to king dealt out
badly betrayed.	on queen's orders.
Avenging wife	Noble prince
laid ambushes,	was pierced with spear
for drunken lord	on ancient shores
a death prepared.	of Stiflusund.

there exist also lives of saints, homilies, sagas based on early Germanic legend (like the Old English *Beowulf* or of the Edda poems), translations and adaptations of foreign works such as Geoffrey of Monmouth's *History of the Britons*, and finally, the romantic sagas or Sagas of the Knights. Tristram, Sir Gawain and the other Knights of the Round Table all appear. Despite their country's isolation, the Icelanders were not ignorant of the great legends of medieval Europe. When, early in the twelfth century, Ari Thorgilsson decided, against the usual practice of the time, to write his *Book of the Icelanders*, a short history of his native land in the vernacular and not in Latin, he could not have foreseen that he was doing something without parallel in the Middle Ages. The *Book of the Icelanders* is the first work known to have been composed in Icelandic, and in it, and in the tradition upon which it was based, can be seen the germ of the greatest contribution Scandinavia has yet made to the world of letters.

The most remarkable literary achievements of the Viking Age were the Poetic Edda, and the poetry of the scalds. The most important source for our knowledge of the Eddic poems is a manuscript, the *Codex Regius*, written in Iceland at the end of the thirteenth century, containing twenty-nine poems and poetic fragments. They deal with mythological and heroic subjects, and many of them must date from the Viking Age. The first poem of the collection has the widest scope: the theme of the *Völuspá* (The Sibyl's Prophesy) covers the history of the Norse cosmos from its creation to the Ragnarök (The Doomsday of the Gods). The seeress who is the narrator of most of the poem presents a series of visions as striking and as vivid as they are fast-moving. She first sees the Universe at the beginning of time: "In the beginning, when Ymir lived, there was neither sand nor sea. The earth was not there, nor the firmament — a gaping gap, with grass nowhere!" Odin and his brothers create the world, and the idyll of the gods' primeval existence is described. The gods also create man: on the sea-shore they find two tree-trunks, Ask and Embla (" Ash " and " Elm "):

Breath they lacked

and spirit they lacked

blood and voice

and warmth of life

Breath gave Odin

and spirit Hoenir

blood gave Lodur

and warmth of life.

Next follows a description of the stupendous World-Ash, Yggdrasill, which is "always green and steeped in white dew". The central part of the poem contains an account of one of Thor's many fights against the giants, and the tragic murder of Baldur, the purest of the gods. But the *Völuspá* is best known for its long and intense apocalypse describing the last vain struggle of the gods against the powers of evil. When that time comes, the cock of Valhalla will crow to awaken Odin's warriors; it will be ominously echoed by the "soot-red" cock of Hell. The watch-dog Garm adds his baying to the cacophony and breaks his bonds. Now men become depraved and live in adultery and incest. A new, vicious age begins — " a spear-age, a sword-age, a wind-age, a wolf-age. No longer is there mercy among men." The gods take council and prepare for battle, their watchman Heimdall blows his horn. The World-Ash shakes and "the Giants" get free. The World-Serpent writhes in its rage. The catastrophe

KING MAGNUS DESTROYS THE WENDS

The following verses are taken from a famous poem addressed by the scald Arnor Thordarson to the Norwegian king Magnus, who died in A.D. 1047. The part quoted here tells how Magnus, having established himself as king of Norway, sailed in his ship *Visund* or *Bison* past Stafang — that is Stavanger, in the south-west of Norway — across the Baltic, to destroy Jomsborg, a Viking fortress that was then held by the Wends, one of the Slavic peoples.

Sithen, south along the homeland
sailed the king with many warships;
scope then was there given for skiffs to
skim the seas — ran Visund southward.
Ordered he his men to every
oar-bench, helmet clad; 't was fearsome
— shapely seemed the ships with Russian
shields — for men to see such war-gear.

Hatefully the spume and spindrift
spattered 'gainst the poop and rudder,
gusts of wind did shake the galleys'
gold-decked railings, low them bending,
as you steered past Stafang southward
steadfastly — the water parted —
up above there burned like fire
burnished mastheads — towards Denmark.

intensifies: the sky reddens with fire, the firmament is cloven in two. The powers of evil, led by traitors, fire-demons and giants, converge on the home of the gods. Freyr slays the giant Beli but falls to the fire-demon Surt. Odin is swallowed by the Fenris-Wolf; his son avenges him. But when Thor and the World-Serpent slay each other, the end has come: " the sky blackens, the stars are gone, the earth sinks into the sea. Steam there is, smoke and fire: the flames play against heaven itself. " The destruction is complete.

Here the sibyl stops for a moment, and when she continues, it is in a calmer strain. In a quiet epilogue she foresees how even after this last holocaust, a new green earth will rise out of the sea, how gods and men will return to their old homes, and how all ills will be repaired:

She sees a hall

lovelier than the sun,

roofed with gold in Gimle.

The noble warriors

there shall dwell,

enjoy eternal pleasure.

Just as the seeress speaks in *Völuspá*, so in the longest poem of the *Codex Regius*, the *Havamal*, the god Odin tells of his personal experiences. He tells how he seduced Gunnlöd and so won the mead of poetry from her father, the giant Suttung (Odin is the god of poetry), and how he was crossed in love by "Billing's maid". Most of the poem, however, consists of a series of precepts for behaviour in what seems to have been a lawless, suspicious and cynical society: " He who wishes to rob another of his property or to take his life should get up early; the lazy wolf will get no meat nor the sleeping man victory". The audience is particularly advised to avoid over-drinking: " There is a bird called the heron of forgetfulness which hovers over the ale-bout. It robs a man of his wits. With the feathers of this bird I was fettered at the house of Gunnlöd. " Most dangerous of all, however, is the deceitfulness of woman-kind: " To have the love of a deceitfully-thinking woman is like driving a frisky two-year-old stallion over slippery ice when it has not been broken in; or like steering a boat without rudder in a wild wind; or like trying to catch a reindeer on thawing fells when one is lame ".

In contrast, scaldic poetry was deliberately elaborate, elliptical and complex. Tradition tells that before the battle of Stamford Bridge in 1066, the Norwegian invader of England, King Harold Hardrada, declaimed two verses to his waiting troops. The first was as follows:

We stride forward,

fighting bravely,

Hear now how the scion of heroes
harried on the Wendish homelands,
in this burden; fortune-favoured
fared his ships from shipyard rollers;
hardly ever had a ruler
highborn launched more ships — 'twas ruled
rued by Wends — the foaming main to furrow,
frosty-prowed — against the folk-land.

Skylding king! With fire then fell you
furiously upon the heathen,
made great carnage, keen-eyed rapine —
queller, bloody, south by Jomsborg;
heathen hosts durst nowise shield their
halls within the ample breastworks:
fire and hurtling flame, high-blazing,
frightened townsmen, king, awe-stricken.

though byrnie*-less,

'gainst blue-steel swords.

Helmets do shine —

I have not mine:

our armour lies

below in the ships.

After this, he said: " This is crudely composed poetry. I shall now make a second, better verse. " He then recited the following: " In battle, we cringe not from the clashing of weapons in the shelter of shields — the valkyrie of the hawk's ground, true of word, exhorted me thus long ago. The necklace-bearer, in days gone by, bade me bear my helmet-support high in the din of metal, where the ice of battle and skulls meet. " The distinction Harold was making was between the relatively simple, Eddic style of the first verse and the so-called " scaldic " style of the second verse. It provides some relatively simple examples of kennings, or metaphors. " The helmet-support " is the head and " the ice of battle " is the gleaming sword. " The hawk's ground " is the arm, a term taken from falconry. The kenning can be considerably more complicated and abstruse. For example, in the poetry of an eleventh-century Icelandic scald, the following paraphrase for a warrior appears: " the slinger of the fire of the storm of the troll of the protecting moon of the boat-house's steed ". " The steed of the boat-house " is a ship. " The protecting-moon of the ship " is a shield, a reference to the fixing of shields along the gunwales of Viking ships. " The troll of the shield " is the sword, " the storm of the sword " is battle and " the fire of battle " is again the sword. Finally, " the slinger of the sword " is a warrior.

The ornate effect produced by the kenning is increased by the intricate scaldic verse forms. The so-called "Court Measure" cultivated by most scaldic poets is one of the most complicated metres ever used. Like the Eddic metres, alliteration is part of the structure, but in addition it demands set internal rimes and assonances, a six-syllable line and an eight-line strophe. Composing scaldic verse according to the rules must have been very much like constructing a crossword puzzle.

The poems were sometimes misunderstood even by the saga writers. A famous example of this is in Snorre's Saga of St. Olaf. He quotes a poem of the scald Sighvat Thordarson which described Olaf's sixth battle, in which he attacked London Bridge and " offered Ygg's strife to the English ". The meaning is clearly that Olaf was fighting against the English, but Snorre believed and wrote

* Byrnie: a coat of mail

KING HELGI SAILS FOR THE LAND OF HUNDING

From *The First Lay of Helgi the Hunding-Slayer*

Rose the din of oars, of iron clashing,
crashed shield 'gainst shield with shock of rowing,
as dashed through the waves the warrior's fleet;

the staunch wave-steeds[†] stood out to sea.
It burst on the ears when, buffeting,
the long ship keels met Kolga's sister[o],
as if surf with cliff did clash in storm.

Then higher Helgi bade hoist the topsails —
the crews shunned not the shock of billows —
when the dreadful daughter of Aegir
would overwhelm the hawser-steeds.[†]

But Sigrun[‡] on high hovering above
did shield them stoutly, and their ships also;
the king's brine-hogs[†] out of Ran's[8] clutches
glided safely at Gnipa Grove.

[†] Kennings, or poetic metaphors, for ships.
[o] A daughter of Aegir, the sea-god, *i.e.* "the wave".
[‡] A valkyrie.
[8] Aegir's wife.

in his history that Olaf was always on the side of the English king Ethelred. He therefore has Olaf and Ethelred as allies jointly attacking London Bridge in an attempt to dislodge the Danes from London.

Even so, a good deal of scaldic poetry is simpler, and easy to enjoy even today. The Icelander Egil Skall-Grimsson, of all the scaldic poets, most successfully mastered his medium. Egil's greatest poem is the *Sonatorrek* (The Irreparable Loss of Sons). After many adventures, including two successful encounters with his enemy Eric Bloodaxe, king of Norway, he eventually returned to Iceland and settled down. But then he lost his two eldest sons within a very short space of time. One is taken away by illness, the other, his favourite, was drowned in the fjord near home. At first Egil is inconsolable. He takes to his bed and refuses to touch food and drink, intending to starve himself to death. But his daughter persuades him to tell his sorrow in poetry rather than succumb to it. This is the occasion for the *Sonatorrek*. The poem begins slowly, with an expression of grief and loneliness:

Tardily takes

my tongue to move,

and to stir

the steel-yard of song:

hopeless is't

about Odin's-theft,

hard to draw

from the heart's-fastness!

(Odin's theft is poetry.) The pace quickens as the poet declares how he longs to wreak vengeance on the sea-god Aegir and his wife Ran:

Sorely Ran

has smitten me —

left me bare

of bosom-friends;

the sea snapped

my sib's tight links —

a strong strand

is stripped from me.

If my suit

with sword I could press,

all over

for the ale-smith were it:

could I kill

the storm's kinsman,

THE HEAVENLY MAIDENS

Viking-Age metal figures such as those in the drawing above represent the Valkyries, the legendary beings whose duty it was to carry the souls of warriors killed in battle to their last resting-place, Valhalla, and who feature frequently in Viking poetry. These stout, homely and apparently middle-aged ladies bear little resemblance to the popular, heroic Wagnerian conception of Valkyries.

Aegir's might

I would meet as foe.

(The ale-smith was Aegir, who was also the brewer of the gods.) But, the poet realizes, he is too weak for this: he is just a luckless old warrior. All that is left for him is to find consolation in poetry, and await death cheerfully:

Hard my lot;

for Herian's-foe's-

stern-sister

stands on the ness.

Gladly, though,

and ungrudgingly,

with light heart

Hel I will bide.

" Herian " is a name for Odin, and his " foe " is the Fenris-Wolf who swallowed him in the Ragnarök, as is related in the *Völuspá*. The Fenris-Wolf's sister is Hel, the death goddess. The allusion to the fate of the god of poetry is particularly appropriate here. " The ness " is Digranes, where Egil's father and sons were buried.

A WOMAN ON A BUCKLE

It is true that the Vikings were notable craftsmen, but they seldom went further than purely ornamental art within a fixed framework. The unique buckle on the right is therefore all the more remarkable, for it represents human beings in an almost naturalistic form. Fashioned in bronze, the buckle shows the strong face, powerfully carved, of a woman with a carefully elaborate hair arrangement apparently held in place by a frontlet.

DAILY LIFE —
DOMESTIC ARTS, TOOLS, CLOTHES, AND
CRAFTSMANSHIP FOR PEACE AND WAR

Much modern knowledge of the Vikings' daily life has been reconstructed from the rich finds at Oseberg and Gokstad. They provided a full range of utensils for kitchen and table, tools for spinning and weaving, shoes, combs, wagons, and sledges. Hunting and fishing supplied the food that the farm did not yield, while the skins and wool of animals reared on the farm supplied material for clothes and shoes. Buildings, tools, shoes and cloth were made on the farm. The Eddic poem *Rigsthula* provides evidence which helps piece together the daily life of the Vikings. The thrall had unskilled duties: carrying burdens, fetching firewood, spreading dung, feeding and herding pigs, cattle and goats, digging peat. The freeman worked as ploughman, smith and carpenter, among other jobs. Nobles passed the daylight hours practising with weapons, swimming, riding, hunting to hounds, playing chess, making war and winning wealth. Most houses had a single room, where people cooked, ate, slept and worked. The Vikings cultivated oats, barley, rye, and probably wheat and peas. Cereals were used for porridge as well as baking, and malted barley for brewing beer. They had milk, and so, no doubt, cheese and butter. They ate beef, mutton, bacon, fish, game and poultry. *Rigsthula* tells us of some of the dishes typical of the different classes — meat broth and hard bran bread for the thrall; boiled veal for the freeman farmer; white wheaten bread, chicken and wine for the nobles. The centre of family life was, as described in *Rigsthula*, the open hearth, which was probably placed in the middle of the floor. The fire provided most of the heat and gave light for the household, but oil lamps existed for extra illumination. People retired indoors as daylight faded, and gathered around the fire. *Rigsthula* describes a typical indoor occupation of the freeman — making the warp-beam for a loom — while the earl in his house is shafting arrows and making a bowstring.

One Gotland picture-stone includes the little illustration above of the workshop of the legendary smith Völund or Wayland. The tongs and hanging hammers are, however, realistic enough.

THE TRAIL OF VIKING RELICS

The most important of the finds which have helped scholars to build up a composite picture of daily life among the Vikings are concentrated in Scandinavia, as the map opposite shows. Among them are the ship-burials at Oseberg, Gokstad and Tune near Oslo, at Ladby and Skuldelev in Denmark, and at the towns at Birka, Hedeby and Kaupang. The ship-finds at Hjortspring and Nydam in south Jutland are pre-Viking. Rich Viking finds are conspicuous by their absence in the areas of Nordic settlement in the British Isles, probably because of the strength of the native English culture. Even Iceland, a place where the Vikings found no competing culture, has produced little in the way of spectacular finds from the Viking period, perhaps because Icelandic Vikings were settlers rather than notable plunderers and traders like their relations in Scandinavia, and never had kings and other men as rich as these.

ICELAND

REYKJAVIK

Ship finds
Important Viking graves
Viking military camps
Viking-Age towns
Post-Viking towns

Faroe Is.

Hebrides
Shetland Is.
JARLSHOF
Orkney Is.

NORWAY

SWEDEN

FINLAND

OSLO
OSEBERG   BORRE
GOKSTAD   TUNE
KAUPANG

VENDEL
VALSGÄRDE
TUNA   Åland   HELSINKI
OLD UPPSALA
BIRKA
STOCKHOLM

DUBLIN   MAN

YORK

ENGLAND

AGGERSBORG   LINDHOLM

FYRKAT
MAMMEN

DENMARK

JELLING

LADBY   LEJRE
COPENHAGEN
HJORTSPRING   TRELLEBORG   LUND
NYDAM
HOLLINGSTEDT   HEDEBY

Gotland

Öland

The Baltic

Bornholm

GROBIN

LONDON

DORESTAD

WOLLIN

WISKIAUTEN

TRUSO

HUNTING AND FISHING

With agriculture, hunting and fishing of different types were the most important occupations in Denmark, and also in some parts of Sweden and Norway. Without literature and archaeological finds, it would be impossible to piece together precisely how and why these activities were carried on. The great forests were full of game. Traps were used for small game, though none has yet been found, but deer, bears and boars were hunted with bows and arrows or with spears; that is to say, normal weapons also served as hunting implements. Fishing, on the contrary, must have demanded special equipment: nets, fish traps and hooks, but very few of these have been found. A specialized form of hunting was the pursuit of the big sea-mammals such as whales, seals and walruses. The walrus was particularly sought after. Almost every part of it could be used: the teeth were valuable as a substitute for ivory, the meat was eatable, and the best ship-ropes were made of strips of walrus skin. Other game, like bears and otters, was hunted for its fur, which the people of Southern Europe found very attractive.

Fowling was particularly widespread in the northern parts of Scandinavia, where there are still enormous colonies of seabirds. If present-day fowling on the Faroe islands is anything to go by, a team of Viking fowlers would first climb the landward side of the cliffs overlooking the sea. The birds were nesting on narrow ledges below. A man was lowered on ropes, and caught the birds partly with his hands and partly by swiping at them with a long-handled net. Feathers and down were, of course, gathered by hand. One can assume that in the areas where this difficult and dangerous sort of hunting was practised, a certain section of the population became specialists. There may also have been professional fishermen, but even these no doubt possessed a bit of land which they cultivated.

HUNTING IN ARCTIC NORWAY

*The wealth of Norway in the Viking Age was
based largely on the export to continental Europe
and the British Isles of Arctic products from the
northenmost parts of the country. Lying on a
sheltered coastal route, these areas were comparatively easy and safe to reach. The trader Ottar,
who lived in those parts, told King Alfred of
Wessex that among the most important goods were
down collected from so-called "bird-mountains"
— small islets on which birds nested or rested
on sheltered slopes (right foreground of drawing),
and blubber obtained from birds and from sea-
mammals like walruses (centre background) and
whales. There is no evidence that the Vikings har-
pooned whales. Instead the technique presumably used was one that is known today in the
Faroes: the whales are driven into narrow creeks,
and there slaughtered (left background). Sometimes, of course, whales simply became stranded,
and died.*

THE VIKING AS FARMER

It is clear not only from common logic but also from the poem *Rigsthula* that the population of Scandinavia during the Viking Age consisted mostly of farmers. In one of the poem's stanzas many of the farmer's activities are listed. He "tamed the oxen and tempered ploughshares, timbered houses, and barns for the hay, fashioned carts and followed the plough".

That the true plough with mouldshare was known in Europe during the later part of the Viking Age appears from representations in the Bayeux Tapestry, and from Anglo-Saxon manuscripts. A unique discovery at Lindholm Höje in Denmark shows, however, that this plough was also in use in Scandinavia, at least by the beginning of the eleventh century. At about that time a sandstorm struck Lindholm. It was so violent that some of the village fields were covered with more than a foot of sand, and had to be abandoned. They lay untouched until they were uncovered during archaeological excavations in 1955. The field had undoubtedly been ploughed with a true mouldshare plough. It looked like an enormous wash-board, being composed of parallel banks about three feet broad separated by furrows. This appearance can only have been produced by cutting a straight furrow the length of the field, then turning round and driving another furrow back beside the first. A Swedish description of Polish farming of about 1757 exactly fits the method which was used at Lindholm Höje in the later part of the Viking Age.

Between the farm and the field at Lindholm Höje was a carriage-road worn down to a depth of nine inches. It, too, was filled with sand, forcing the farmer to drive across his field. This, his last drive over the field which was sentenced to death, also left its mark on the borders, where the wheels pressed the sand down into the newly ploughed mould. These slender traces of his two-wheeled cart are a living illustration of the words of the Eddic poem. Contemporary accounts do not mention harrowing, but traces have been found of this process also. Sickles and short scythes were used in harvesting. Rakes may also have been known, as they are found in remains from the previous period. Threshing may have been done with flails, though no flail has yet been found.

A VIKING-AGE FARM

On the left, a Viking farmer grazes his livestock in his fields, which run down to the edge of a river. His animals include horses, cattle, goats and sheep. Between them and the farm buildings in the background are the cultivated fields ploughed in deep, parallel furrows with a mouldshare plough. Agricultural implements were, for the most part, made of wood — men would go into the forest, taking note of young trees with a shape suitable for making a plough, a pitchfork or the handle of a sickle, and wait perhaps for years until the material had grown to appropriate size. The iron heads and blades were hammered out by the village smith.

Viking-Age houses in Scandinavia were built mainly of timber. Since wood is perishable, archaeologists usually find only "negative" traces of early Norse houses: holes where posts had been sunk, grooves where walls had been, the remains of stone foundations. Little that is definite can be proved, except on the basis of a few instances where, under special circumstances — like dampness of soil — large sections of house timbers have been preserved. Hedeby, a characteristic Viking-Age site including houses where this was the case, has already been mentioned (page 55).

In the pre-Viking Iron Age, the most common type of house in Scandinavia was a hall-like building, sometimes more than 150 feet long, with a double row of wooden supports to carry the roof, and with walls of earth, turf or so-called "plaited work". This consisted of a frame of vertical posts through which rods and brushwood were woven, the whole being then coated with mud: in other words a sort of wattle-and-daub construction. These were all-purpose houses, with both human beings and animals under one roof.

With the coming of the Viking Age, buildings began to be grouped together to form towns at certain geographically favourable places, to promote trade and industry. Hedeby was such a place. Individual houses also underwent a change. There was specialization, each building being designed for a specific purpose, so they were therefore made smaller. The biggest verifiable house in Hedeby is about 15×50 feet. Most of the other houses there are considerably smaller. Because of this, only in exceptional cases was it necessary to have posts inside to help to support the roof. All the houses are four-sided, and have straight walls into which support posts are built. These carry the roof, and were probably connected by longitudinal beams. The largest of the Hedeby houses have wattle-and-daub walls, and in this respect they differ little from the normal practice of the early Iron Age. They also had an entrance in each gable. But instead of using the old Iron Age solid-post construction, builders seem to have experimented at Hedeby with several sorts of plank work. The idea seems to have been to form a framework of sufficient stability by joining upright planks, set in the earth, to horizontal planks at ground level and roof level. The spaces between the upright timbers were then closed by walls of mud-coated wattle-work. The roof was presumably covered with straw. The hearth, simply a pit dug in the floor, sometimes plastered with mud or stone-lined, is situated in an unusual position, the centre of the house, where two pairs of vertical posts — presumably roof-supports — sometimes also occur. Smaller wattle-and-daub houses are also found at Hedeby, the smallest

A WARLIKE WEATHER-VANE

Before being used as a weather-vane on a Swedish church, the gilt bronze standard opposite flew at a warship's prow.

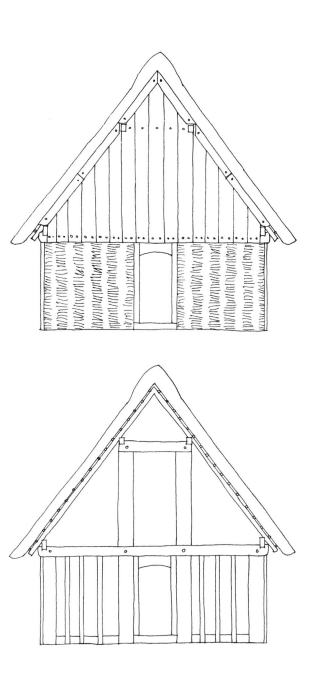

HOW HOUSES WERE BUILT

At left is a detailed reconstruction of the interior of one type of Viking house, divided into rooms. The hearths are in the centre of the floor. Above one, food is being cooked in a large hanging cauldron. Smoke from the fire escapes through an open gable. The walls have sleeping recesses. The drawings directly above show what the gables of a house in Hedeby probably looked like. The top drawing shows the exterior, where wattle-and-daub has been applied over planks. Below it is a sketch of the internal construction of the gable. Horizontal and vertical timbers were joined by wooden nails.

measuring 10 × 13 feet. A special type of Viking construction had wattle-and-daub walls faced on the inside with boards — the walls having a layer of stones as a foundation. This wattle-and-daub construction, incidentally, is an ancestor of that used in the half-timbered houses of Elizabethan England.

The walls of some houses at Hedeby were built entirely of timber. They are all very small. Presumably it was too wasteful of material to build big houses in this way. Two types of wooden construction occur. One used a frame which, in principle, is the same as in the plaited-work construction, but the actual wattle-work is replaced by horizontal planks nailed or pegged to the vertical timbers. In the other method of construction — called stave-construction — the whole wall consists of upright planks or staves standing side by side, with their ends sunk into the ground. The Hedeby house thus constructed measures only 10 × 10 feet, with a hearth in one corner and an entrance at the other. Similar construction made its appearance in western Europe as early as the New Stone Age, at Aichbühl in Germany for example. Then it seems to have disappeared until it turned up again at Hedeby, but was mostly used for much larger buildings like the stave-churches dating from the end of the Viking Age, which exist at Lund in Sweden and at Urnes in Norway. In these later buildings, the staves are usually jointed into one another, which helped to make the building more windproof.

Curiously enough, during the late Viking Age a strikingly severe standardization of house-types sometimes occurred, when individual houses were all built according to one standard pattern and show a quite amazing resemblance to each other. Such houses are found in the great Danish military camps excavated at Trelleborg, Aggersborg and Fyrkat (page 63). The houses in each of these camps are exactly the same size, but house-sizes differ somewhat from camp to camp. In Trelleborg the houses are exactly a hundred Roman feet long. At the widest point they measure twenty-six feet across. The gables are straight, and the long sides are sections of an extremely regular ellipse. The construction of the walls, as was the case in one of the houses found at Hedeby, is double: there is the wall proper, and then, outside it, at a distance of three feet, a row of posts running parallel with it. At Fyrkat and Aggersborg the actual house walls consisted of wattle-work, and the outer posts leaned inwards, thereby strengthening the wattle-work and helping buttress the weight of the roof.

The builders at Trelleborg evidently felt a real need for houses with a large open space in the middle. This was achieved by eliminating the series of support posts inside, which had been obligatory in the older design, and by giving the walls their ellipse-like shape. Questions of economy may have dictated

171

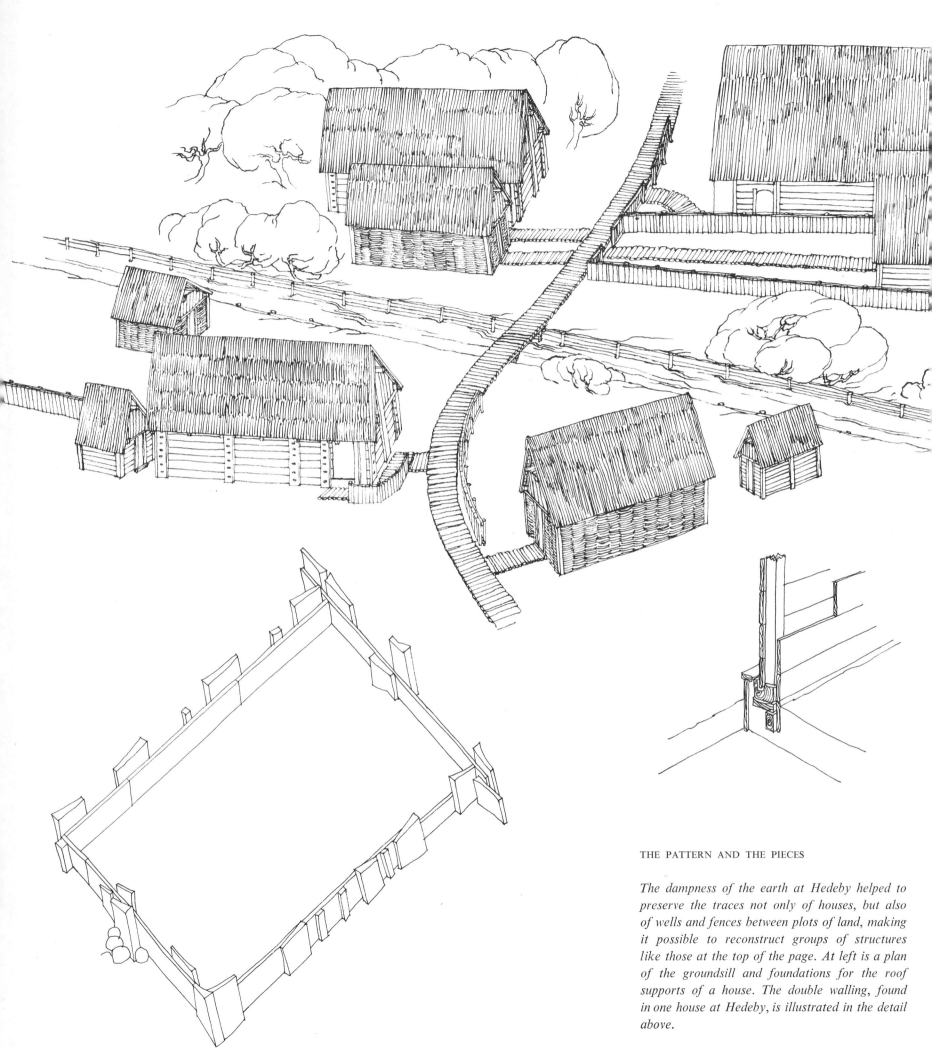

THE PATTERN AND THE PIECES

The dampness of the earth at Hedeby helped to preserve the traces not only of houses, but also of wells and fences between plots of land, making it possible to reconstruct groups of structures like those at the top of the page. At left is a plan of the groundsill and foundations for the roof supports of a house. The double walling, found in one house at Hedeby, is illustrated in the detail above.

the new house-design, for it allowed a saving in timber. But the need for a free space in the middle of a house was evident earlier in the Iron Age, and was achieved by construction on the same principle used in Trelleborg houses. What seems to have been a sixth-century ship-house — a so-called *naust* — has been excavated to the south of Bergen in Norway. Ninety-two feet long by twenty-three feet wide, the house had to be big enough to hold an entire longship. The building material most readily available dictated the building methods used. In the coastal areas of north-western Europe suitable timber was scarce, and as a result wattle-and-daub construction predominated there until superseded by half-timbering. In more heavily forested areas such as eastern and central Europe, it was not only possible, but usually necessary, because of the severe winters, to build houses that were more solid. Construction methods requiring an abundance of timber — such as cross-timbering — naturally occur in these areas. No cross-timbering exists at Hedeby, however. It is still not known when this technique first gained a foothold in Scandinavia. It is found in the burial chambers in the early Viking Age graves at Oseberg and Gokstad in Norway, but no other definite instances of early cross-timbering are known. One difficulty is that houses so built are not sunk in the earth, so that it is virtually impossible to be sure when traces of them have been found. The investigation of farms undertaken recently on Helgö island in the Mälar district of Sweden may help clear up the question. The main period of settlement on this site was, as noted earlier, immediately before the Viking Age. Though the houses generally are long and hall-like with rows of posts inside, foundations of stone have been found which can hardly be anything but bases for cross-timbered houses. Their excavation, however, is not yet complete.

HOMES IN HEDEBY

Danish houses at the Viking town of Hedeby included several designs and types of construction. Above, a house with holes under the roof-peak to let out smoke. Below, a house built wholly of timber. The horizontal planks are fastened to vertical ones.

173

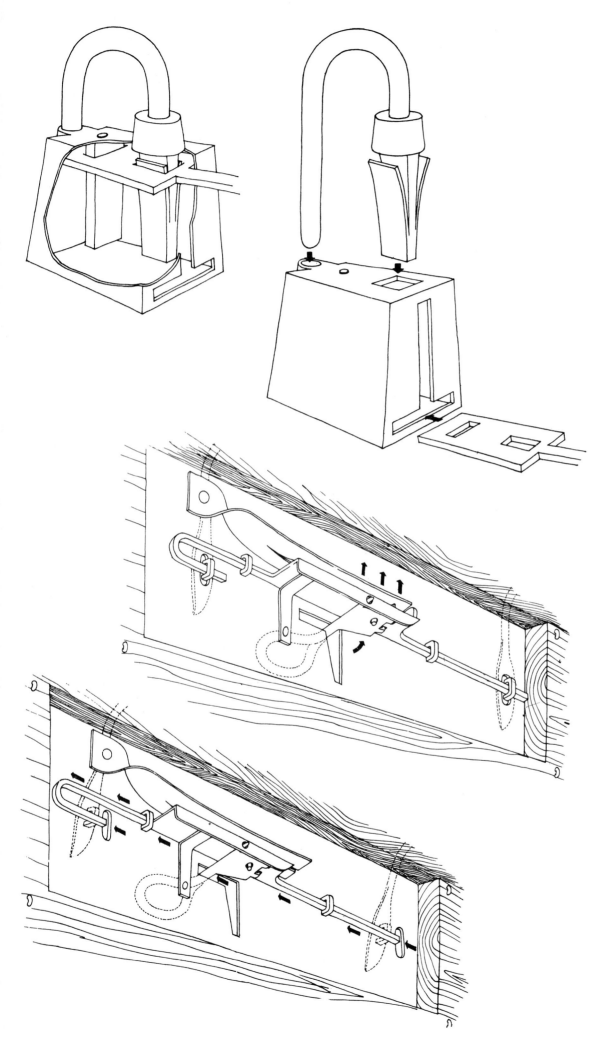

DETERRING THE THIEF

The Vikings had much more need of locks than did their forefathers. In their new trading towns, there were more expensive objects to steal, and many strangers to steal them. Viking locks are skilful adaptations of the Roman locks preserved in western Europe. Roman locks, however, had far too many details requiring precision work to be easily and cheaply manufactured. The Vikings very cleverly simplified their construction, as is shown in the two drawings of locks on the right. The lids of Viking chests were locked in much the same way as a modern suitcase: there were hinged mounts which had eyes or little lugs fitting into the lock proper. But whereas modern man has to use both hands to unlock his suitcase, because it has two separate locks, the Viking could unlock (or lock) his chest in one operation. Padlocks were common during the Viking Age. Their method of construction was well adapted to the abilities of a country smith. As in the case of the chest-lock, a maximum of security was achieved with the minimum of intricately-shaped details. Viking smiths, in fact, provide an object-lesson in how to construct an entirely adequate padlock while using nothing but plain pieces of iron. When found nowadays Viking padlocks are almost always locked. The reason for this is that the bow or hoop of a Viking padlock — like most other early locks of the type — is not hinged or pivoted as it would be in a modern one, but is a separate, removable piece. To avoid losing this piece, one had, therefore, to lock a Viking padlock immediately after use.

TWO CLEVER LOCKS

The spring mechanism of a Viking padlock (top drawings) seems simple, but was an irritating deterrent to anyone without the right key. The hole at the shaft end of the blade of the spadeshaped key engages and compresses the double-bladed spring on the bow, so that the bow can be withdrawn and removed. The slot at the end of the blade fits over a specially-shaped piece of iron inside the lock, thus preventing the use of unauthorized keys. The chest-lock (shown below) works in another way. The key is shaped more like a modern one, and is intended to be twisted. When this is done, its prongs slip through the holes of the locking bar, and lift the spring on the upper side. A lateral movement of the key in the keyhole, and the chest is open.

WALLET, WEIGHTS AND MEASURES

This skin wallet of fine workmanship (1), with many practical pockets, was needed by its owner, a Birka merchant, to keep silver coins of different values separate. When found, it contained a few of these, and also some small weights. A small portable set of scales (2) was part of the necessary equipment of the tradesman in Viking times — not for weighing merchandise but for weighing the payment, silver. But such scales were sensitive articles which had to be stored and transported carefully. This illustration shows how the scales were folded up (3), the pans placed inside one another (4), the whole thing put in a round metal box with a cover (5), and, finally, the box stowed in a skin bag (6, 7).

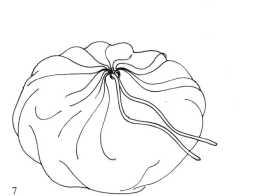

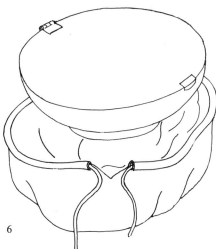

SIGNS OF WORLD-WIDE TRADE - AND LOOT

In the tenth century hundreds of thousands of coins like those on the left poured into the Baltic region, and their presence bears witness to Viking skill at trading, and fighting, in the farthest reaches of the known world. Some coins are from as far away as Samarkand, Tashkent, Bokhara and other Muslim mints more than 2,000 miles away across the forests, steppes and deserts of Central Asia. With the rare exception of coins minted at Birka and at Hedeby, the Scandinavians did not produce currency themselves until the eleventh century. Instead they continued to use this imported coinage in its original form. At present, about 85,000 Islamic and Persian coins have been found in Scandinavia, mostly struck by the Samanid dynasty which ruled in Turkestan in the tenth century. There are only slightly fewer German coins, mostly of the eleventh century, and from England there are at least 50,000, almost all minted between 990 and 1050 A.D. Most consist of tribute extorted from the English. The Anglo-Saxon Chronicle reports the payment of over 200,000 pounds weight of silver to the Vikings between 991 and 1018.

MAKING CHANGE - AND WEIGHING IT

Barter was no longer the only means of exchange, but pure-metal weight, assessed on scales like those illustrated at right, was the only wholly reliable monetary standard. To the dealer of skins in Birka or Kaupang, a silver coin was worth exactly the same as an equivalent weight of uncoined silver — unlike today, when silver is worth considerably more uncoined than coined. Therefore, he did not hesitate to split the coins into small segments when change was needed. Arm bracelets or unworked silver rods, spirally shaped and securely fitted around the wrist — for pockets did not exist — were another form of working capital. A piece could simply be cut off and weighed when needed. The box at the lower edge of the picture is a case for a folding balance of this kind — functional, elegant, and not much larger than a pocket watch. Marked weights of iron and bronze of oriental design, the property of the merchants, are often found in Birka graves.

In Viking houses, most of what little furniture there was, was built permanently into the house, and consisted mainly of fixed benches on which to lie on to sleep. Large decorated beds were used in the royal households of Gokstad and Oseberg, as can be seen from the finds, but it is not known if they were common. The benches and beds were furnished with heavy blankets like those found at Oseberg. There, and in a few other instances, the remains of feather pillows have been found, so it is possible that the Vikings sometimes slept under eiderdown covers.

A rich Danish grave from the late Viking Age contained fragments of a small wooden table. On the table was a shallow bronze dish, and the whole may have served as a wash-stand. The ordinary household table of the Vikings would probably look like the long narrow tables known from the Middle Ages, and depicted on the Bayeux Tapestry. In the Oseberg ship burial was found the only known chair of the period.

Articles not in use were kept in wooden chests and boxes. Several splendid chests were found in the Oseberg ship, and locks, keys and hinges have survived in many graves even when the wood has long since crumbled away. The locks are often of ingenious construction, and many of the small boxes must have been intended for valuables. Some of the Oseberg chests are veritable strong-boxes, heavily iron-bound, while others have only the minimum of iron mounts to hold them together. The keys to the various locks would hang from the housewife's belt, as a symbol of her social status. In old Norse laws, it is stated that a woman has the right of divorce if her husband denies her the keys of the house.

A large trough from the Oseberg ship still contained remains of cereals, and was surely used for kneading dough. Flour for bread and porridge was ground in hand-mills, a tedious task taking up much of the time of the domestic servants. Bread was probably baked on small round pans, which are often found in Viking graves. Many of them can be rotated on a central rivet to avoid burning the bread: see illustration on page 180. Kettles were hung from chains above the open hearth. Viking-Age kettles were of riveted iron or copper sheet, or carved from soapstone. Most of them have a capacity of between seven and eleven pints. Soapstone is soft and easily carved, and retains heat for a very long time, so it is a good material for cooking vessels. The soapstone vessels, at any rate, must have been very popular, for a great many have been found. Wooden ladles were used for stirring and pouring, and several have been found in the Oseberg ship.

A BUCKET WITH BRONZE TRIMMINGS

This bucket from the Oseberg find contained wild apples when found — part of the food for the voyage to the land of the dead. The engraved openwork hoops do not resemble the decorative style generally used by the Vikings, and the bucket is probably imported. It may have come from the British Isles. A richly decorated object like this was probably part of the "tableware" used in the Oseberg household.

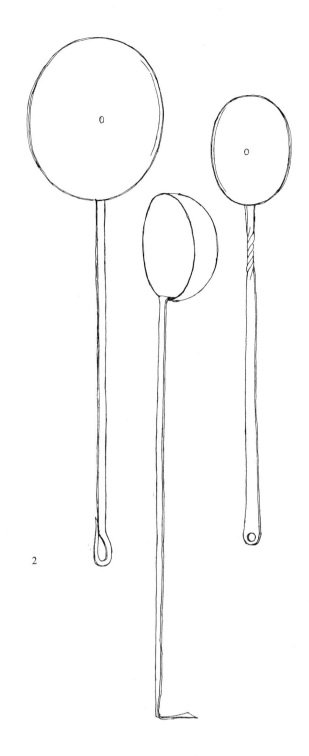

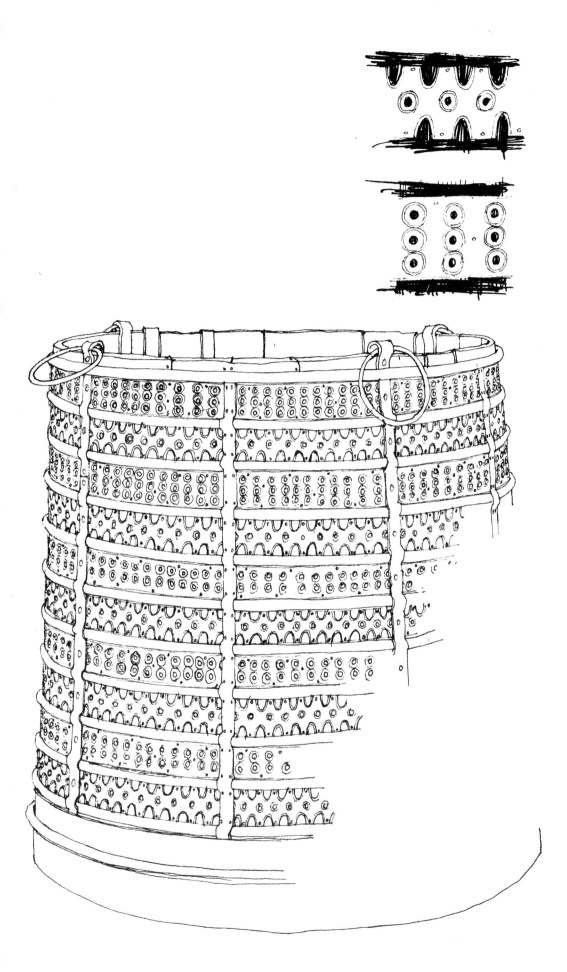

DOMESTIC IMPLEMENTS

1. Details of the bucket found at Oseberg (see page 178).

2. Simpler than the bucket, but very practical, are the two frying irons with their revolving discs, and the long-shafted scoop, which could also be used for heating drinks.

3. Iron implements for frying meat and fish.

4. This iron kettle, with a collapsible stand supported by clawed birds' feet, was probably used as a camping utensil only. It stood firmly on the ground over a fire at a temporary camp-site.

Meat and fish could be grilled or boiled. The grill forks and spits found in many graves point to the popularity of grilled food, then as now. Some graves have large forks, for picking choice pieces of meat or fish from the cooking-pot. Much fish and meat was undoubtedly preserved for use in winter or on long sea voyages, in much the same ways as those used in later times: by salting, smoking and drying. Well-worn carving-boards for cutting up dried fish or meat were found in the Gokstad ship, and in the Oseberg ship a large table knife lay among the other cooking implements. For eating, every man, woman and child had his or her own knife, and spoons of horn or wood. Otherwise, they ate with their fingers. Ordinary axes were used for butchering animals and cutting up meat. Two such axes were found in the Oseberg ship. Well-made, decorated troughs and trays from the Oseberg find were probably the "table-ware" of the royal household. In the Gokstad ship were flat round wooden disks, which probably served as plates.

By the standards of the modern housewife, used to stainless steel and electricity, a Viking housewife's kitchen equipment would seem appalling. But though the implements were few, even in the Viking Age their shape and function had been tested for many centuries, and they are as practical as anything of the sort made today. Some of the large buckets found at Oseberg and Gokstad may have been used for brewing beer, and others as containers for salt meat. One smaller bucket is fitted with a lock in the lid, and must have been intended as a container for other things than food. When found, it held weaving tools.

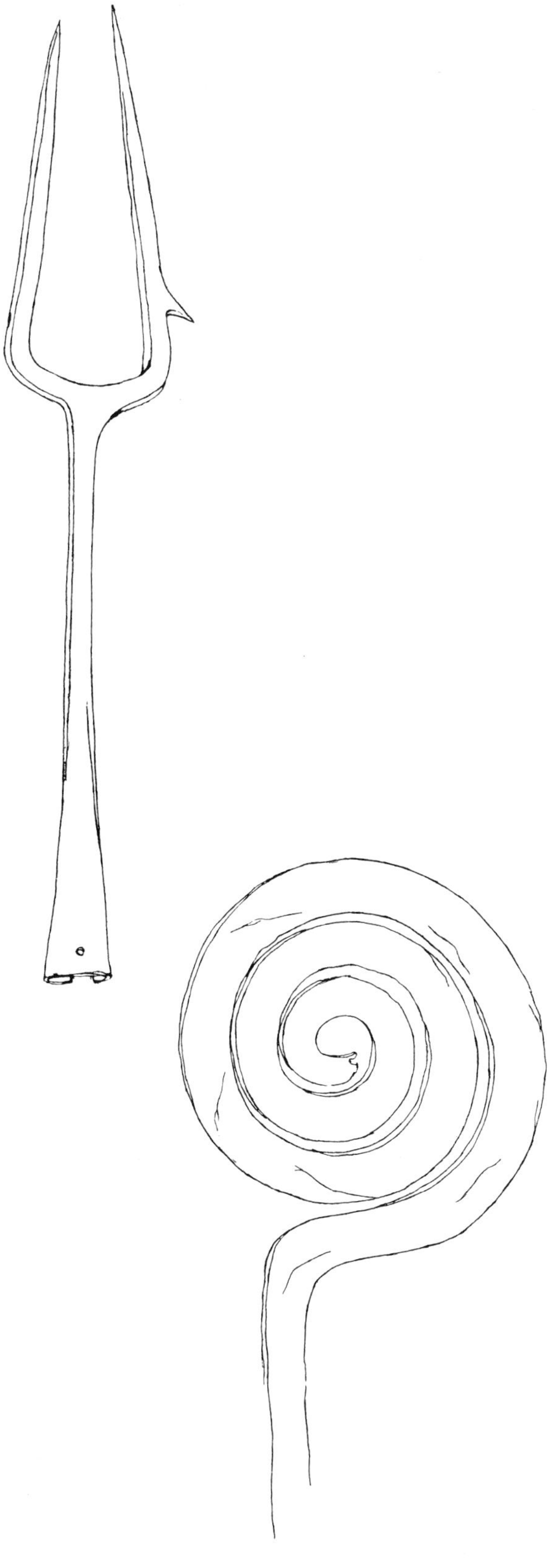

3

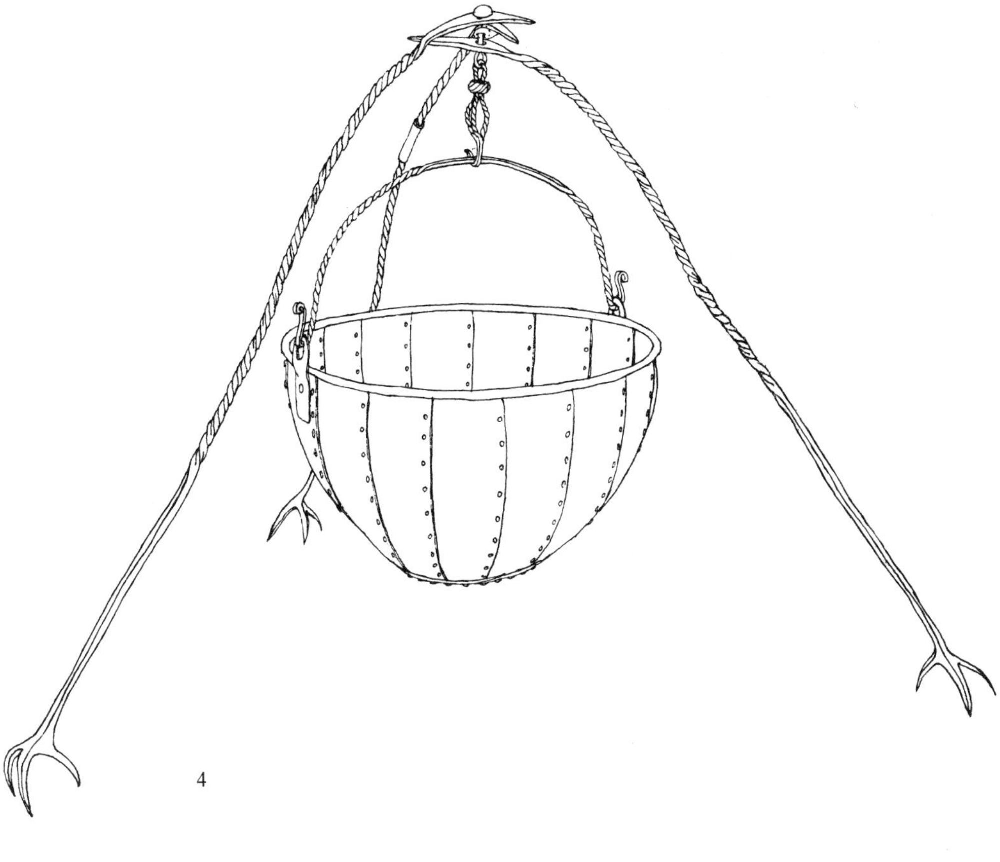

4

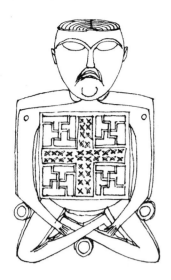

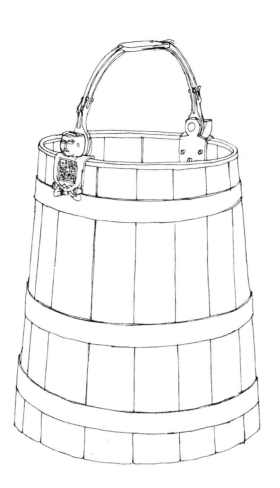

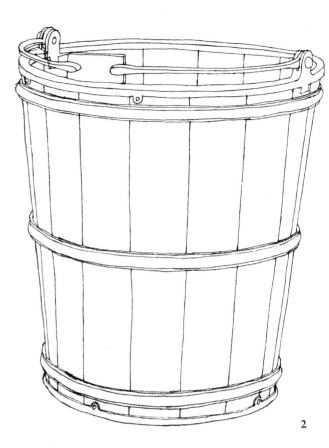

1

2

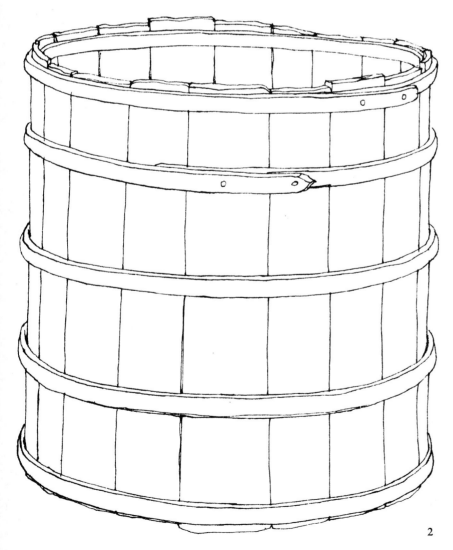

2

TROUGHS AND A BUCKET

1. Wooden bucket from the Oseberg ship. Made of yew-wood, with hoops and mountings of yellow metal, probably brass. The small male figures have enamel inlays. The bucket was most probably made in Ireland. It is the finest ever found and was obviously a prized possession of its Viking owner.

2. Other buckets from Oseberg.

3. Wooden containers from the Oseberg ship. The lower one, which in the grave held weaving tools, has a lid that can be locked in place. The upper one is decorated with criss-cross knife marks.

4. Details of the decorations on two small troughs. It is characteristic of the Viking's love of show and ornamentation, that even simple everyday articles were decorated.

5. Troughs from the Oseberg ship. Both have been cut from single blocks of wood. The large one was used for kneading dough. When it was found, there were still remnants of dough in it. Several small decorated troughs, probably used for serving food, have also been found.

3

4

5

3

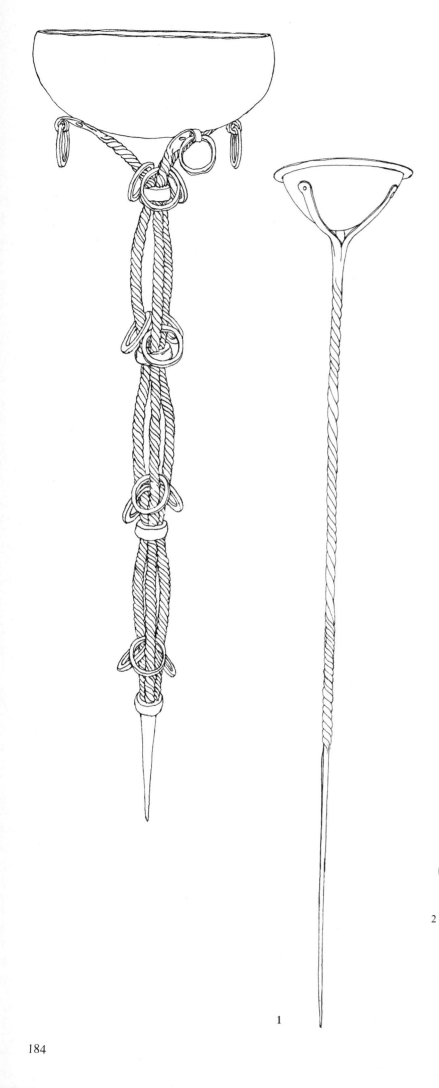
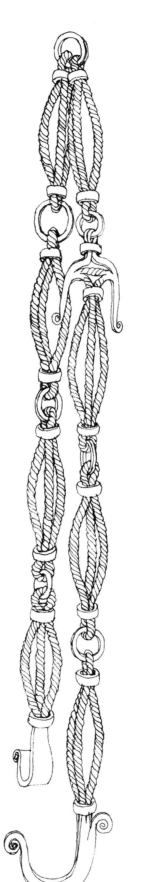

3

HEATING, LIGHTING AND COOKING

1. Iron lamps from the Oseberg ship. They burned tallow or fish oil, and probably used a wick of moss. They are pointed at the lower end so that they can be stuck into the ground or the clay floor of a house.

2. Iron chain for hanging a kettle over the fire, found in the Oseberg ship. It can be shortened to regulate the heat.

3. Steels for firemaking. They were struck against a piece of flint to give sparks.

4. Soapstone vessel from a Viking-Age grave. Soapstone is a soft, easily carved material, and it was popular for cauldrons, net sinkers and many other things. In some places it was mined extensively, and in Viking times had become an important Norwegian export.

5. Wooden ladle and trough from the Oseberg ship.

6. Carved serving tray of wood and a large kitchen knife, from the Oseberg ship.

7. Stirring ladle of wood from the Oseberg find.

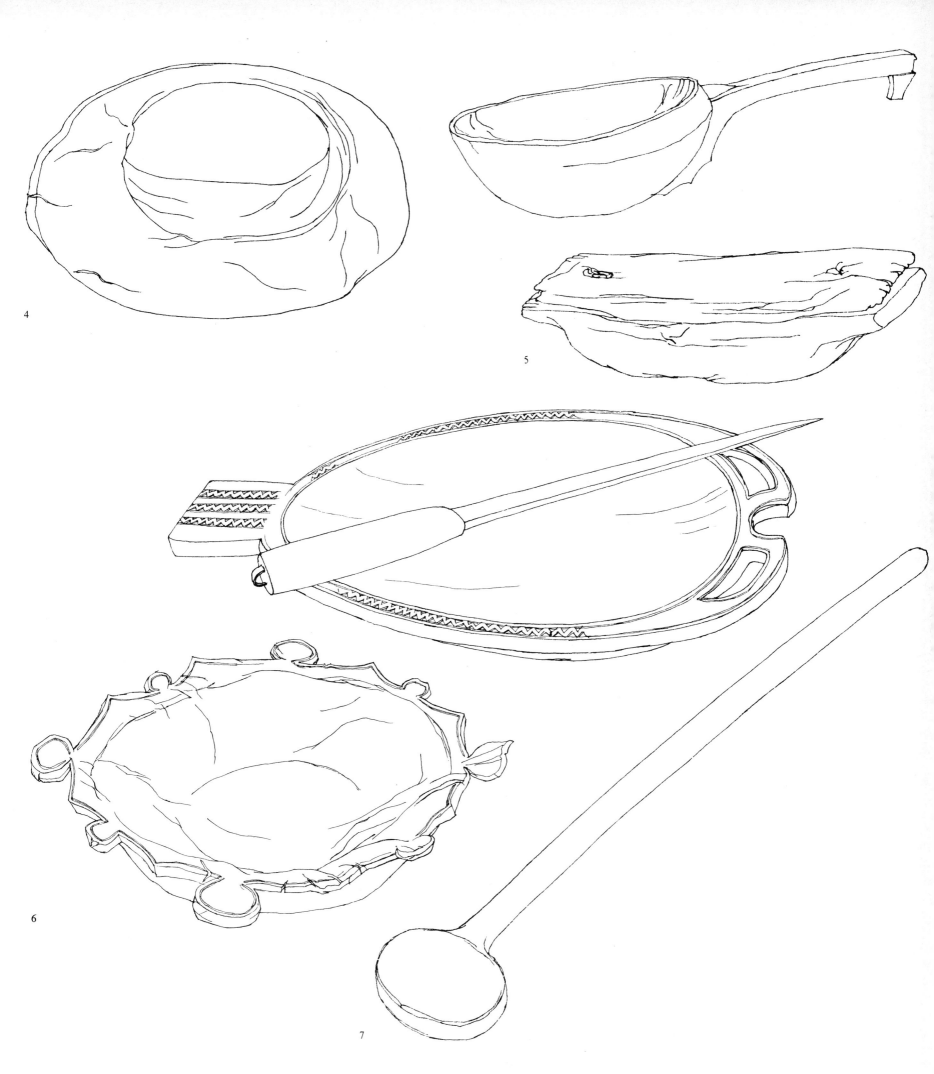

4

5

6

7

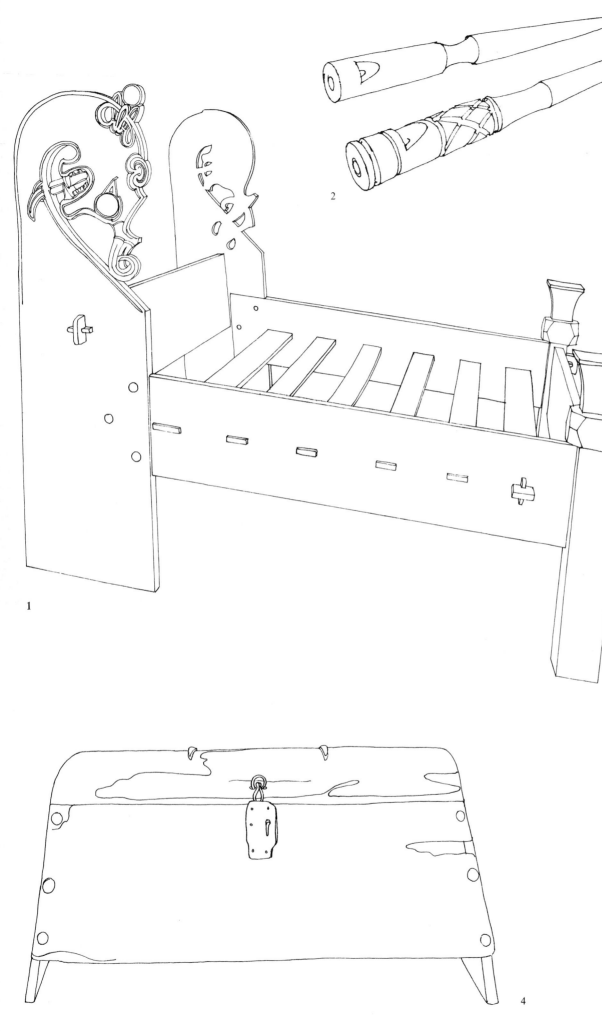

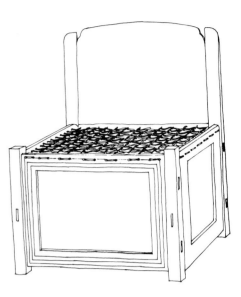

1

4

AN OSEBERG MISCELLANY

1. Big decorated beds were found in both the Oseberg and the Gokstad ship, together with plain ones. The beds can be taken apart for use on voyages. The largest measures six by seven feet, so they were surely not intended for use on board, where they would take up too much room. When a tent was pitched on shore, beds would probably be set up there, permitting the chief to sleep in a manner suitable to his station.

2. Two carved whistles.

3. The little chair is puzzling. Unlike chairs in contemporary or medieval illustrations, or others that have been preserved, which are often so high that there is an extra bar as a foot-rest, this one is remarkably low, less than 15½ inches. Possibly it was intended for a child.

4. Iron-bound chest. Chests of this kind must have been an important part of the furniture in most Viking-Age houses. This chest is exactly the right height to serve as a rowing bench on a Viking ship.

A CHEST FROM THE OSEBERG SHIP

This chest, of a type the Vikings used to store domestic implements, is about four feet long, and sixteen inches high. It is made of oak reinforced with iron bands. The end battens, or "legs", on which the chest stands are pegged into the bottom plank. The lid is secured by a padlock, which has survived, though the key has been lost. Each of the lock hasps is shaped like an animal's head. The decoration of the chest consists of iron plates ornamented with tinned nail-heads.

IRON CAULDRONS

That Viking smiths could handle sheet-iron is proved by the two iron cauldrons shown here. The smaller one is fashioned by hammering a flat piece of sheet iron into shape. The larger is composed of several hammered sheets riveted together. Iron cauldrons are less frequent in Viking-Age graves than soapstone ones, presumably because they were more expensive to manufacture.

BLACKSMITH'S TOOLS

Anvils, hammer and tongs; the favourite tools of the smith. Such tools developed a functional shape long before the Viking Age, and they have barely changed today. If the smith is handy and has a sure eye, he does not need other tools for much of his work. The Viking smith's work was based on 1,000-year-old traditions in the handling of iron, and his best craftsmanship can hardly be copied to-day.

A CARPENTER'S SKILL

An axe or a broad-axe — the latter being a variation of the axe in which the edge is only ground from one side — has until recent times been the woodworker's most important tool. With this implement, walls, posts and planks for houses and furniture were cut, and stocks were split for floors in storehouses where earthen floors were not possible because of the rats. With the axe, all the wooden parts of a ship were hewn — later, of course, they could be decoratively carved — and with it the blocks intended for wooden tools and shafts were given a rough shape which could then be evened off with a knife. To " yxa till " in Swedish (to make with an axe) still means to rough something out crudely and quickly so that it meets the basic need, having a proper form but not a proper finish.

In the Viking Age, as today, many things were made on a " do it yourself " basis. The Viking farmer made many of his farming tools himself, and repaired his wood and metal utensils. Most men owned a few tools — a hammer, firetongs, an axe, a knife.

From other grave-finds it is clear, however, that highly-skilled craftsmen did the jobs that no average man could manage. The quality of the discoveries from Oseberg and Gokstad shows that well-trained smiths and carpenters, wood-carvers and boat builders were employed by royal households. A Norwegian grave in Telemark revealed a great number of smith's tools and other implements. The specialized range of tools suggests that this man was solely a smith, probably concentrating on high-class weapons. The spearheads with silver and copper inlays were probably his own work. A tool chest lost during the late Viking Age was found at Mästermyr on the Baltic island of Gotland. The hundred so different implements in it give a clear picture of a travelling craftsman, who would stay some time at different farms, doing all sorts of jobs. He had a wide selection of wood-working tools, and good iron-working equipment, and seems occasionally to have worked as a coppersmith as well.

For shaping wood, his main tools were axe, adze and knife, with scrapers instead of planes for smoothing. The well-made planks of Viking ships show how efficient such tools were in the hands of a skilled man. Special scrapers were used for hollowing-out, and for decorating. Holes were bored with augers of different sizes, and there was a selection of chisels. Viking Age saws are rare, but the "Mästermyr man" had two, one used for wood, the other probably for metal. Files for use on wood or bone have been found.

The most common iron-working tools in grave-finds are the hammer and blacksmith's tongs, the latter used in handling hot iron. The better-equipped smiths' graves have hammers and tongs in several sizes. Anvils have been found — they are often shaped like a modern anvil — but are all surprisingly small. When hammering out large pieces, the Viking smith therefore probably used a stone anvil. Shears for cutting thin metal are sometimes found, but they are rare, and seem to have been a tool for the specialist, not the average blacksmith. Smiths working in precious metal had crucibles for melting silver or bronze. The silver was often cast into ingots in soapstone moulds. Filigree work was much practised by the Viking Age, and several drawplates for drawing wire have been discovered. Punched decoration was common too. The "Mästermyr man " had punches among his tools.

A charcoal fire was used for heating metals, with bellows supplying air. There

189

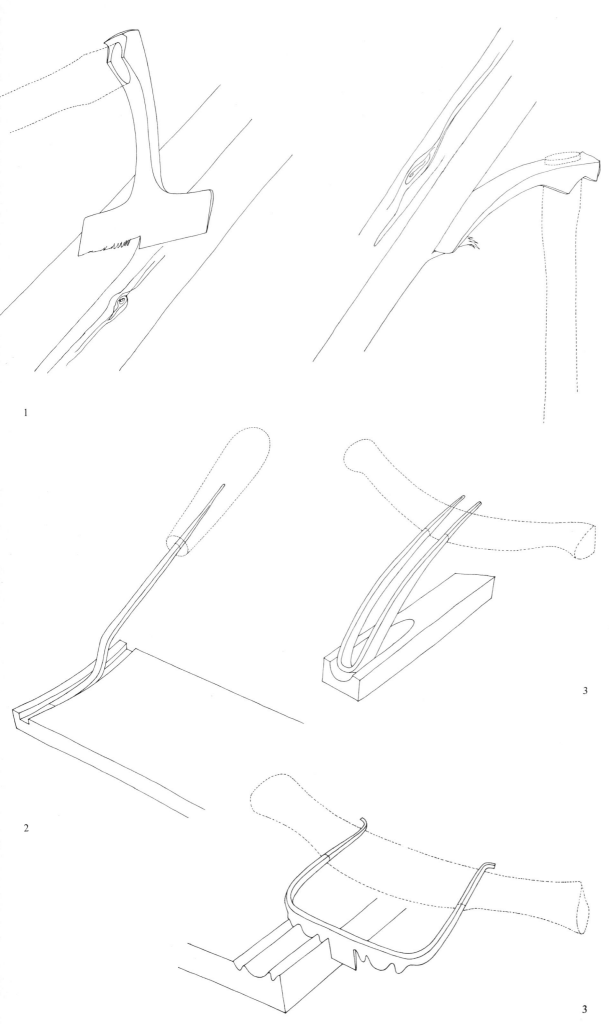

1

2

3

3

CUTTING AND SHAPING TOOLS

1. Axe and adze for woodworking. They were the most important tools of the craftsmen in wood. The T- shaped adze is probably a boatbuilder's tool.

2. Chisel for woodworking. Carpenters in the Viking Age, as they do today, used chisels in many ways — for hollowing out, to shape holes for dowels, and so forth.

3. Scrapers, used for hollowing out and for decorating. The decorative mouldings on the planks of Viking ships were made with such scrapers. Others, with a straight edge, took the place of planes for smoothing wood.

4. Coarse file for working horn or wood. The files for metal found in smiths' graves have much finer teeth.

5. Saw for metal. Saws were very rare in the Viking Age, and were seldom used by the average craftsman. One type of craftsman who could not do without the saw was the combmaker, who needed it to cut the teeth of combs made from bone, horn and wood.

6. A knife, the most versatile all-round tool in woodworking. However poor otherwise, nearly every Viking grave contained a knife.

7. Augers of different sizes, for boring holes in wood. The handles are reconstructed.

is reason to believe that Viking-Age smithies very much resemble those shown in existing medieval illustrations. The fire was tended by an assistant who handled the bellows, while the smith worked by the anvil, which was sunk in a large block of wood in the middle of the floor. The redhot iron from the hearth was gripped with the tongs and hammered into shape. Finishing was done with file and whetstones, and the latter were also used to sharpen the edges of cutting tools.

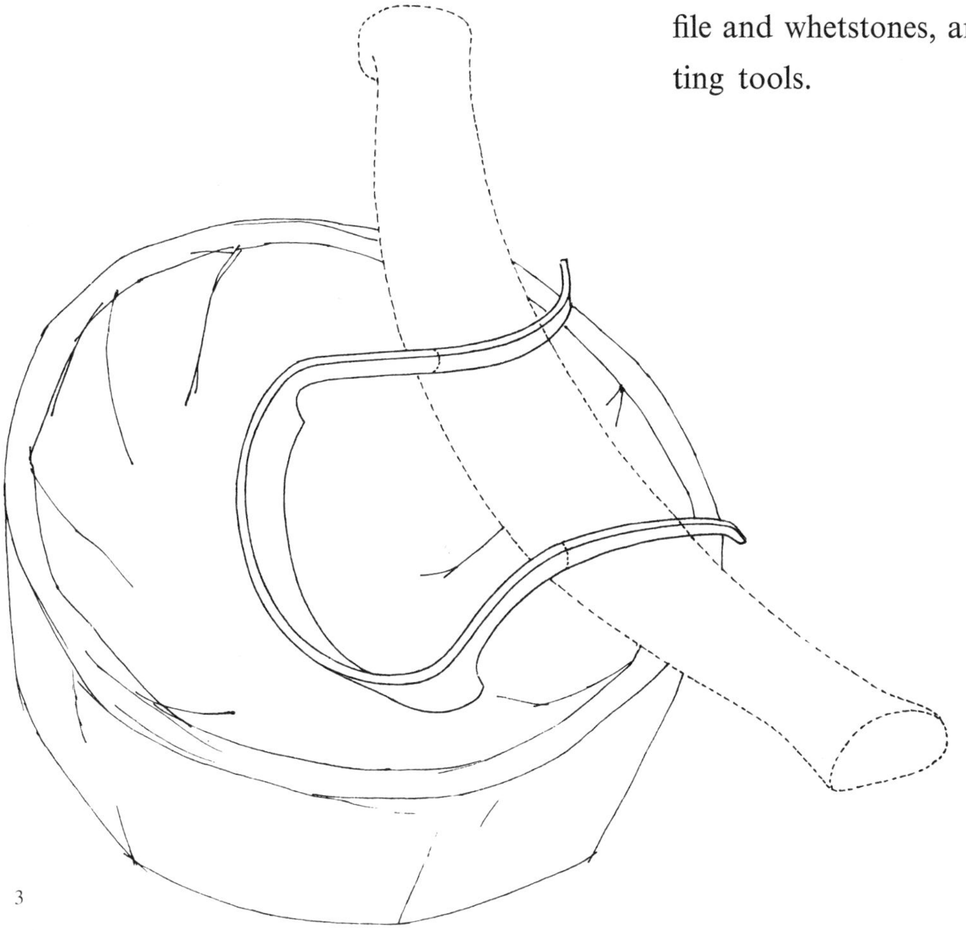

3

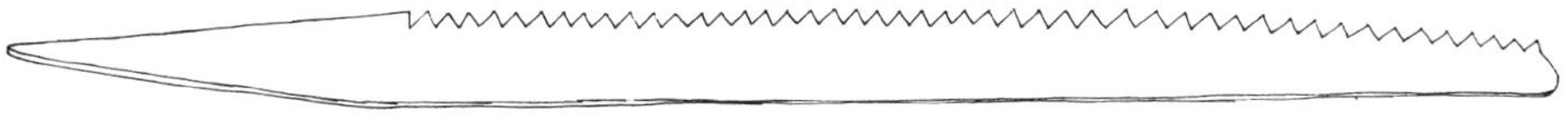

4

5

6

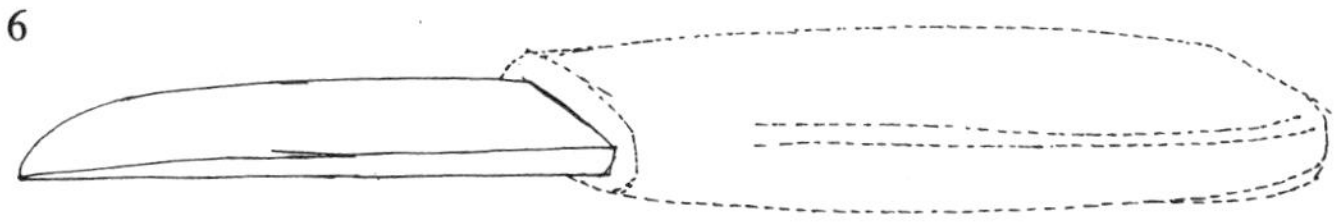

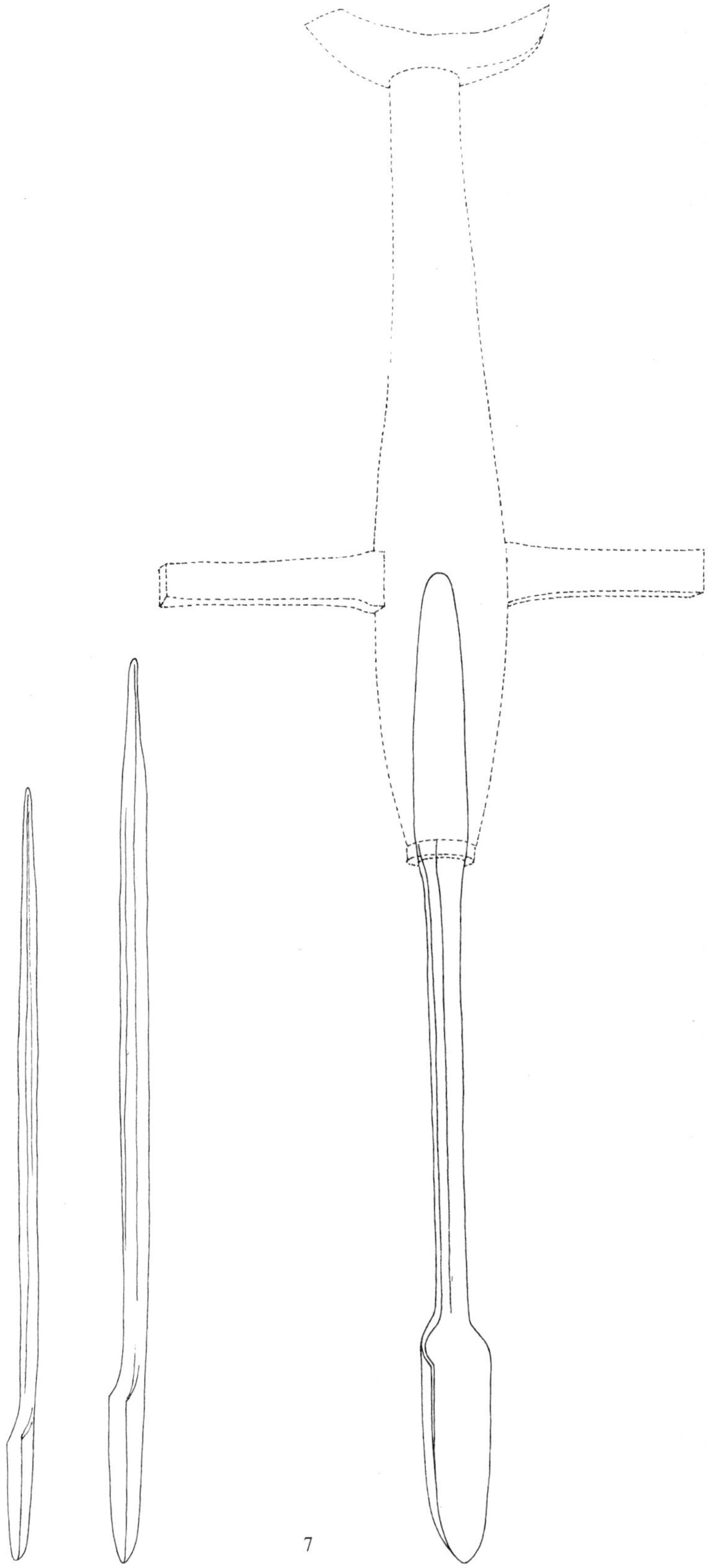

7

3

2

1

METAL WORK

1. Smith's tongs. Tongs come in many sizes, like hammers, for handling different pieces of iron. A few have a different shape of jaw, and are intended for drawing gold or silver wire.

2. Smith's workmanship: chains, probably for dogs.

3. Hammers. Viking-Age hammers differ in weight and size, from the smallest goldsmith's hammers to a large sledge weighing many pounds.

FORGING A SWORD

On the far left are details carved on a stave-church portal at Hyllestad in Setesdal, Norway, dating from the end of the twelfth century. The pictures illustrate the saga of Sigurd Favnesbane. In the scene at bottom, the sword Gram is being forged. The smith, to the left, is holding a piece of red-hot iron in his tongs, hammering it out on the anvil with powerful strokes. Beside the anvil, a large hammer lies ready for use. An apprentice is tending the bellows. Between the two men the woodcarver has depicted a torch, illuminating the smithy. In the upper scene the finished sword is tried on the anvil, and breaks.

A GIRL SPINNING

Spinning on a distaff was an art which every girl had to learn. The distaff or hand spindle consisted quite simply of a rod passed through the centre of a weight called a distaff wheel. Distaff wheels could be of burnt clay or stone (often soapstone), and are quite common finds. The wool or flax that was to be spun was wound around a large, often ornate stick which was held against the body by the right upper arm. The end of the thread was fastened to the distaff wheel, which was set spinning. As material was drawn little by little out of the flax or wool, the thread grew longer. Each time it reached the floor, it was necessary to stop work, wind up the thread onto the distaff and start again.

By far the greatest number of cloth pieces from the Viking Age found in Scandinavia are wool, because it survives better in the earth than vegetable fibres like linen and hemp. But small bits of cloth made from vegetable fibres have occasionally come down to us because of the chemical action of metal patina or rust. It was in this way, for instance, that pieces of fine linen were preserved on the underside of brooches in graves at Birka. In addition to such native materials, fragments of expensive imported silk materials have been found, and embroideries and lace-work in gold and silver thread. Some graves held woollen goods of almost incredible fineness — with as many as 125 or more threads to the inch. This may be the famous "Frisian cloth", spun and woven in the most favourable climate imaginable — the humid coastal areas of the North Sea. Before spinning, the wool was combed with iron combs. When wool was cut, or the flax prepared, it was spun on a spindle (see drawing opposite), wound into skeins, and kept as skeins or balls of thread. Distaff wheels and skein-winding tools have been preserved. Skeins and balls of yarn have also been found in a few places. How was weaving done in the Viking Age? A passage in *Njal's Saga* explains:

"On the morning of Good Friday, it happened . . . that a man called Dorrud . . . saw twelve riders approach a woman's bower and disappear inside. He walked over to the bower and peered through the window; inside, he could see women with a loom set up before them. Men's heads were used in place of weights, and men's intestines for the weft and warp; a sword served as the beater, and the shuttle was an arrow. And these were the verses they were chanting:

Blood rains

From the cloudy web

On the broad loom

Of slaughter.

The web of man,

Grey as armour,

Is now being woven;

The Valkyries

Will cross it

With a crimson weft.

The warp is made

Of human entrails;

Human heads

Are used as weights;

193

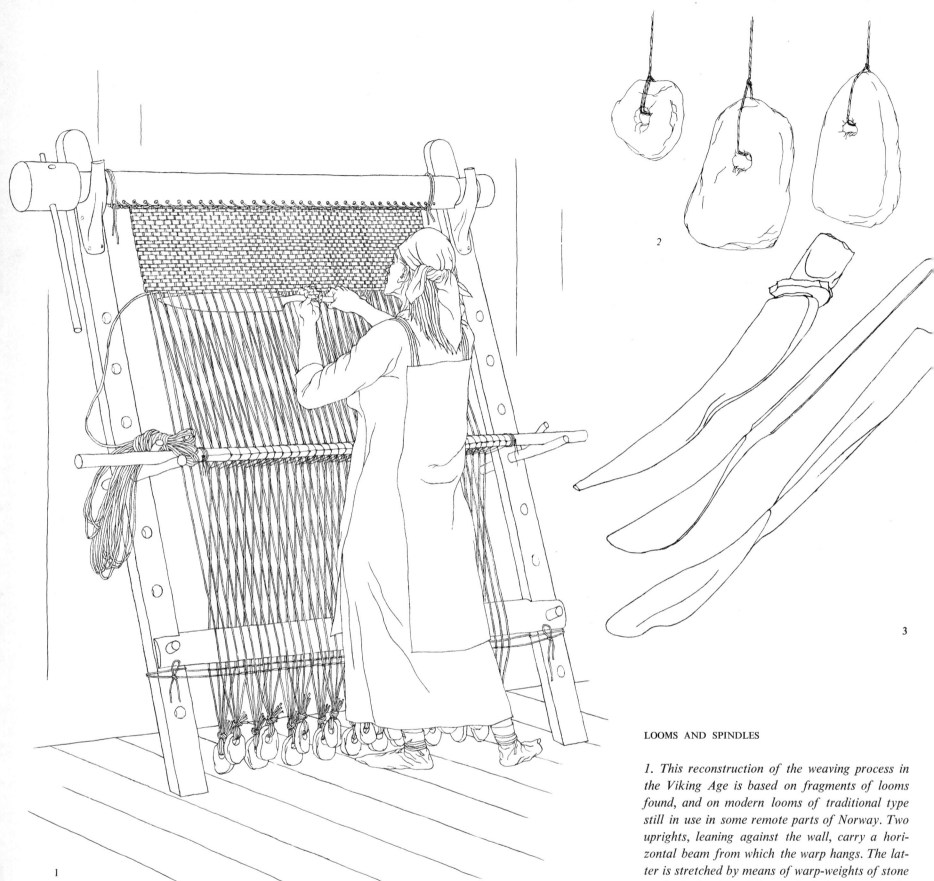

LOOMS AND SPINDLES

1. This reconstruction of the weaving process in the Viking Age is based on fragments of looms found, and on modern looms of traditional type still in use in some remote parts of Norway. Two uprights, leaning against the wall, carry a horizontal beam from which the warp hangs. The latter is stretched by means of warp-weights of stone or fired clay. The different sheds (openings in the warp through which the shuttle is thrown) are made by threading the warp-threads through heddles (looped cords) attached to movable heddle-rods. 2. Soapstone weights for warp-weighted looms. The upright warp-weighted loom was the only one known to the Vikings. To keep the warp straight, loom-weights of soapstone or baked clay were used.

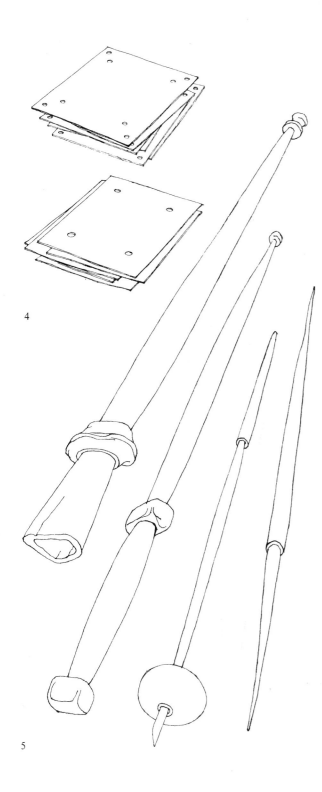

The heddle-rods
Are blood-wet spears;
The shafts are iron-bound,
And arrows are the shuttles.
With swords we will weave
This web of battle."

These bloody stage-properties notwithstanding, this rather macabre description of an ominous vision gives a quite graphic account of how Viking-Age women worked at their looms. Their methods were the same as those followed in the Bronze Age in Scandinavia, and in earlier antiquity. The same methods survived in Norway and Finland within living memory, and even into our own day. A vertical-warp loom, of the kind known as a warp-weighted loom (see drawing page 194), was the most usual in Viking times. The warp is kept taut by means of a number of free-hanging weights. The weaver walks to and fro while at work, and the weft is beaten upwards.

By means of a four-shed construction, one could weave both ordinary equilateral plain twill, and also produce more decorative results such as lozenge twill, chevron twill and so forth. More resplendent tapestry patterns could be achieved by inserting coloured threads by hand in the course of weaving. Because the warp was kept taut by weights dangling round the weaver's ankles, and because of the lack of any proper reed to keep the threads at a uniform distance apart, the warp is unevenly spaced in cloths woven in this way. Still more conspicuous and readily understandable is the unevenness of the weft, particularly in cross-striped materials. The weaving proceeded from the top downwards and the weft was beaten upwards by means of a quite short sword-beater — or simply with the hand. No two people have exactly the same touch, so that with two weavers or more working as a team it is easily seen that the weft could occasionally become uneven. But how in fact can anything be known about Viking weavers — even, for instance, that several of them worked simultaneously at one weaving? The evidence lies in the cloth itself. Examination of prehistoric woven textiles shows that two weft threads sometimes run towards each other from opposite sides at exactly the same level, then cross and continue on the line immediately below. And if three threads that meet all the time consistently cross, and continue on, that means that there were three weavers working together. The sagas tell how different kinds of cloth were used in a room — large wall hangings, above them a long narrow tapestry, and pillows on the benches. Small tapestry fragments from Oseberg show battle scenes and religious processions originally depicted in many colours.

3. Small wooden tools from the Oseberg ship, probably used in tapestry-weaving.

4. Wooden tablets from the Oseberg ship, used for weaving bands by the "tablet-weave" technique. A tablet-woven band was often used as a starting-border. A warp-thread was twisted through each hole, and different sheds were formed by twisting the tablets a quarter-turn each time.

5. Spindles from the Oseberg ship, one with a distaff wheel of stone. The spindle was used for spinning yarn — the Vikings knew no other tools for this operation.

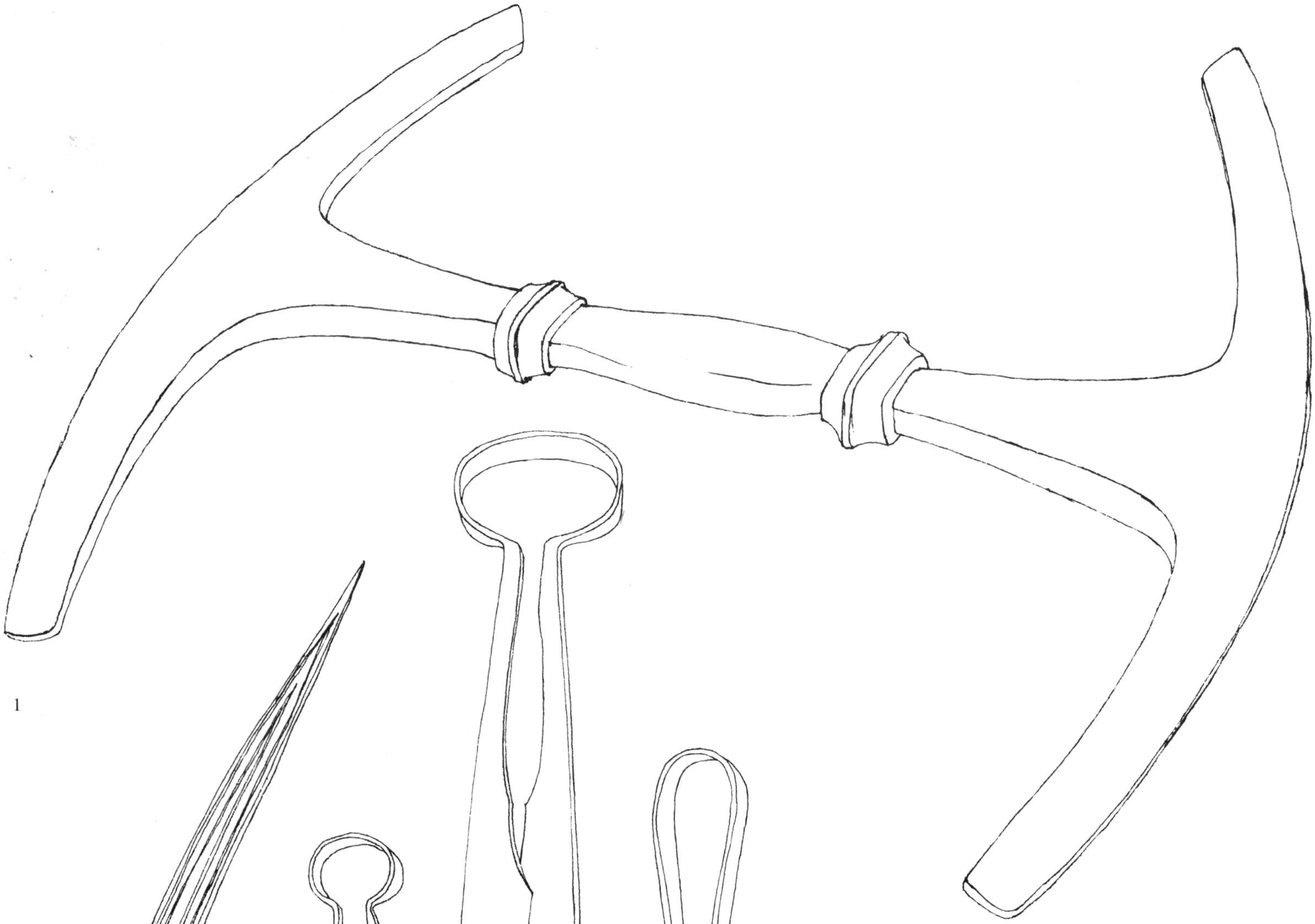

WEAVING ACCESSORIES

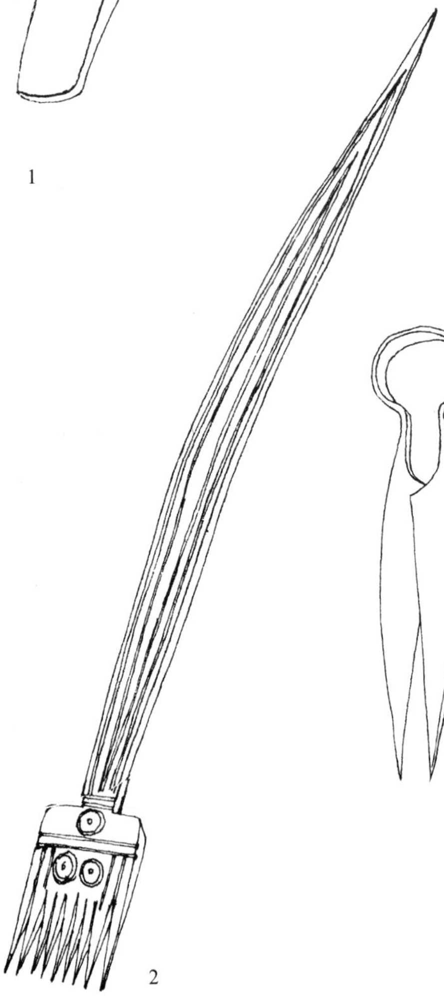

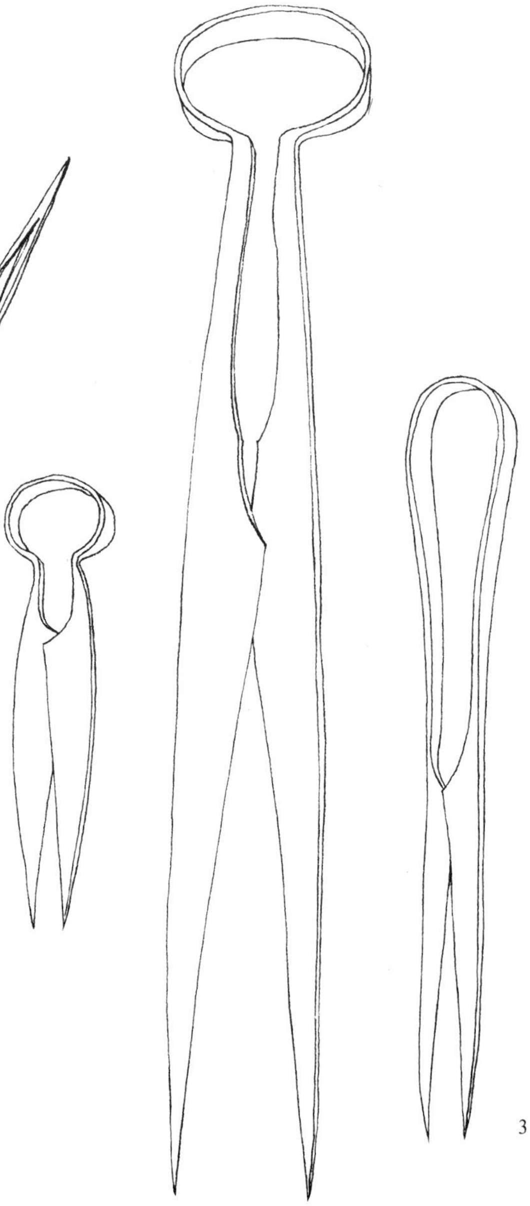

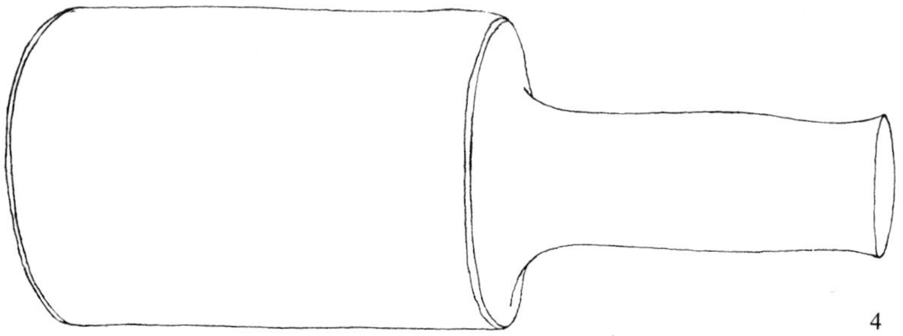

1. Skein-winding reel of beechwood from the Oseberg ship. Used when the necessary amount of yarn for weaving was to be rewound.

2. Weaving comb from the Oseberg ship, presumably used for beating together the weft in finer textiles.

3. Three pairs of shears from different Viking graves. The larger one is for cutting wool, the smaller for sewing.

4. Wooden mallet from the Oseberg ship, probably used in one of the stages of preparing flax.

A FRAGMENT OF HISTORY

The tapestries from Oseberg have lost most of their original colouring, and are a dull greyish-brown, but on the piece shown here a beautiful reddish colour can still be distinguished. The width of this tapestry is only between seven and nine inches, but a great multitude of people and events are depicted.

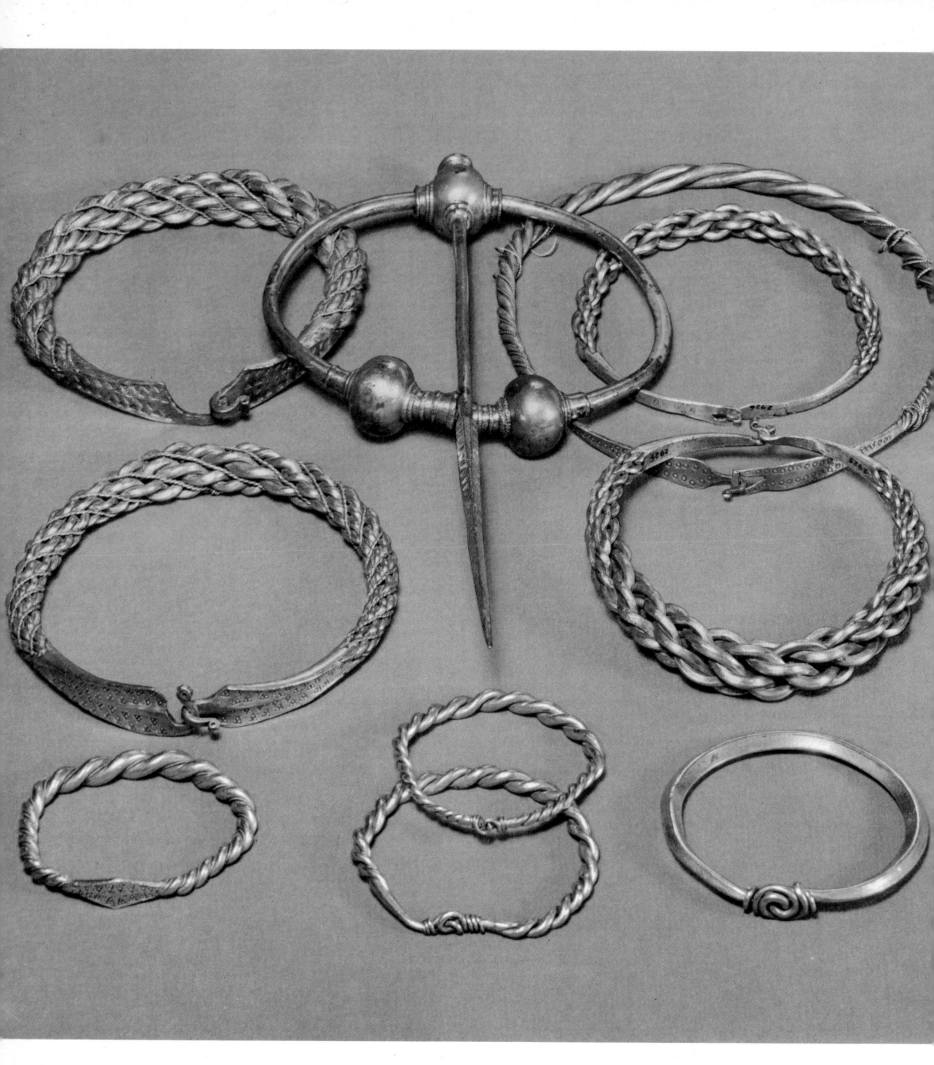

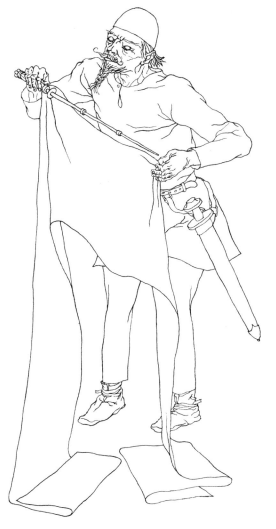

MEASURING BY FOOT AND THUMB

All the old measurements of length have names that tell how they originated. An aln *(ell) is the distance from the elbow to the fingertips; a* famn *(cord) is the distance between the fingers of both hands when the spinner stood with the hands spread wide apart; a* spann *(bucket) — which in later times became a cubic measure as well — is the distance spanned by the outstretched fingers of one hand; a* fot *(foot) is the length of the foot; and finally a* tum *(inch) was originally equivalent to the width of the thumb. But all arms are not the same length, nor all hands the same size, so it soon became apparent that suitable measuring rods of iron approved by some authority would be more convenient, and avoid the worst disagreements.*

A NORWEGIAN TREASURE

The find on the facing page, from Vullum in the north of Norway, consists of silver necklets and gold armlets. It is dominated by the enormous ring-and-pin brooch, made of silver in a design which, for Viking workmanship, is unusually plain.

PETTICOATS AND BROOCHES

Most clothes were probably made on the farms, by the housewife and her helpers. Viking women wore an undergarment (petticoat, shift or chemise), but it was apparently the height of fashion to let this hang down as far as possible beneath the outer garment — to "have one's slip showing", as it were. This idea of wearing a linen petticoat was new in Scandinavia, for earlier, women seem to have worn only coarse woollen clothes, just like the early Romans, who learned the idea of wearing linen undergarments from the Celts. In another respect, too, the Viking Age petticoat was rather smart: it was pleated. This meant that it was wide enough to allow the formation of a sort of sleeve, just like the early Greek pleated tunic or *chiton*.

This petticoat was probably sewn together or drawn close at the neck with a ribbon or draw-string. Women's clothes had no buttons, hooks or lacing. The outer garment was held up, not by the waist, but by straps over the shoulders, these being fastened by a pair of the oval brooches which are extremely common in women's graves of the Viking period. A practical explanation of this otherwise apparently complex arrangement would be that it allowed easy breastfeeding of an infant even with a garment that reached so far up the mother's body. The brooches were very elegant, in that the pin was completely hidden under the hollow convex shell of the brooch. This was made possible by the use of special shoulder straps, which could easily be caught by the pin (see pag 202). In order to prevent the straps or garment from being cut by sharp edges, the brooches were provided with flanges which were made increasingly broad as time went on.

The oval brooches found in graves show a strange tendency to be uglier and uglier the more recent they are. Is this to be explained as simply a degeneration in style or is it one of the evil effects of the then-new custom of clustering together in towns, where rapidly-changing fashions would have induced Viking womenfolk to keep asking for more and more new brooches? If so, their husbands, in turn, would have begun asking the bronze-smith for cheaper and cheaper articles, which the bronze-smith would try to provide by mass-producing second-rate stuff. Attractive as such speculation is, the real reason for the increasing ugliness of the oval brooches may more likely have been changes in dress. The brooches were no longer meant to be seen because they came to be hidden by a third garment, the shawl. This was an imported idea: shawls were used in Byzantium as well as among the Frisians. And Frisian women used an extra brooch — often rectangular or with symmetrical "wings" — to keep their shawls fastened. Brooches of precisely this sort, transferred

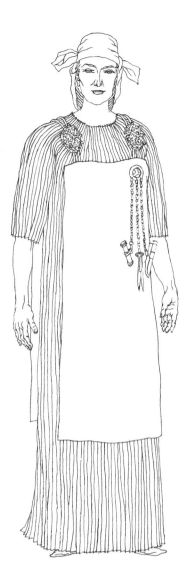

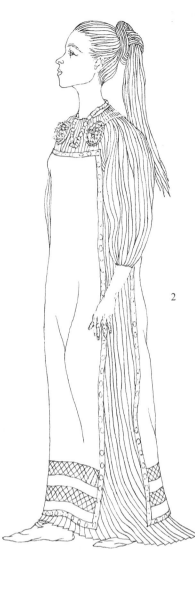

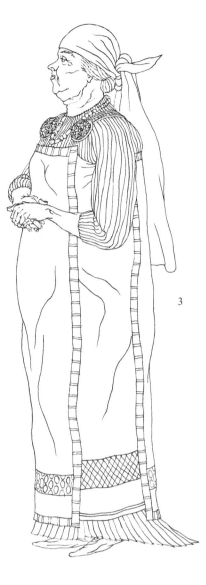

1

2

3

4

FEMININE FASHIONS

Tailoring in the modern sense was unknown in the making of women's clothes. Over a pleated linen petticoat, rectangular sheets often of very expensive cloth were worn, just as in latter-day Russian folk costume (2, 3). They were joined by oval brooches (far left) at the shoulder. The result was maximum accessibility when a child had to be breast-fed (4). Sewing implements were always ready to hand, being carried on the person, hanging on chains (1), which may have been suspended from pins like that illustrated on the left. Bracelets, some of which opened (above, left), were also worn.

THE SHAWL

In the Viking Age, the shawl — in later times a garment for the poor — seems to have been very fashionable. As so often happens in the case of fashions, it was of foreign inspiration (in this case Byzantine). It could be worn either hanging down straight (2, 3, 4), or folded into a triangle (1), and fastened by a shawl brooch, illustrated between (1) and (2). Little is known of Viking women's headdress. Contemporary pictures show a large knot which can either be a hair-knot (1) or a knotted head-scarf. In those days a married woman had to cover her hair.

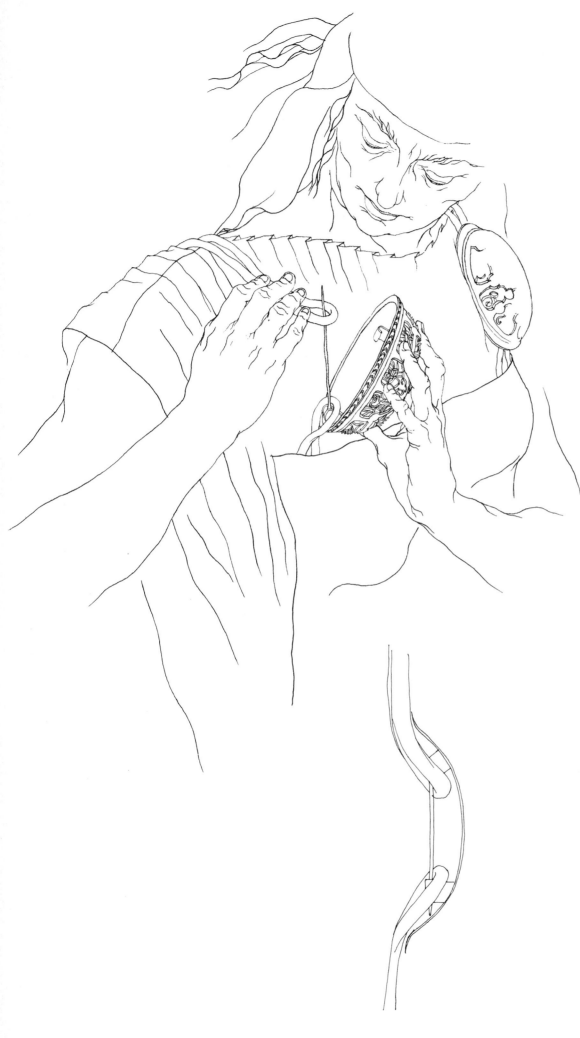

HOW BROOCHES WERE WORN

A Viking woman fastens the front and back sections of her outer garment (see page 200) with a hollow convex brooch. The sections were fitted with looped shoulder straps specially designed for this purpose. After being passed through each loop, the pin of the brooch was fastened (left). Above, the brooch has been used to fasten cloth instead of shoulder straps. The pin is invisible beneath the shell of the brooch when the latter is fastened. On the right, a woman is wearing a shawl, which could be fastened at the front either by a normal general-purpose convex brooch (1) or by a special winged shawl brooch of a type that originated in Frisia (2). As a rule, much care was lavished on the decoration of brooches worn with shawls.

to Scandinavia, were sometimes better ornamented than the original oval brooches, obviously because they were worn where they could be seen. On Gotland in its boom period, shawl brooches were covered with silver plate or even gold. Beads, too, were arranged in a practical way: they were concentrated in the opening at the point where the shawl was fastened.

Viking men generally had to be content with the age-old Teutonic costume, which included narrow trousers combined with stockings, or full-length trousers open at the bottom, and a wide tunic reaching just below the hips. No buttons were needed, though there might be a bead acting as a shirt-button at the neck. This type of dress is curiously reminiscent of modern skiwear. It is, moreover, a costume worn by Roumanian peasants right down to 1939. The third item in men's dress was the cloak. This was not, as sometimes depicted, worn symmetrically over both shoulders. This was a Byzantine fashion introduced to the upper classes of medieval Europe, perhaps as a result of the Crusades. The Viking cloak, instead, was fastened over the right shoulder (sometimes at the right hip), to leave the sword-arm free. Cloaks were held in place by the so-called "penannular" or semi-circular brooch or by a ring pin (see page 208), both of Irish-Scottish inspiration, which in the Viking period spread rapidly as far as the eastern Baltic. Some picture-stones from Gotland suggest that cloaks may sometimes have been very wide. They were probably made of fine cloth, and, on the evidence of some of the finds from the graves at Birka, perhaps even silk.

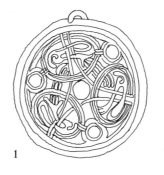

1

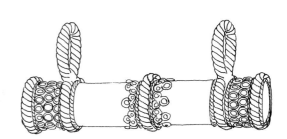

2

203

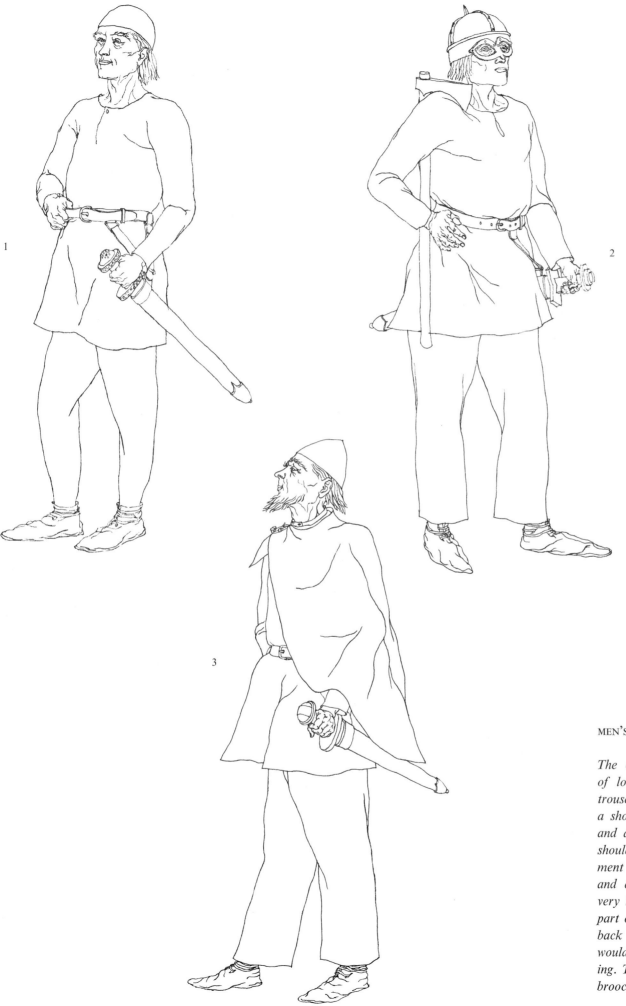

MEN'S DRESS

The ordinary Viking "battle-dress" consisted of long trousers, tight-fitting like modern ski-trousers (1) or else loose and open-bottomed; a short tunic more or less like an anorak (2); and a cloak which was fastened over the right shoulder, giving the sword-arm freedom of movement (3, 5). The cloak, sometimes made of light and elegant imported material, could be worn very long. When riding, however (4), the longest part of the cloak had to be worn at the front — back to front, as it were — otherwise the rider would sit on it and rip it from the shoulder-fastening. This fastening, a penannular (semi-circular) brooch, could also be worn at the hip (6).

4

5

6

FASHIONS FROM FAR AWAY

Buttons were not a part of the Vikings' native dress, but they have been found in graves. In the drawing (1), the man is wearing only one, at the neck: a small shirt-button consisting of a glass bead. Some Vikings wore more ornate dress with very wide, baggy Turkish style trousers, very like those still worn in Crete (2).

In contemporary illustrations, men's beards are often shown plaited (2). There is probably a direct connection between normal Viking dress and Lappish dress (3). Both, for instance, have narrow trousers and a belted tunic. But the exact cut and ornamentation of Viking dress is not as well known as these features of Lappish costume. Contemporary tunics in western Europe had the same shoulder-cut as the Lappish.

A GOLDSMITH'S MASTERPIECE

This splendid round buckle was found at Horne-lund in Denmark. It is decorated with different types of filigree and granulation. Filigree work is done by imposing patterns of very fine wire threads on various backgrounds. Granulation is a coating of small metal grains, often of gold. These threads and grains are soldered to the object. On this buckle the decorative effect has been further enhanced by making the ornament resemble a pearl necklace in miniature. Acanthus and braid-like patterns were often used — apparently because they were easy to fashion out of thread.

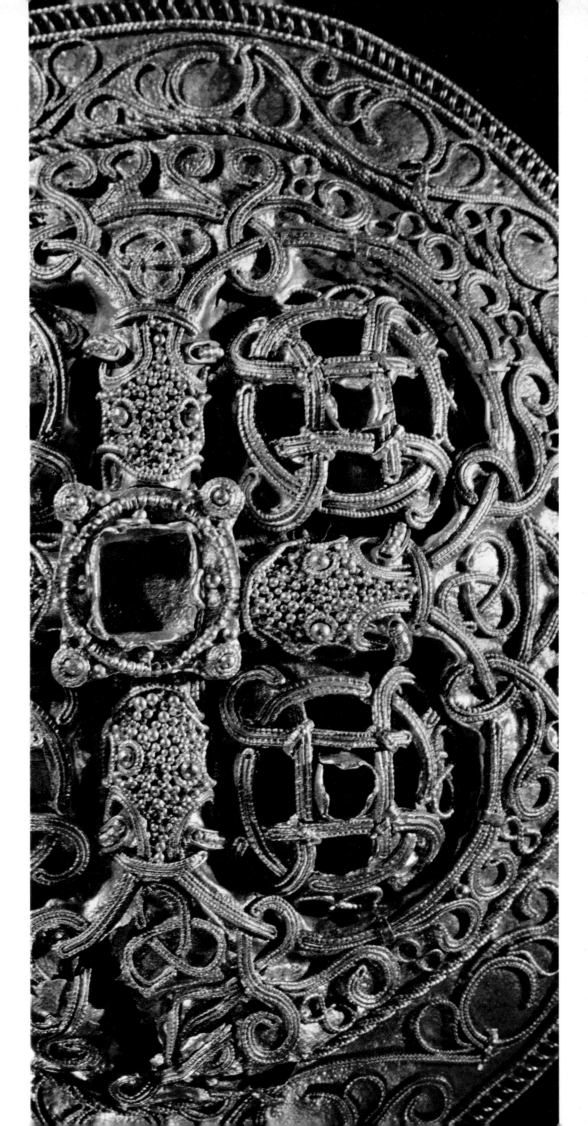

FOUR FINE BROOCHES

The splendid penannullar (semi-circular) brooches shown at the top of the illustration above are both cast in bronze, the one on the right also being gilded. Both have ridges and other sections covered with welded-on sheet-silver, which in turn is decorated with black niello. The Gotlanders could afford sheet-silver thick enough to be grooved and filled with the contrasting black niello, which consisted of a mixture of copper and silver sulphate, fused to the metal.

HOW A BROOCH WAS MADE

Viking women loved gaudy ornaments. To supply them relatively cheaply, craftsmen resorted to something very like a system of mass-production, whose separate stages are illustrated here. From a lump of clay laid on a flat board, the bronze-smith fashioned a detailed model of the oval brooch to be cast. In order to make a mould from it, he first coated the model with white of egg, preventing adhesion of clay to clay.

1. The upper part of the two-part mould was formed by pressing the clay on the coated surface of the model. When it had dried, it could readily be removed from the model, which shrank a little in the process.

2. Into the concave upper part of the mould, the smith next pressed a thin layer of cloth and clay. Its thickness determined the eventual thickness of the casting. To keep the casting light and cheap, it was obviously desirable to use as little metal as possible. During the casting process, therefore, the surface of the convex or lower part of the mould had to fit as closely as possible to the concave half. The interval required was achieved by pressing clay or other mould-material against the layer of clay-impregnated cloth. Traces of this cloth layer are clearly discernible on most of the finished objects.

3. The two parts of the mould now being ready, they were separated to allow the removal of the layer of clay-filled cloth. They were then placed together again, and the space formerly occupied by the cloth was filled with molten metal, poured through holes cut in the rim of the mould, the desired interval now being maintained by flanges around the edges of the mould sections. Even two-part moulds had to be broken in pieces to remove the metal casting. This explains why only fragments of such moulds have been found at places like Birka. In theory a mass-producer should be able to turn out endless numbers of absolutely identical objects. In fact, however, Viking-Age castings always differed somewhat. The explanation seems to be that with every new casting, the initial clay model was slightly damaged and had to be rebuilt to some extent.

4. The finished brooch.

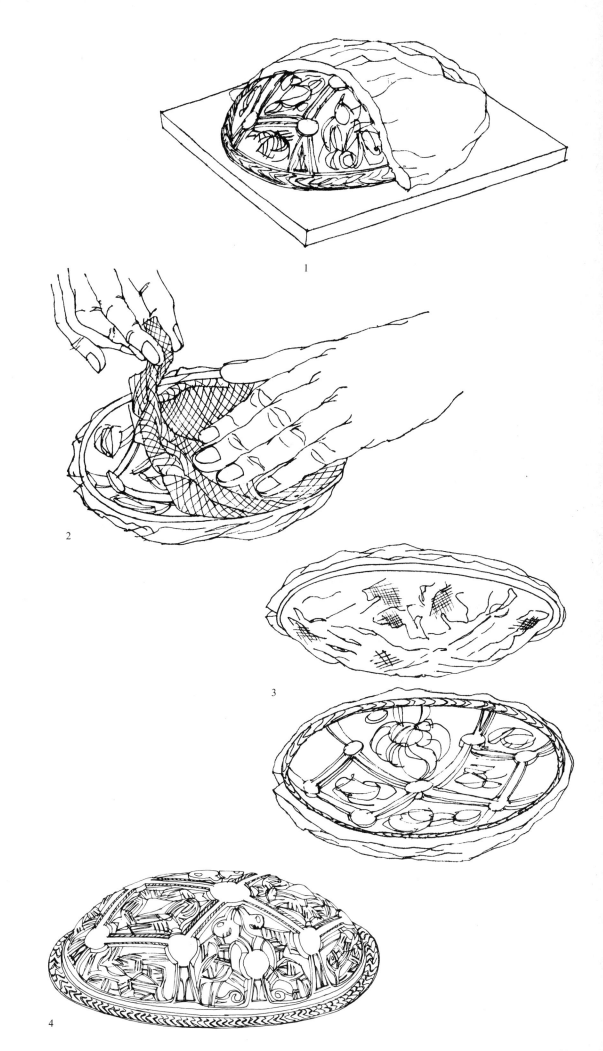

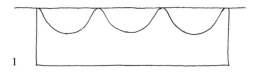

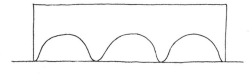

1

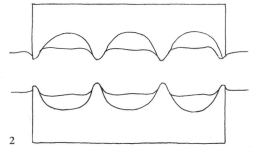

2

3

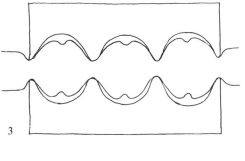

4

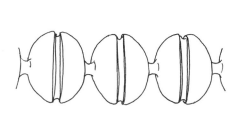

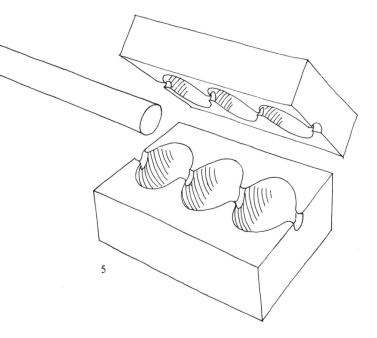

5

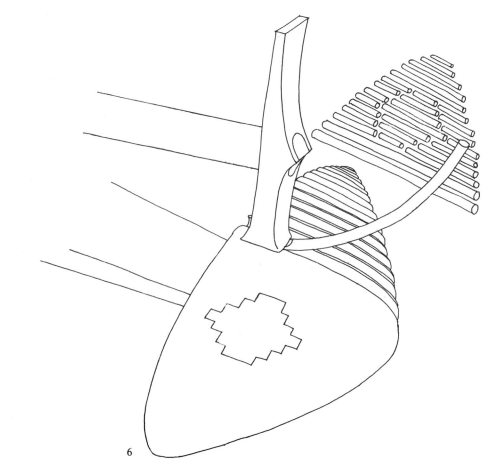

6

FINE WORKMANSHIP IN GOLD

The fine filigree wire used in the most delicate goldsmith's work, which was probably made in the stages shown above (at left), was shaped like a string of beads. Directly above (5) is a piece of wire about to enter the mould. All-over patterned ornamentation of precious metals on iron, for example on sword mounts, could be made in the manner shown on the left (6). Parallel grooves have been chiselled into the piece of iron, and silver and copper wire is being hammered down into the grooves. Silver and copper are soft metals, easy to hammer into a smooth surface. Other methods of ornamenting metal with metal are shown on the following pages.

A GILDED GOTLAND SPECIALTY

Box-shaped shawl buckles like the one shown at right served as formal-dress ornaments for the wives of well-to-do Gotland merchants, and were proudly worn in the middle of the bosom. This buckle is about two inches in diameter. With its rich decoration and handsome granulation, it looks as if it has been worked from pure gold and silver. In fact the goldsmith was much more economical. The framework of the ornament is bronze. It is covered by only a very thin coat of precious metal.

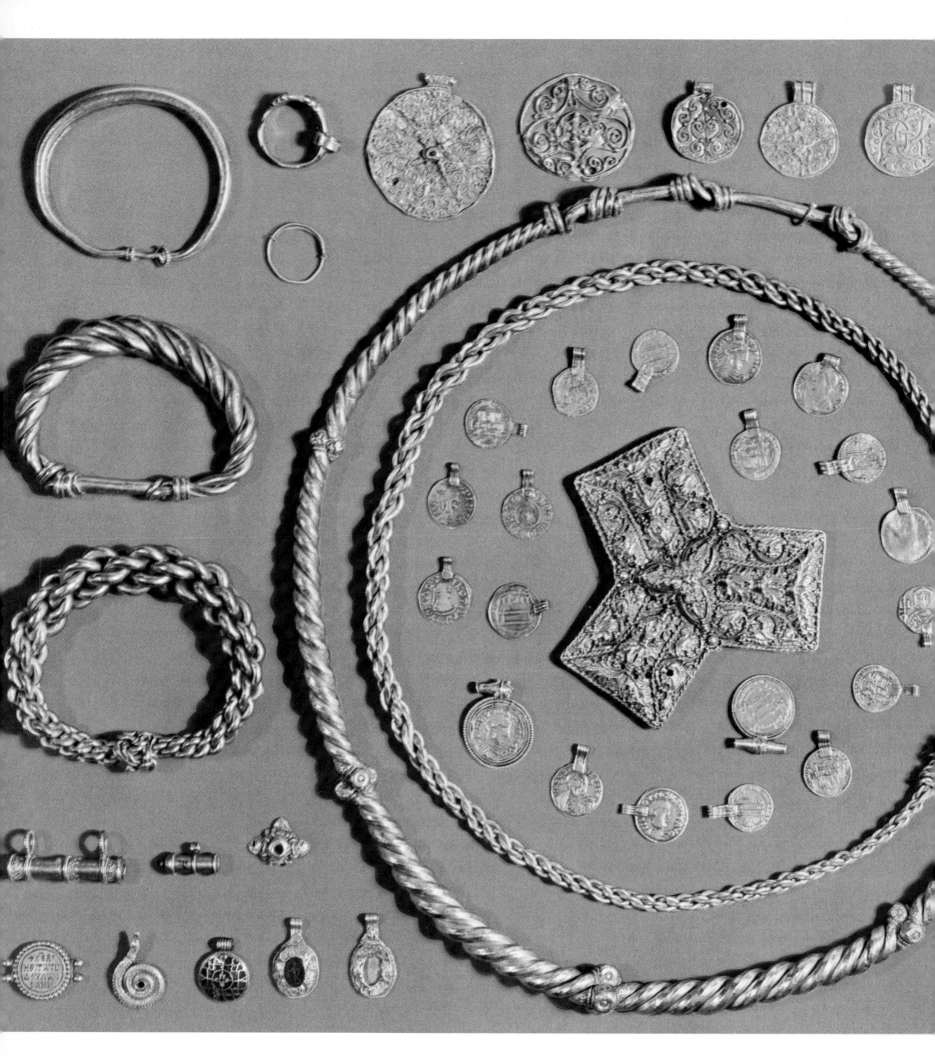

TREASURE FROM NORWAY

In 1834 this remarkably rich collection of jewellery was found in a grave at Hon, not far from Oslo. The treasure consists almost entirely of golden objects and weighs more than 5½ pounds. The biggest of the neck rings alone weighs more than 2½ pounds. Arabian, Byzantine and Frankish coins, all equipped with loops for use as ornaments, are represented, though most of the articles in this treasure are of Frankish origin. The central object, not only in this picture, but also of the treasure itself, is the large three-tongued mounting from a Frankish sword-belt. In Scandinavia such mountings were often remade into shawl clasps by simply adding a pin at the back. The Franks thus indirectly set the pattern for the native three-tongued clasps with purely Nordic ornamentation, which are common grave finds from the Viking Age.

213

1

VIKING CRAFTSMANSHIP IN METAL

The various objects illustrated on this page represent craftsmanship on a large and on a minute scale, applied both to everyday and to very special objects.

1. A small stag made of silver, found at Birka.

2. A reliquary for storing holy relics — Danish workmanship of about 1000 A.D. It is particularly interesting because it seems to represent the special type of house found in the Danish military camps built at about the same time (see page 63).

3. A tiny piece of gold foil from the eighth century, on which two lovers are represented in close embrace.

4. An ear-spoon and nail cleaner carried on a chain round the neck, or attached to a woman's dress. Contrary to what is usually thought, the Vikings, though fierce, were very particular about personal cleanliness.

VIKING JEWELLERY

The ordinary Viking woman had to be content with a necklace of gaily coloured and ornamented glass beads (bottom row, in picture at left). Only rarely would it include some beads of silver or gold (centre right in the second row from the bottom). The rich Viking-Age merchants of Gotland in the Baltic, however, could afford to spend money on what we would call real jewellery for their wives. The gaudy sectioned necklace of silver gilt shown in the centre is one example, and the exquisite silver-mounted rock crystal spheres or lens-like pendants are even more luxurious items.

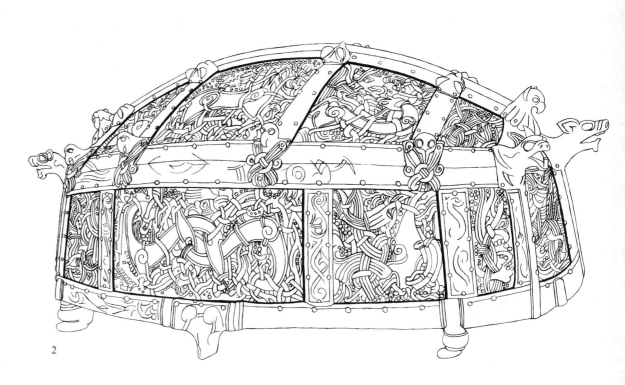

2

3

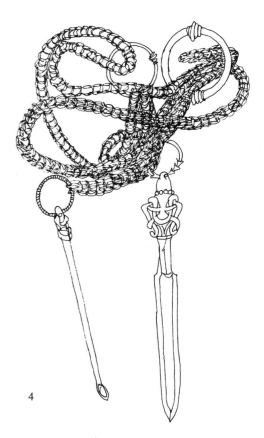

4

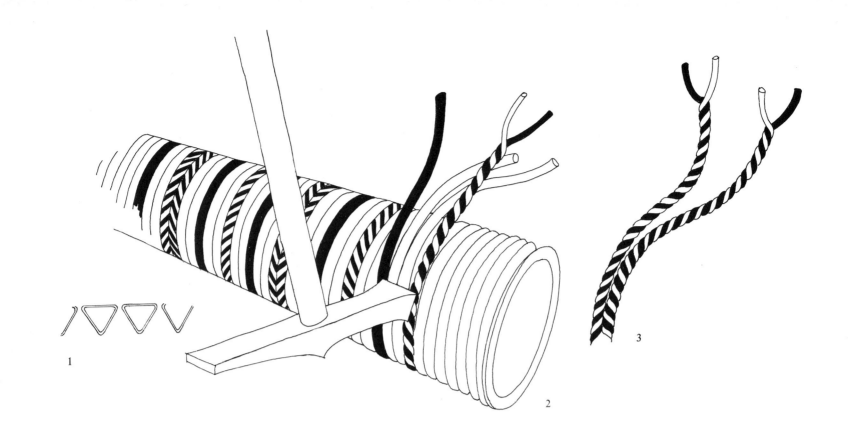

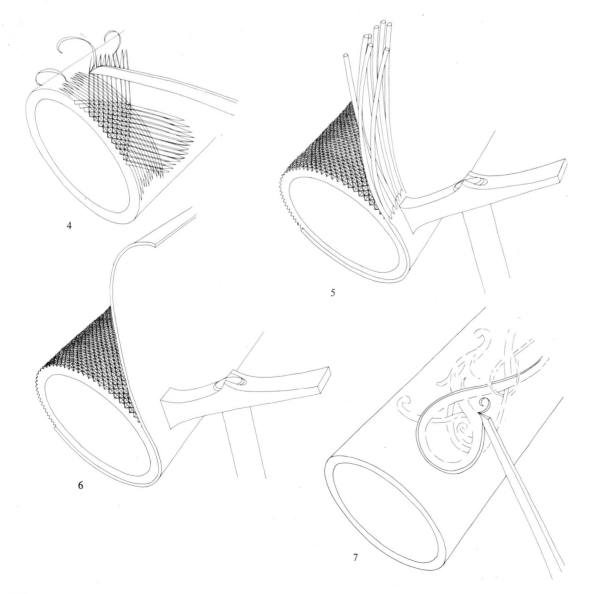

INLAYING METAL OBJECTS

In the upper illustrations (1, 2, 3) an inlay of two kinds of wire is being formed. The inlay consists of pure copper wire and a thinner wire of each kind twisted together which are being hammered into grooves in the iron object to be decorated. The patterns will be simple but often very ornamental. In the lower illustrations an iron surface which will receive inlay has not been grooved but merely roughened (4), so that a simple silver inlay will adhere to it. Then there are two possibilities: either silver wire is wound closely around the article and then hammered into a smooth surface (5), or a silver plate is applied (6). On the silver a decoration is engraved (7), and in order to heighten the effect, it is filled with black niello (see page 208).

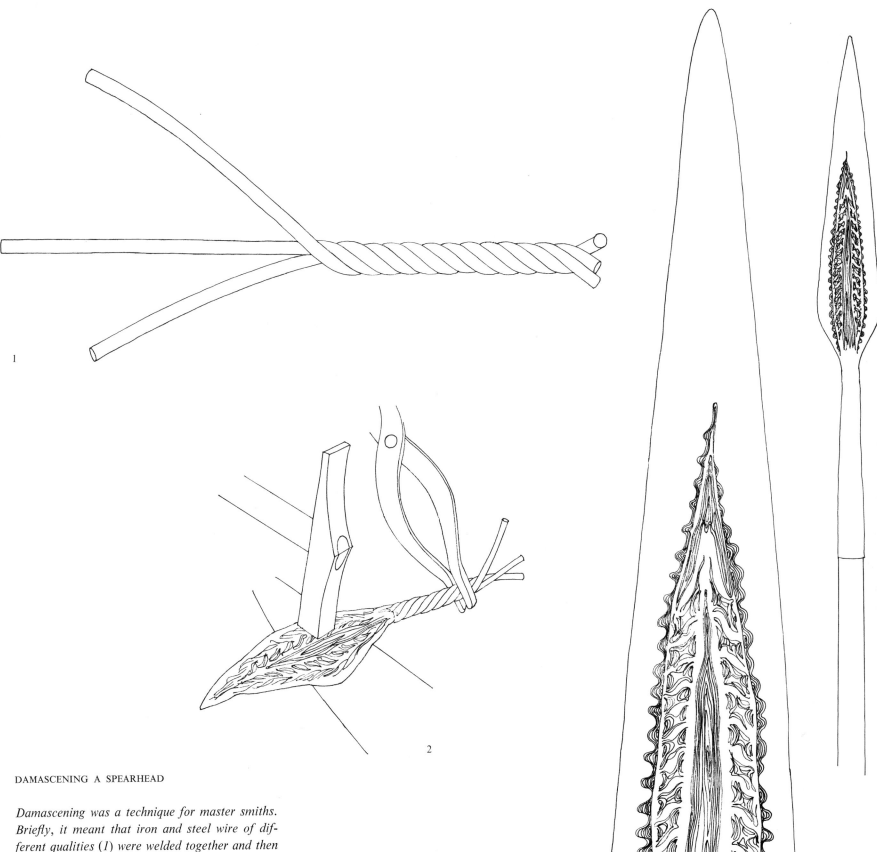

DAMASCENING A SPEARHEAD

Damascening was a technique for master smiths. Briefly, it meant that iron and steel wire of different qualities (1) were welded together and then hammered into sword-blades and spear-heads (2, 3, 4). The technique was one of the specialities of the Franks, from whom the Vikings probably learned it. Sometimes Frankish smiths even signed their work, by putting their names into the damascening. The technique got its name from the town of Damascus — but the word does not occur until the Renaissance in Europe, and it is not clear whether the art of damascening first developed in Damascus or not.

217

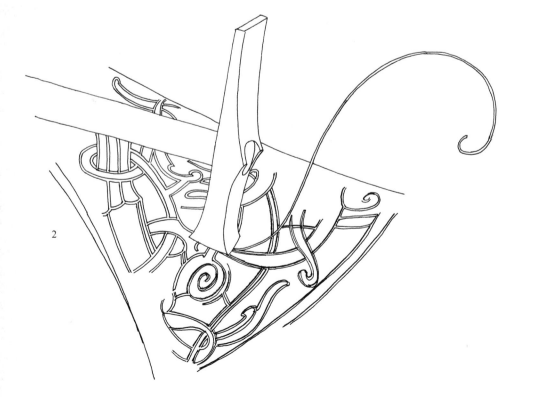

A DECORATED BATTLE-AXE

The iron battle-axe from Mammen in Denmark, seen on the right, was decorated by a technique known as "encrustation". The term is a trifle misleading because it really means inlaying a precious metal into patterns carved into iron. Grooves were cut in the ordinary metal (1, left) deep enough to hold the inlay — in the case of the axe shown here, silver thread. Gold inlays were often made too. A variation of the technique entailed the cutting of closely-placed grooves which did not form a pattern, but merely acted as slots to hold the inlay in place. Once in place the inlay was hammered (2, left) so as to spread and so cover a greater part of the surface. It was an economical way of achieving a silver-plated effect. This technique was extensively used in decorating Viking military equipment such as spear-head sockets, swordhilts, stirrups and spurs. On the European continent the term used for the technique is Tauschieren, *a derivation from an Arabic word meaning "to colour".*

The Viking's weapons were very different from, and much better than, those of his immediate ancestors. The latter had reflected a nostalgic memory of times past. The Vikings' forebears used swords with intricately ornamented gilt bronze hilts, obviously made in imitation of the solid gold hilts (each requiring literally pounds of gold) which came into fashion just after the sack of Rome in the fifth century. In Denmark and Sweden at least, such imitation "Golden Age" swords were used right up to 800 A.D. Then, suddenly, as the Viking Age began, new swords appeared. The change from the eighth to the ninth century is just as dramatic as that from eighteenth-century aristocratic trinkets to the functional iron objects of the nineteenth.

The new swords had iron hilts that would not break in battle like the imitation gold ones. They had new and better blades that were damascened — that is, decorated with different qualities of iron and steel wire welded together (see page 217). As they sometimes even have trade marks in the damascening — the Frankish swordmaker's name — it is easy to see that this was the type of sword used by Charlemagne's victorious armies and also imported by the Vikings, who successfully turned the weapons against their makers. Frankish-style swords were exported as far afield as Russia.

Viking helmets were equally useful — and unglamorous. The horned helmets which turn up so insistently in films about the Vikings were never even seen, still less worn by them. Only their forefathers in the Bronze Age, some 2000 years earlier, wore horned headgear. In the case of helmets too, however, nostalgic memories from more recent times lingered on until the start of the Viking raids. Helmets found in boat graves from the centuries immediately preceding the Viking Age (800 A.D.), are in a late Roman style (page 15) that went out of date about the year 500 in its area of origin. Both the Roman and the pre-Viking headgear was of iron, covered with silver or ornamented bronze plate. Like pre-Viking swords, it was less functional than decorative. A Norwegian helmet from the Viking Age shows the puritanical tendencies of Vikings at work. It is of plain iron without embellishment. No other complete Viking helmets have been found in Scandinavia: only fragments are known. But a few Russian finds are contemporary specimens of a conical type that is known from the Norsemen's own pictures of themselves — for instance, those shown on the Gotlandic picture-stones and the Bayeux Tapestry (page 220). These may have been imported from Scandinavia, or been copied from Viking models brought by traders. Another Viking-type helmet is preserved in Prague as a relic of St. Wenceslaus, patron saint of the Czechs, together with a Viking sword-hilt of horn or walrus-tooth.

INFANTRY AND CAVALRY EQUIPMENT
SHOWN IN THE BAYEUX TAPESTRY

The Bayeux Tapestry was a long historical picture story, embroidered to commemorate the exploits of Duke William, who defeated the English at Hastings in 1066 and became their king. It presents with exquisite skill and careful richness of detail persons and events from the then-immediate past. In this section we see heavily-armed Norman cavalry clashing at Hastings with equally well-equipped infantry of King Harold's household troops. The body protection on both sides—sleeved knee-length mail coats with legs, conical helmets with nose-protectors, and kite-shaped shields—is very similar. The mail coat of one stricken man, who is just collapsing, extends over his head like a hood. The respective weapons most prominent here, however, are different. The Norman horsemen use javelins and stabbing spears in the charge, and have just accounted for at least one Englishman, who falls forward. The foremost of his comrades, who sports a long moustache, wields a great two-handed axe borrowed from the Danes, which may have beheaded the man lying at the bottom right of the picture. A standard-bearer stands beside him. A hedge of English spears points forward over their heads.

The objects which the archaeologist usually lumps together under the single heading "spearheads" should probably be divided into two groups according to the diameter of their shafts. The thinner, lighter weapon was the javelin, which was thrown, while the heavier lance was used for thrusting. In histories of Western European warfare and of feudalism, lances have been closely connected with the first use of the stirrup — a post-Roman idea introduced by Eastern horseman like the Avars. According to this theory it is necessary to have stirrups in order to be able to thrust one's lance into an opponent without being lifted out of one's own saddle by the force of the collision. Thus, it is said, with the introduction of stirrups heavy feudal cavalry, which depended on the lance, first became possible. But the first people known to have employed heavy cavalry, the Parthians and Sassanids of Persia, are often shown on their stone reliefs as throwing their enemies out of the saddle with lances, without the aid of stirrups. Conversely, on the Bayeux Tapestry, the stirrup-equipped, heavily-armed Norman cavalry at Hastings (1066 A.D.) is still shown throwing javelins as well as charging with the lance. These Normans are also wearing chain-mail armour covering arms and legs to the knee as well as the body — a form of protection that did come to northern Europe from the Sassanids, via the Romans. So are some of their English opponents, though they are foot-soldiers. The Viking ancestors of the Normans had mail-coats too, but only the richer warriors could afford them, unless they captured them in battle. The Vikings used foot-archers, as the Bayeux Tapestry and written sources prove. (see page 223).

The Bayeux Tapestry, so reliable in matters of detail, also shows the rightly-dreaded Viking axe. This triangular-bladed weapon (which, incidentally, is still borne as insignia by the Yeomen Warders at the Tower of London), is shown being wielded not by the Norman horsemen, but by their English enemies, who fought on foot. They had probably adopted the Viking weapon at the time when the Scandinavians conquered England at the beginning of the eleventh century. It is just because they fought on foot that they were able to use this broadaxe. It took two hands to wield this axe, and no rider could spare more than one hand for his weapon. Accordingly the broadaxe remained an infantry weapon and disappeared with the final domination of the battlefield by feudal cavalry. The blow of such a cutting edge fixed to the end of a long handle must have been terrible indeed. There is little doubt that it was the thing with which to kill a horse; though the ranks of the axebearers would have to be kept unbroken in order to withstand the weight of a cavalry charge.

SPEARHEADS OF DIFFERENT PATTERNS

These iron spearheads have shaft sockets decorated with inlaid silver. This decoration is comparable with that on the sword hilts seen on page 222, but is more distinctly Nordic in character. The third head from the left has two mysterious projections on the shaft socket. No one knows what they were for. The wooden shaft was so long that they can hardly have acted as protection for the owner. They are not barbs, either. Perhaps their function was to allow the spearhead to penetrate an enemy's body just deeply enough to wound him mortally, while preventing this elegant and expensive weapon from becoming too far imbedded for easy withdrawal. The idea may have been derived from the hilt of a dagger.

A GOLDEN SPUR

The golden spur from Rød in south-east Norway, shown above, is one of the most costly survivals of the Viking Age, with its rich ornamentation in filigree and granulation. Even the mountings on the stirrup are made of gold. It must be borne in mind, however, that such a piece of jewellery — and in this case a spur can rightly be classed as jewellery — was not found on every Viking heel. Most horsemen had to be content with much simpler accessories.

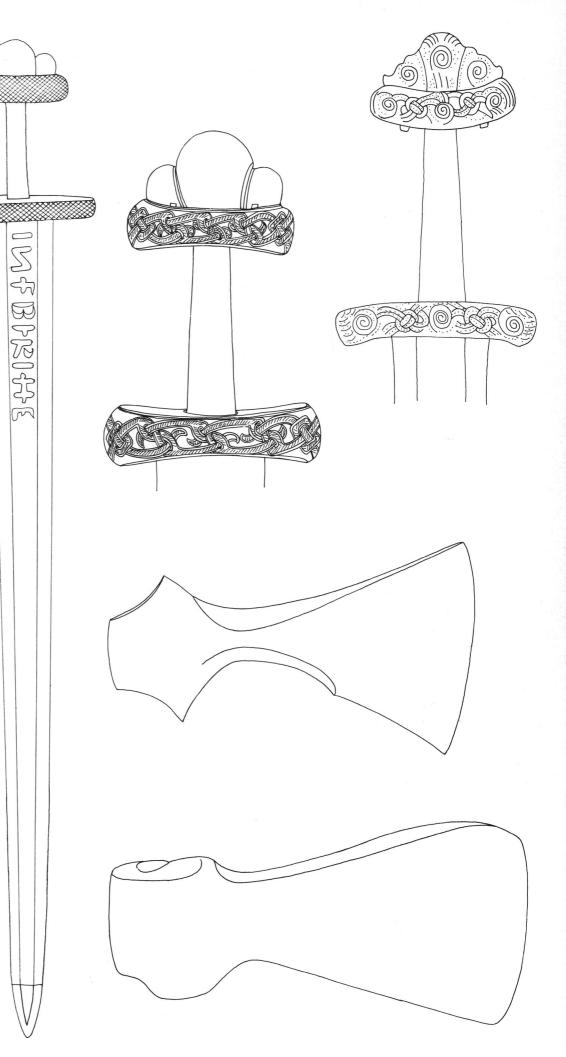

VIKING WEAPONS

The spearheads illustrated above were found at Gjermundbu in Norway. They and the other weapons shown here are much corroded now, after ten centuries in the earth, but still retain their deadly functional lines. Some are elegant, too, like the broad-bladed spearhead above, left. The slim blade in the centre of the three shows a strong contrast with the broad and strong neighbour to its right. The swords are of similar type, though they were found in different countries. The complete sword (right) was dug up in Denmark. Its blade is engraved with the characters INF BERHT, perhaps the signature of the swordsmith, probably a Frank whose work was imported into Scandinavia. The sword hilt next to it is from Gjermundbu, and is decorated with engraved ribbons of silver and other metal. The weapon whose hilt is shown at the far top right was unearthed near Södertälje in Sweden. Both the axe-heads are from Gjermundbu. The narrow neck of the lower one is decorated with small vertical grooves.

Because it lay closer to the Christian West, Denmark has fewer heathen graves of the Viking Age than any other country of the old Scandinavian north. Of these, the earlier examples mainly contained only very simple equipment. Then, suddenly, from the middle of tne tenth century onwards, comprehensive riding equipment — stirrups, spurs, and bridle-bits — appears in Danish warriors' graves, and some even contain a horse buried at the dead man's feet. Remarkably often, the spurs and stirrups are splendidly inlaid with silver and copper, and there are richly ornamented mounts for the stirrup-leathers. Every one of the bridle-bits found in Denmark has the same peculiar T- or H-form. Such a form is something previously unknown in Scandinavia. But in Hungary, the Magyars used their exact counterparts. These Magyars were a horse-riding people who came originally from the steppes of Asia. From the later part of the ninth century onwards they ravaged the eastern parts of Europe, attacked Byzantium, and, as soon as they had established themselves in Hungary, set off on a series of rapid robber raids against the north-west. By the year 908 they had gone as far as Bremen. Like the Vikings, they owed their successes mainly to mobility. The Magyars knew the art of attacking and fighting on horseback in very great numbers. As fighting cavalry they behaved, not as disorderly hordes, but as disciplined troops.

This explains why the Hungarians remained undefeated for so long. It was not until 933 at Merseburg in central Germany that the German king seems to have been able to stop the Magyar armies effectively. It would have been virtually impossible for him to do so, had he not formed and trained cavalry of his own. If this is in fact what happened, then such a troop may have been incorporated in the army with which the king conquered the south Danish commercial town of Hedeby in the very next year, 934 A.D. It was probably on this occasion that the new bridle-bit of Hungarian type was first introduced to Denmark.

In the Hedeby area, rich horsemen's graves of the type later found all over Denmark already occur at this stage. They contain not only Hungarian bridle-bits, but also Hungarian-type stirrups. But there is more to it than that. The Magyars were experts in the use of the bow and arrow from horseback, and arrows of types known in Hungary begin to turn up in Scandinavian sites of this period or later — in the Danish Viking fortress of Trelleborg, for instance, and in horsemen's graves at Birka in Sweden. As in the case of many of the Danish and Hungarian horsemen's graves, the latter have a horse, or several horses, buried at the dead man's feet.

BORROWED PLUMAGE: A COMPOSITE PORTRAIT OF A VIKING RIDER

This drawing bears little resemblance to the traditional — and completely false — picture of a so-called Viking, decked out in a horned helmet from the Bronze Age and sounding a Bronze Age horn. It also has little in common with the true everyday dress of the Viking. It is a careful reconstruction, nevertheless, based on archaeological finds and contemporary illustrations, of the gear that some Viking horsemen are thought to have possessed. The horse has bridle and stirrups of the Hungarian type. The stirrups were probably borrowed from the Germans — the Magyars did not descend to wearing such things. The wide trousers of Oriental cut have been taken from the rune-stones of Gotland. The coat is Oriental, too, with buttons from chin to waist. The bands across the chest strengthen the thin silk in the close-fitting parts of the garment. The cap has silver mountings, and braids with silver lace balls hanging down.

In certain graves at Birka, as at other Swedish burial sites, bronze buttons for fastening clothes are also found. As finds go, these might seem insignificant. In actual fact, however, it is a very remarkable thing that buttons should turn up among Viking Age finds. Throughout the entire period of the Roman Empire and the Middle Ages, buttons were all but unknown in Europe, being essentially oriental things. It is usually suggested that the Viking Age buttons found in the graves at Birka may have come from Russia, but they have exactly the same shape as the buttons found in the graves of the Magyars in Hungary. In a late nineteenth-century photograph, shown on page 232, a young cavalry lieutenant, Winston Spencer Churchill, is seen wearing what is in effect a Magyar uniform, that is a hussar uniform, which along with cavalry of Hungarian type, was introduced and re-introduced to western Europe on several occasions in modern times. A row of closely-spaced spherical buttons runs from chin to waist. Other features include horizontal bands, cruciform loops of golden thread, and plum-shaped pendants of metal thread in the cap. This high-sided fur cap has another feature that is not seen in the Churchill photograph — a triangular piece of cloth that hangs over the side. This triangle is in fact the same thing as the top of the pointed cloth cap for which the conical silver mounts found in Birka graves and Magyar graves in Hungary must have been designed.

A PRECURSOR OF THE VIKINGS

This man is not a Viking. He is a chieftain from Vendel or Valsgärde in Uppland, Sweden, of the period 200 years before the Viking Age. He looks quite warlike, but to a genuine Viking his equipment must have resembled fancy-dress costume, rather as a pre-war cavalryman in full dress looks to a present-day paratrooper. His armour and weapons and his horse's harness glitter with gilt and red semi-precious stones, but his handsome sword is not a very serviceable weapon, and the design of his elegant helmet is several hundred years old. One reason for the Vikings' effectiveness in battle was that they ignored all old traditions concerning battle equipment, adapting or deriving for themselves.

THE EVOLUTION OF A VIKING COSTUME: WINSTON CHURCHILL AS A CAVALRY LIEUTENANT

A turn-of the-century British hussar's uniform, worn in the photograph by Winston Churchill when he was serving in India, has features in common with Viking horsemen's equipment based on Hungarian models that have been found in Viking graves of about 1000 years earlier. By Churchill's time the earlier strengthening braids across the tunic chest have developed into an even more extensive adornment, and have lost almost all practical function. The coat of Lieutenant Churchill's uniform happens to have cloth-covered buttons, but small cast metal buttons, like those found at Birka, were also used around 1900. His hussar cap has a wider fur band, and the point of the original cap has shrunk to a hanging flap, though this does not show in the photograph.

NORMAN CAVALRY IN ACTION

This section of the Bayeux Tapestry shows Norman cavalry riding against the English, with archers on foot in support. The Latin text above tells how Duke William inspires his troops for the coming battle. In everyday life, the Normans, like their Viking ancestors, were rugged individualists who hated discipline. But when they went into action, the horsemen illustrated did not behave like a mob of freelances; their alignment, and their control of their animals seem perfect. Such discipline must have been the result of long experience of working closely together in battle on the other side of the Channel. Their good order is not a result of artistic simplification on the part of the women who embroidered the Tapestry, for there is no sign of mechanical repetition in the scene — each horse and each rider has its own individual character, and the obvious aim was to portray the cavalry as it really was: a formidably professional force.

RA NCI: INPRELIO :⋅:

THE WEAKNESS OF CAVALRY

This extremely lively scene from the Bayeux Tapestry, portraying an isolated incident in the battle of Hastings, shows one of the great weaknesses of cavalry: the difficulty of attacking infantry when they have made a stand on a hill. On the steep ascent, the Norman cavalry charge loses its main advantage, its impetus. Many of the mail-clad Normans die ignominiously at the hands of unarmoured Saxons.

HARNESS BOWS

These fancy harness bows (right) for two horses yoked in pair were found in Søllested in Denmark. They have richly decorated fittings of gilded bronze. The harness bow, with a pair of supports which did not survive the ages, rested on the back of the horse. Its function was to support the traces and keep the reins together. Even though there is so far only one wagon find from the Viking Age — the one from Oseberg on page 236 — these harness bows reveal that horses were used not only for riding, as was usual in contemporary Europe, but also (and far less usually) as draught animals yoked before a sleigh or a wagon.

The Oseberg wagon is the only complete wheeled vehicle preserved from the Viking Age. The "road system" being what it was, until the advent of rune-stone "bridges" in the eleventh century (see page 151), it is not surprising to find that the wagon's under-carriage was generously provided with handles to carry it with whenever it got stuck in the mud. The body of the wagon has a curious tub-like cross-section, and the sides are riveted together with almost exaggerated care. The explanation is that this part was really a waterproof container intended to be lifted bodily into the middle of a boat (see page 238) into which it would have fitted exactly. The only means of holding the container in place on the bumpy roads of Scandinavia were ropes fastened round the hook-like beards of the carved heads on the supports that carry the body.

A close look at the Oseberg wagon also shows that it could not have been steered by its shaft, because, to obtain lightness of construction and flexibility, the shaft was not fixed rigidly to the pivoted axle, but was joined to it by means of loose wooden pivots. The actual steering must have been done by the traces that ran from the ends of the wooden axle to the horse's harness. Such traces may be seen on the Oseberg tapestry (page 240). This must have been the purpose of the hitherto mysterious Viking-Age objects collectively known as *rangel* (pages 240-241). These consist of two conical iron mounts connected by a six-foot rope, one mount being equipped with a large hook obviously designed to guard against its becoming unhitched. Now certain Viking Age finds have also included other mounts having at one end a large eye which would fit ideally around a fixed axle, and at the other a smaller eye which fits the hook described (pages 240-241). The other mount of the *rangel* had a large, more or less oval ring with a series of smaller rings attached to it. The large ring would have been suitable for attaching to the harness, as the tapestry shows. In the course of time the *rangel* underwent changes that made it still better suited to its function. For instance, one side of the large ring became flattened, which must have made life more comfortable for the horse. Strangely enough, one can still find a rather similar mode of construction on Persian wagons. It is possible, therefore, that the origin of the *rangel* is connected in some way with the Orient. It seems natural to assume that the *rangel* was a result of the Viking contacts eastwards, but those found so far actually date a bit earlier than the period of the main Viking expansion towards Russia. They are, however, contemporary with earlier trade contacts on the Eastern shores of the Baltic. It is interesting to note that mounts for traces at the end of an axle are still known in the eastern Baltic area.

THE RICHLY CARVED OSEBERG WAGON

The ornate, complex decorative carving on the Oseberg wagon is clearly seen in these photographs. On the end of the wagon the carving illustrates the torment of Gunnar in the snake-pit, a well-known story of Viking times. Also seen are the bearded heads to which were fastened the ropes holding down the removable body.

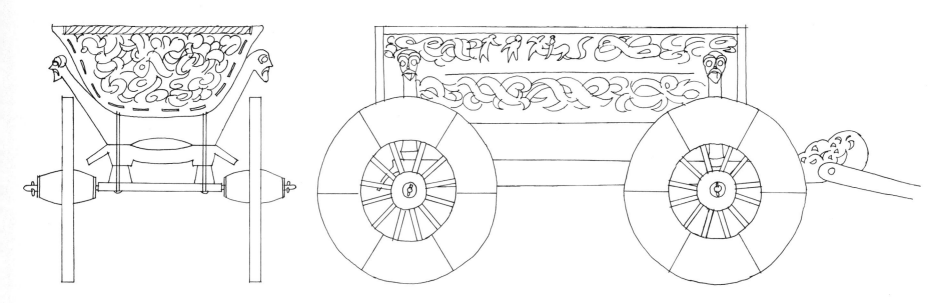

A SENSE FOR THE PRACTICAL — AND FOR THE ORNAMENTAL

The Oseberg wagon, drawn here along with various details and figures, seems clumsy at first sight, with its big lumbering wheels and its trough-shaped carriage body. But the wheels were made for the roads of the Viking Age, which were anything but smooth. The rich and sometimes exaggerated decoration suggest that this wagon was intended, if necessary, for the transportation of passengers. A well-wrapped-up noble lady could be as easily manhandled aboard as the bundle of goods being heaved into the wagon at left. The details of the carved heads (above and to the right) with their extended chins and beards, are on the body supports, and served as rope-hooks. The wagon tongue shaft shown below the heads is also carved with a man's face.

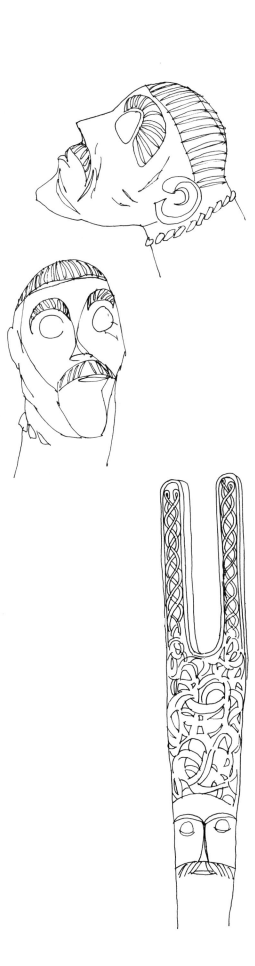

Beautifully made sledges have been found in the great Viking ship-burials at Oseberg and Gokstad. At Oseberg no less than four complete specimens were preserved, three of them with superb carvings. As these extended even over the sledge-runners, they were provided with an extra piece that could be replaced when worn, like a tyre. The runners splay sharply outwards, no doubt to improve the sledges' performance on curves. On the top of the sledge is an unfixed, bottomless box-like frame for the passenger (see page 245) who must have travelled on the sledge-top in a half-reclining position. In later times the driver of such a fine vehicle was placed on a platform at the back, but at the rear of some Viking sledges there is only a light wooden panel. It has very fine open-work ornament, and would have broken under a man's weight. If the passenger was a lady of high degree — as was certainly the case at Oseberg — she could hardly have driven herself. Where, then, was the driver placed? Such sledges were drawn by a pair of horses on either side of a pole or shaft. On one side of the sledge there is an iron mount with a few links of chain. The reason for there being a mount to which to attach a trace only on one side may have been that the driver was mounted postillion on the other horse; an arrangement that is known from sixteenth-century Russia, and even from present-day royal state coaches, where each pair of horses is handled by a rider on one of them. Right up to the sixteenth century, a carriage was a luxury like the Rolls-Royce today. Thus it was no mean thing that the richest Viking ladies, as is shown on a tapestry from the Oseberg ship-burial, could travel in such comfort. The idea may have been borrowed from the horse-loving inhabitants of the British Isles — Picts or Celts — who possibly had a tradition in this respect from late Roman times.

HARNESSES AND HOW THEY WORKED

1. A passenger wagon, illustrated on the tapestry fragments found at Oseberg. The steering traces, running from the ends of the front axle to the harness of the horse, can be seen. The reins pass through a harness bow on the horse's back.

2. The rangels: hollow iron mounts for each end of the steering traces. The one on the left was fixed to the horse's harness by means of the largest ring, to which a number of smaller rings are attached. The rangel *on the right held the axle end*

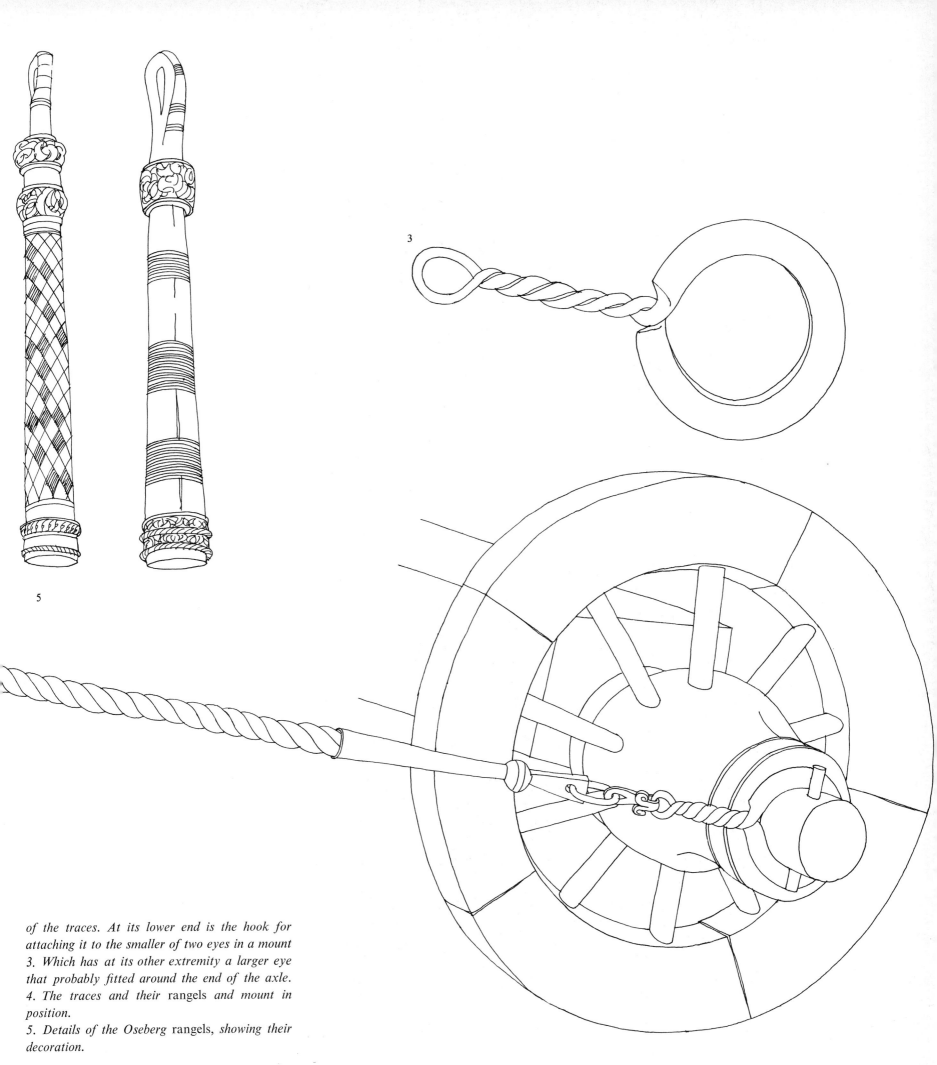

of the traces. At its lower end is the hook for
attaching it to the smaller of two eyes in a mount
3. Which has at its other extremity a larger eye
that probably fitted around the end of the axle.
4. The traces and their rangels and mount in
position.
5. Details of the Oseberg rangels, showing their
decoration.

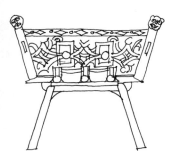

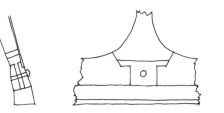

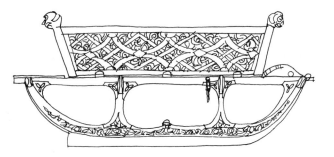

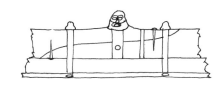

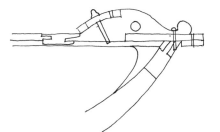

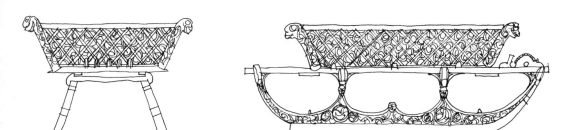

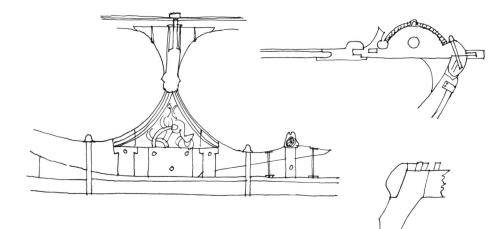

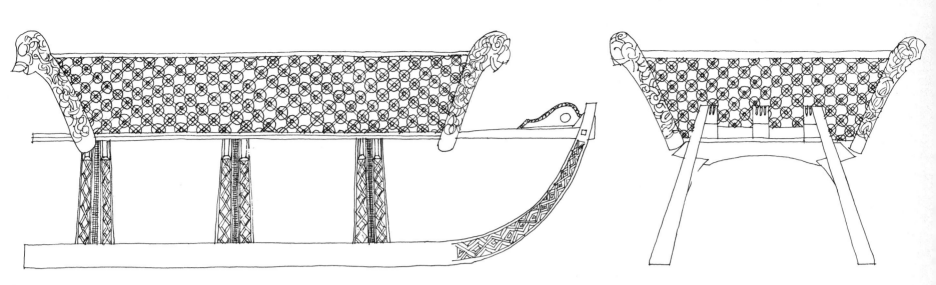

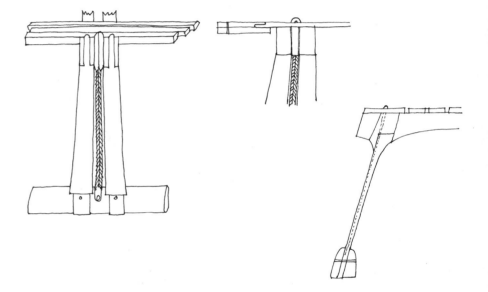

THE OSEBERG SLEDGES

Three of the horse-drawn sledges found at Oseberg, illustrated on these pages, were copiously and elaborately carved. They were transportation for passengers who must have been very important, or they would have ridden on horseback or walked. This explains the decorations. Most of the year, sledges were more suitable than wheeled vehicles for overland travel in Scandinavia in the Viking Age, because runners could ride more easily than wheels over soft ground or snow. On the facing page, on the far left, are front and side views of two sledges, with details of the method of attaching the legs and runners, which have metal reinforcement, and of fitting the detachable pieces protecting the decorated runners from wear. To the right of them are decorative details from the open-work horizontal panels of each sledge. The third sledge, above on this page, has no such panel, but on the right a detail of its paintwork is shown.

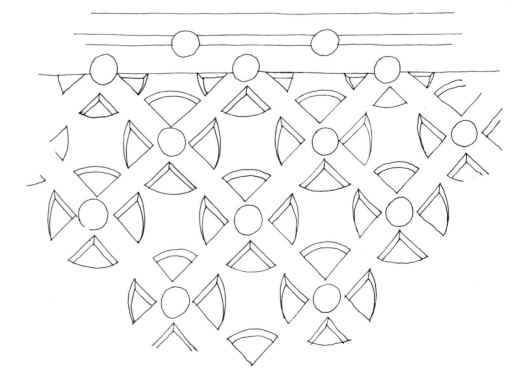

CRAFTSMANSHIP IN WOOD

Above and on the opposite page are details of the carvings on the Oseberg sledges, illustrating Norse mythology. The grotesque head above on the facing page is on one of the corners of the box-frame carrying the passenger, seen in position below it.

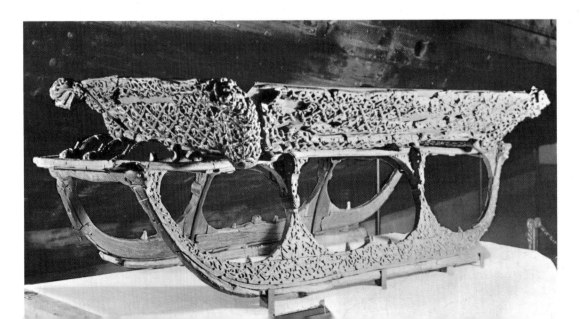

THE FAMOUS VIKING LONGSHIP —
HOW IT DEVELOPED FROM ITS EARLIEST
BEGINNINGS TO ITS GREATEST DAYS

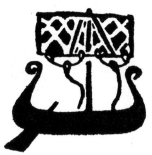

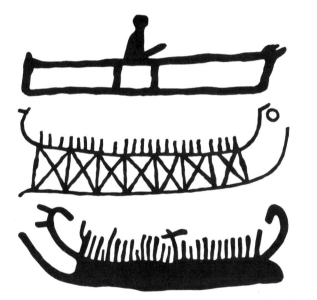

ROCK CARVINGS OF THE EARLIEST NORSE SHIPS

Top: Stone Age picture of a man in his boat, from Rødøy in Nordland, Norway. Below: Two Bronze-Age ships carved at Tanum in Bohuslän, Sweden.

THE GOKSTAD SHIP

The Gokstad grave-ship from Norway, seen on the left, was dug up and restored almost to its original state after a thousand years underground.

It is extremely difficult to obtain accurate knowledge of earlier Scandinavian ships, from which Viking ships evolved. Except for a few dugout boats from Amossen in Denmark dating from the New Stone Age, only rock carvings remain. Among these, the oldest representations of ships (shown at left) occur in Stone Age carvings from northern Norway. Because of a similarity in form, it has been suggested that these are really representations of skin-covered boats not unlike the Eskimo umiak, an open boat about thirty-three feet long and about six feet wide. According to one accepted theory, Bronze Age boats were also skin-covered umiaks originally, and wooden ships resulted when skins or hides were eventually replaced by thin boards or planks, sewn together in the same way as the skins. A counter-theory suggests, instead, that the Bronze Age boat was a version of the wooden dugout gradually developed by fitting additional planks along the sides, so that the original dugout hull was finally no more than the bottom plank of a plank-built boat. The special construction of Iron Age boats, with boards and ribs lashed together, can be used to support both theories. Certainly there are obvious points of resemblance between the Eskimo umiak and the boats represented in the rock carvings of northern Norway. Even more remarkable are the similarities between some of the Bronze Age carvings and Scandinavia's oldest plank-built boat from Hjortspring (page 248).

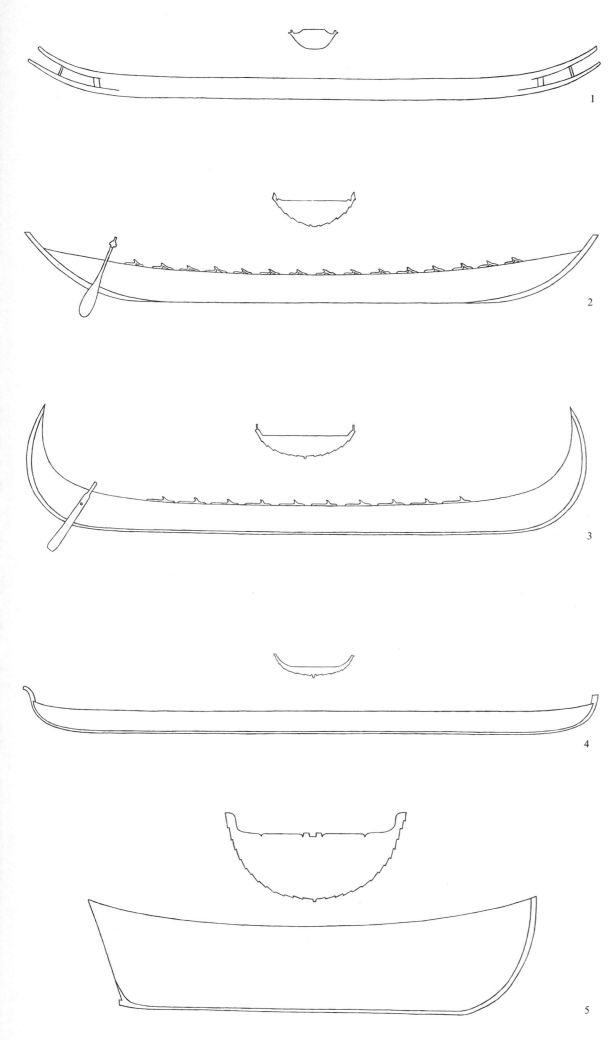

Illustrated at left are five different Scandinavian ships. They range in time from about 300 B.C. to about 1000 A.D. Together they represent a linked chain of evidence about shipbuilding design, before, during and after the Viking Age. (1) is the planked Hjortspring boat, built early in the Iron Age, probably about 300 B.C. It is about fifty feet long and formed of five broad, thin, slightly overlapping boards which were stitched together with hide thongs. These boards and the gunwales were not joined at the stem and stern but were run into hollowed-out end-pieces fixed to the bottom plank fore and aft. The bottom plank and the rails project beyond the boat proper. The boards were laboriously hewn so as to leave cleats on the inside to which ribs of light hazel rods were fastened. The ribs in turn were braced by thwarts or rowing benches supported by vertical props. The boat was propelled by about twenty paddles which did not rest on the rails. The next link in the development of the Scandinavian ship was found at Nydam in southern Jutland on the Flensburger Fjord (2). This ship was built on a truly colossal scale, each plank running the entire length of the hull; more than seventy-five feet. Instead of a prow standing at right angles to a bottom plank projecting beyond the ship proper like that of the Hjortspring boat, the Nydam ship has a true curved prow joined to the bottom plank. Instead of being sewn, the planking is held together by iron rivets. The oaken ribs, like those of the Hjortspring boat, are lashed to cleats carved when the planks were originally hewn. The vessel was intended for propulsion by oars, not paddles. Bent branches tied to the rails probably served as rowlocks. The Nydam boat did not carry a sail. Its bottom planks, moreover, were not strong enough to withstand the impact of waves, and to counteract this the hull was made narrow and the bows rather sharp. The Kvalsund ship (3) was found at Sunnmøre in Norway. It is about sixty-one feet long, broader and apparently more stable than the Nydam ship. Its bottom plank has a spine-like projection along its entire length. This is a development in the direction of a true keel. The rowlocks are fastened by wooden pegs called "trenails". No evidence of a mast was found, but the shape of the hull is such that the ship could have carried a mast and sail. The last two ships represent further advances in shipbuilding. (4) shows the Danish Ladby ship, designed primarily for coastal waters, and propelled by oars only. The Swedish Kalmar ship (5) is an early medieval vessel, deeper and broader than most Viking ships, and intended purely for the carriage of cargo.

CARVINGS IN WOOD AND HORN FROM THE OSEBERG
DISCOVERY

Carved on the underside of a deck plank were found this view (top) of a high-rising ship's stem, and three animal figures. Above, at left, is a dog. Below are two horses facing each other.
A carved sledge-runner gives a good impression of the stems of Viking ships (centre).
On a horn lid is a carving (bottom) which seems to be a construction plan showing how planking was fitted into a ship's stem, and how hull planks were joined to one another.

THE SAILING SHIPS OF THE VIKING AGE:

THE GREAT NORWEGIAN DISCOVERIES AT OSEBERG, GOKSTAD, AND TUNE

Three grave ships found in or around Oslo Fjord, in Norway, have shed more light than any other ship finds on how Viking sailing ships were actually constructed. The first of these grave ships turned up in the parish of Tune, Ostfold, in 1867. The upper planks and stems had decayed, and the shape of the hull could only be roughly reconstructed. As a result it did not provide a complete picture of the Viking ship. But as a complement to the discoveries made during later diggings, it was of great significance in establishing the chronology of early ship-building. The Tune ship is built of oak. Its original length is about sixty-five feet, and its beam fourteen feet. It is flat-bottomed, and for its size it had a very shallow draught. In spite of this the ship was equipped with a sail, and also had eleven or twelve pairs of oars. By the ornamentation on a few excavated wooden articles, the Tune ship has been dated to the latter half of the ninth century.

The second great discovery was made in 1880, in a burial mound on the Gokstad estate in Vestfold. The most important parts of this famous ship were in excellent condition because it was embedded in clay. Only the upper parts of the stems were missing. The ship could therefore be restored to its original condition, although the actual work of restoration was not completed until 1930. The hull was built exclusively of oak, which although it still had a good deal of its original strength, was black from dampness. Even the iron rivets in the planking were relatively well-preserved, and about half of them were used again in the reconstruction work. The Gokstad ship is the largest grave ship yet found. Its overall length is more than 76 feet. The shape of the hull suggests a ship designed for ocean voyages. The construction is considered to be unsurpassed of its kind.

The Gokstad ship dates from about 850 A.D. The last of the great Viking ships was first discovered in a burial mound at Oseberg, in Vestfold, in 1903, and excavated the following year. It, too, was resting on a bed of blue clay, but was covered by peat and a large cairn. The hull had been crushed by the enormous weight, although the oak itself was well preserved. Nevertheless the Oseberg ship was the first grave ship to be restored to its original appearance in every detail.

The building methods and materials used in the Oseberg ship are largely the same as those of the earlier discoveries. Compared to the Gokstad ship, the hull shape is less developed. This, together with other discoveries in the mound, indicate that the ship was built about the year 800. The Oseberg ship

The shipwright in the centre, with raised axe, is in the process of cutting a plank out of a split log. To the left of him, a completed plank is being prepared. At intervals corresponding to the distances between the frames, the plank is kept to its original thickness. In between the frames the thickness is reduced. In the bottom left-hand corner, the cleats are being chiselled to shape, and the man kneeling is boring holes for lashing them to the frames. The man near the stem is giving the plank its simple decoration, by cutting with a shaping iron. The men in and around the ship are bending the last planks to shape, using simple clamps, and riveting them to the planks below.

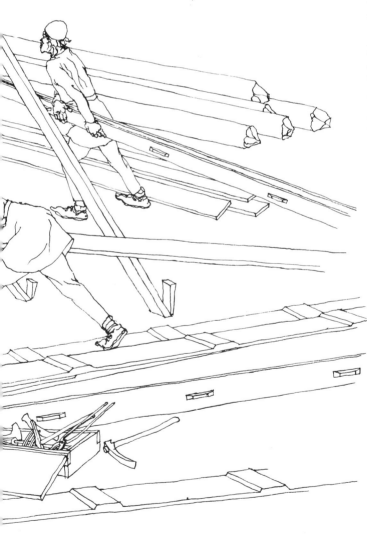

is almost seventy feet long. The ships from Tune, Gokstad and Oseberg are now all kept in the Viking Ship Museum at Bygdøy, in Oslo.

The Norwegian Viking ships found at Oseberg, Gokstad and Tune represent a considerable advance beyond the earlier vessels described on page 248. Many of the parts of the hull in boats at an intermediate stage of development were retained in the ships of Viking times, but with different functions. The keel timber on the Kvalsund ship (page 248) was reinforced along its underside, giving it a T-shaped section. In the typical Viking ship the keel timber was replaced by a keel, and the original flat bottom plank served only as a fastening for the lower lines of planking. In the Kvalsund ship the planks are narrower and therefore more numerous than in the earlier Nydam ship (page 248). Instead of using one single length of timber, several lengths were joined together; an obviously more practical method used throughout Viking ship construction. The planking below the waterline was still attached flexibly to the ribs by lashings, but the hull was greatly changed.

The ship sides were increased in height, so that what was formerly the thick, reinforced rail or gunwale timber, appeared far down along the side of the hull. The extra planking above the waterline was fastened by wooden nails to naturally-bent branches called knees which were fixed to the cross beams. Probably the changes and additions to this and later craft were due to the fact that the ships carried mast and sail. The bottom was strengthened to carry the weight and stresses of the mast, and the sides raised so that the vessel could heel without shipping water. The mast was mounted on a large block of oak called *kjerringa* (old woman) in Old Norse. About six feet long, it was laid along the keel, spanning two ribs. Above the *kjerringa* was the mast partner, called the mastfish from its shape.

The cross beams having lost their function as rowing benches, it was impractical to have the space between them open, so a removable decking was laid over them. The sides of the ship being so much higher, it was no longer possible to use rowlocks along the rails. Instead, holes were cut in the sides at the proper height. The holes could be covered by small wooden discs so that water could not gush in when the ship was under sail.

The keel and the fixed cross beams, which stiffen the hull under the waterline, and the greater breadth make the ship of the Viking Age much more stable than the earlier Scandinavian vessels.

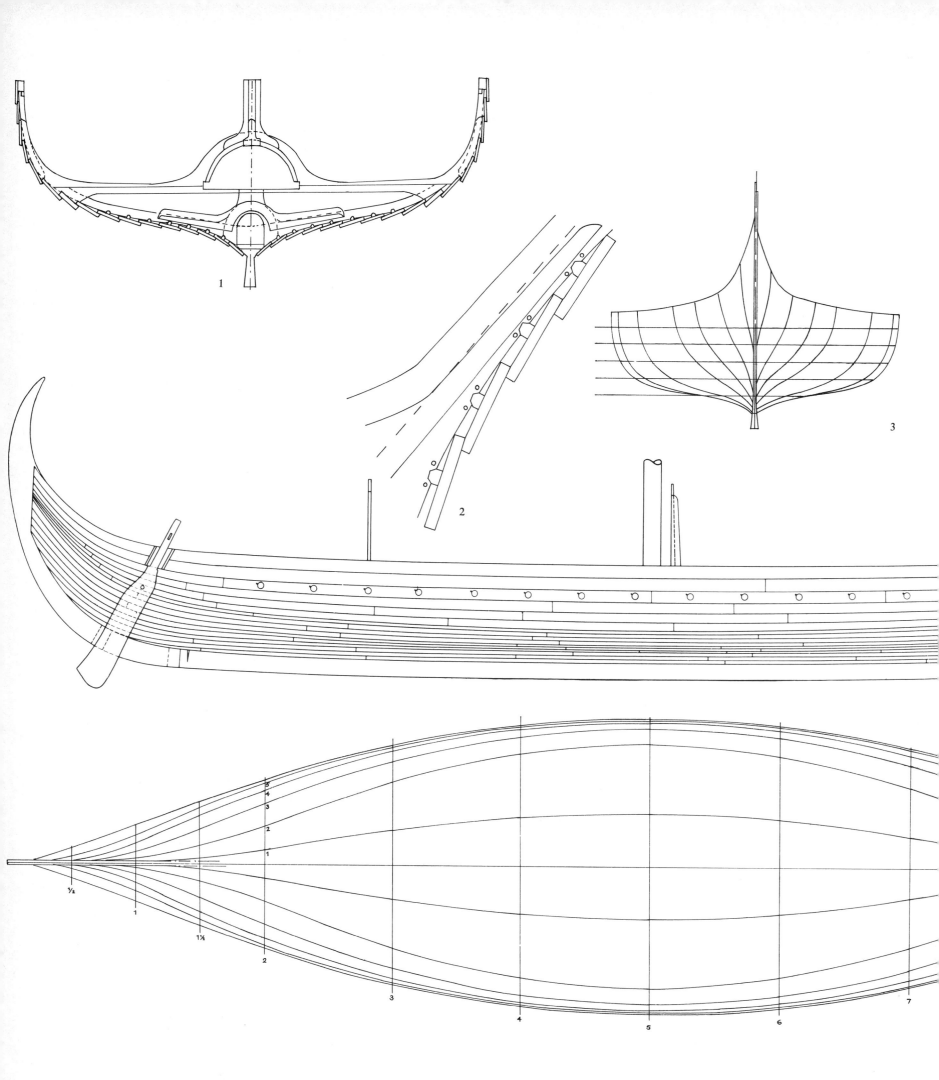

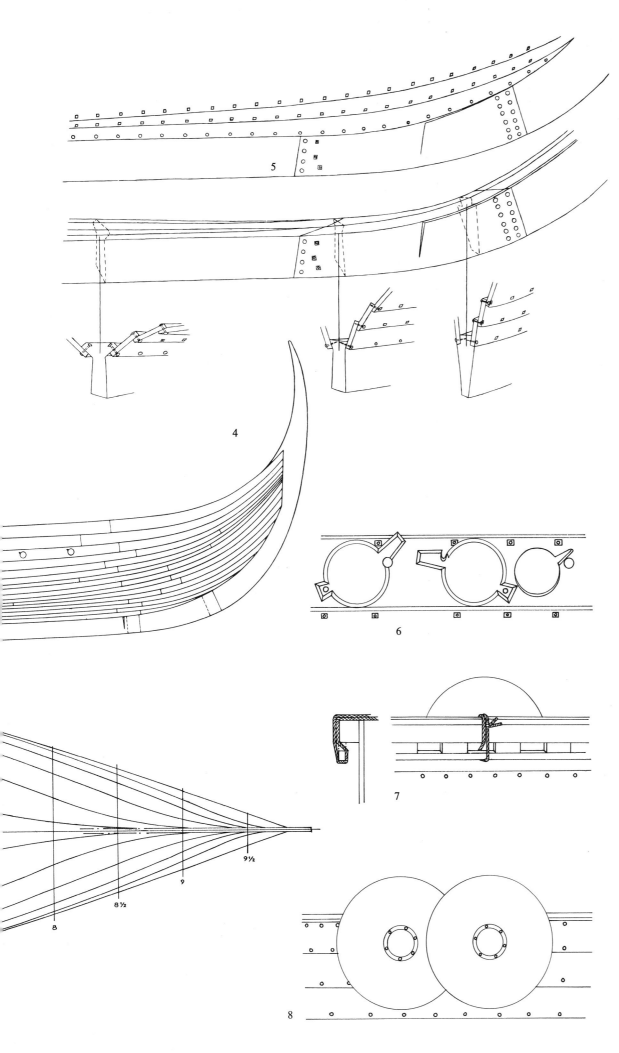

The Gokstad ship was the largest and best preserved of the three Norwegian Viking ships, and it naturally provides the best evidence of constructional details. It is seventy-six feet long, seventeen feet wide and from the bottom of the keel to the gunwale (or rail) amidships measures 6½ feet.

Except for its decking of pine, the ship is built throughout of oak. Its backbone is the keel, which was hewn from a single timber sixty feet long. In cross section (top right) it resembles an elongated letter T (4). The planking consists of sixteen pieces on each side, clinker-built, overlapping slightly and riveted together in strake fashion. Considering the size of the ship, the ribs were surprisingly slight. Except for the bottom board, which is fastened to the keel (5) and the second board, the planking below the waterline was fastened to the ribs with lashings of spruce roots. In other words, the ribs were not joined to the keel. The planking was cut to leave cleats on the inside where the ribs would lie, and the lashings were passed through two holes in the cleats and two corresponding holes in the ribs (2). The heavy board at the waterline, the rudimentary rail or gunwale called meginhúfr in Old Norse, is the tenth plank from the keel. The board under that, the ninth, was not lashed to the ribs but fastened by trenails to each rib. The meginhúfr was also fastened by trenails which pass through the ribs and the cross beams. The planks above the meginhúfr, those above the waterline, were fastened by trenails to wooden knees fixed to the cross beams. These knees reach up to the upper edge of the fourteenth plank (1). The two top planks, the fifteenth and sixteenth, are comparatively thin and reinforced by top ribs butted into the underside of the gunwale (1), and extend down to the upper edge of the meginhúfr beside every other knee. The oar holes, sixteen to a side, are cut in the fourteenth plank. They could be closed from the inside by small, neatly-made, hinged wooden discs (6).

The rivets in the Gokstad ship were driven in from the outside through holes drilled in the planks, and their plain ends were hammered flat over washers on the inside. Trenails in the ribs and cross beams above the waterline were driven in from the outside. They had conical heads which were driven slightly below the outside of the planking. On the inside the trenails were secured by means of a little wedge.

The edges of the cross beams were rabbeted to receive the deck boards, which could be removed for stowing goods or for bailing. The shields (8) were fastened by ropes passed through the shield-grips and a batten on the inside of the rail (7).

In 1893, a few years after the Gokstad ship was discovered, an exact replica was built. It was properly named *Viking*, and a Norwegian sea captain, Magnus Andersen, sailed her across the Atlantic.

"*Viking* did her finest lap from the 15th to the 16th of May, when she covered a distance of 223 nautical miles. It was good sailing. In the semi-darkness the light from the northern horizon cast a fantastic pale sheen on the ocean as *Viking*, light as a gull, glided over the wave-tops. We noted with admiration the ship's graceful movements, and with pride we noted her speed, sometimes as much as eleven knots. . . . We were afforded a first class opportunity of testing *Viking*'s performance when sailing close to the wind. To our great surprise she proved to be in the same class as most modern two-masters". Because of the flexibility afforded by the methods used for lashing the planks to the ribs, the bottom as well as the keel could yield to the movement of the ship, and in a heavy head-sea it would rise and fall as much as three-quarters of an inch. Yet, strangely enough, the ship still remained water-tight. The ship's great elasticity was apparent in other ways too. For instance in a high sea the gunwale twisted out of true as much as six inches. ". . . The rudder is indeed a work of genius. In my experience the side rudder is much to be preferred in such a ship to a rudder on the stern-post; it worked satisfactorily in every way and had the advantage of never kicking, as a stern-post rudder would certainly have done. One man could steer in any weather with merely a small line to help."

Magnus Andersen also relates how well *Viking* fared in the worst sea she encountered, partly under sail and partly using the drift anchor: " . . . A real SSW gale was now blowing. Nonetheless, we found that if the ship could carry sail [in these conditions] she would, of her own accord, progress slightly westwards despite the wind direction, and why should we not make use of it when we could? So we hauled in the drift anchor, hoisted the mainsail but reefed as much as possible. Soon *Viking* was gathering speed, although she could not come closer than six degrees to the wind — but on the other hand she was not carried off course more than four degrees. "

The triumphant *Viking* was taken to Chicago for exhibition at the Chicago World's fair held in the same year as the crossing.

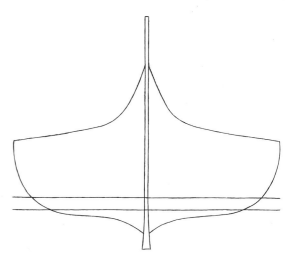

THE SHALLOW-DRAUGHT GOKSTAD SHIP

The sketch above shows the ship's draught, at the two points marked on the displacement curve below.

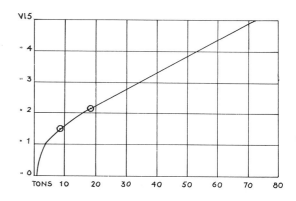

If one measures the volume of timber in the ship and multiplies this by the specific weight of the timber, one arrives at the figure of 15,995 lbs., all included. To this may be added about 2,755 lbs. of nails and gear: a total weight of 18,750 lbs. This means that the ship, when empty, displaced 18,750 lbs. of sea-water. By calculating the volume of the hull up to the various theoretical waterlines, one can draw a graph showing how much water the ship displaces according to her draught at the time — a displacement curve. This shows that a displacement of 18,750 lbs. (8½ tons) of water corresponds to a draught of about twenty-nine inches. (As the distance between the waterlines is approximately one foot, the draught, omitting the keel, would be approximately 1½ feet. The depth of the keel is about eleven inches, which gives the total of twenty-nine inches.) If the ship were loaded with seventy men at 175 lbs. per head, that makes 12,250 lbs. Weapons total 900 lbs., food 2,200 lbs., water 3,300 lbs., and miscellaneous cargo 2,200 lbs. Add the ship's own weight, 18,750 lbs., and we arrive at a total of 39,600 lbs. (eighteen tons), corresponding to a draught of thirty-six inches.

THE GOKSTAD SHIP TILLER AND STEERING OAR
ATTACHMENT

*Decoration of the detail work on the ship is
sparse except for the carved dragon's head on
the tiller with the spigot in its jaws. The head
still has yellow paint on the eyes and neck after
almost 1000 years. The eleven-foot oak steering
oar (right) was fitted on a conical block attached
to the hull, through with passed a rope knotted
inside the hull. The oar was further supported
at the rail by a leather thong.*

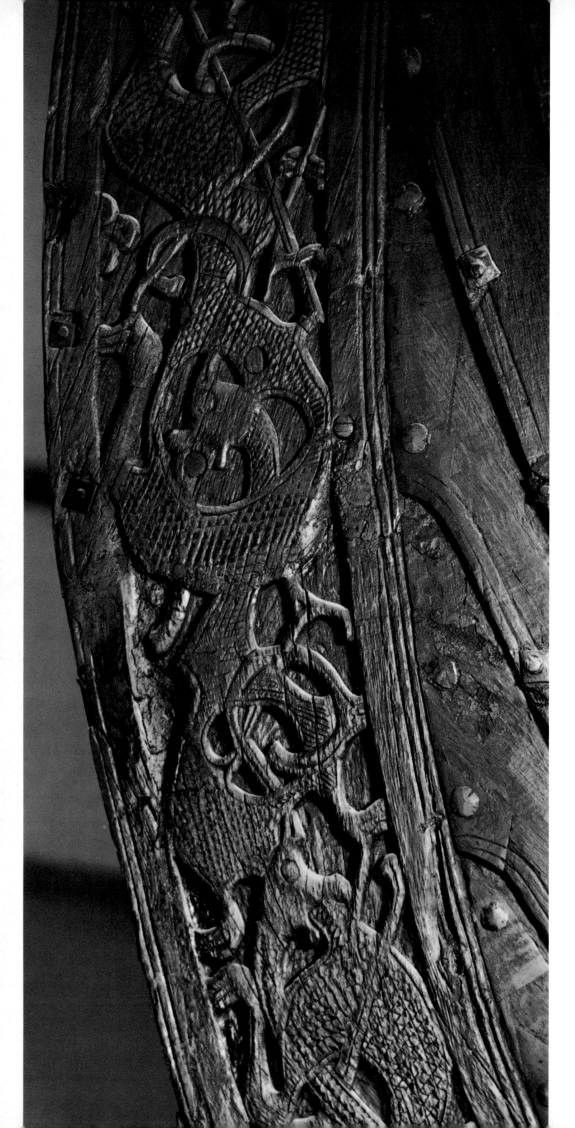

THE OSEBERG SHIP—
SEAWORTHY LINES AND SYMBOLIC STERNPOSTS

In many ways this ship is the most remarkable find from the Viking Age. The ship (right) is richly decorated, with an elegant and attractive design. It belonged to a distinguished person, and the skeleton found with it indicates that this could be the famous queen Asa of the sagas.

On both sides of the stems, at left, carved friezes run from the waterline up to the tops. They represent interlinked fabulous beasts, a decoration which Vikings clearly felt had symbolic and magical significance. The Oseberg ship is the finest example of artistic craftsmanship of the Viking Age.

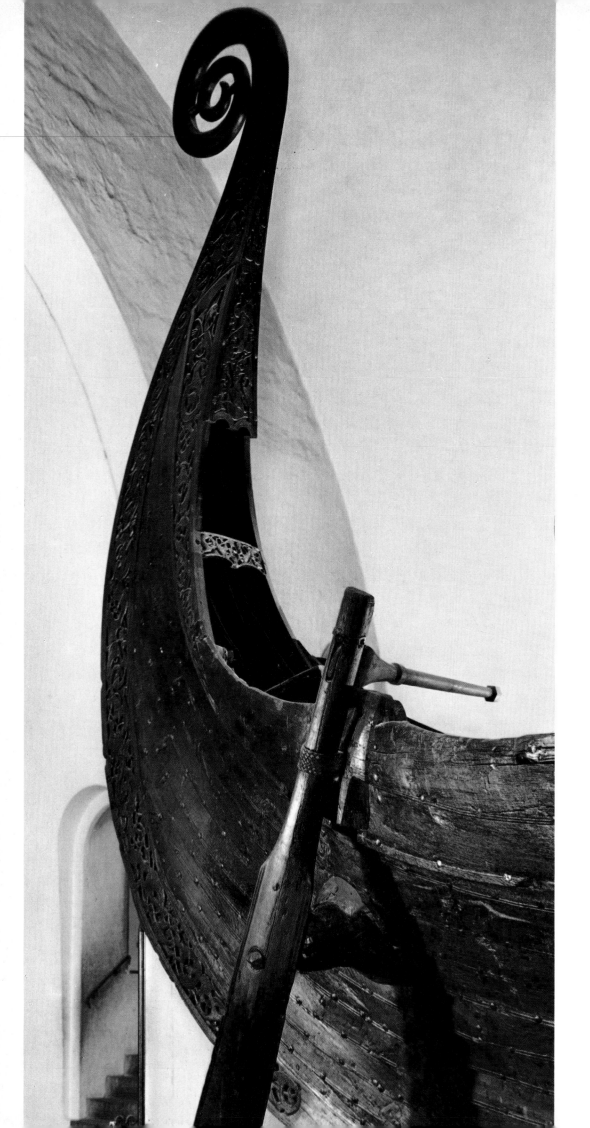

THE OSEBERG STEERING OAR

The function and construction of the Oseberg ship's steering oar is identical to those of the Gokstad ship, but the dimensions were considerably slighter. The tiller was never found, but it was presumably as richly decorated as the rest of the ship. The thong which holds the rudder to the ship's side is of artistically plaited leather.

SHIPS' RUDDERS

The small boats from the Gokstad find carry side rudders of the same type as the large ships. On small boats, however, the rudder was probably used under sail only, not when rowing. The upper picture shows how the withy used for lashing is fastened through holes in the "rudder-rib". The fastening was kept taut with the help of a couple of small wedges. In the lower picture, the rudder is hoisted, to keep it from grounding in shallow water.

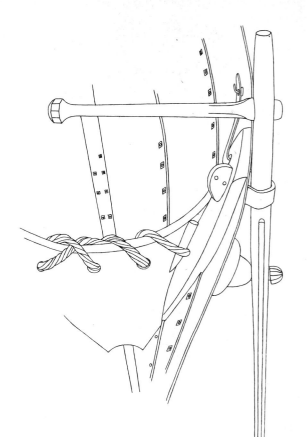

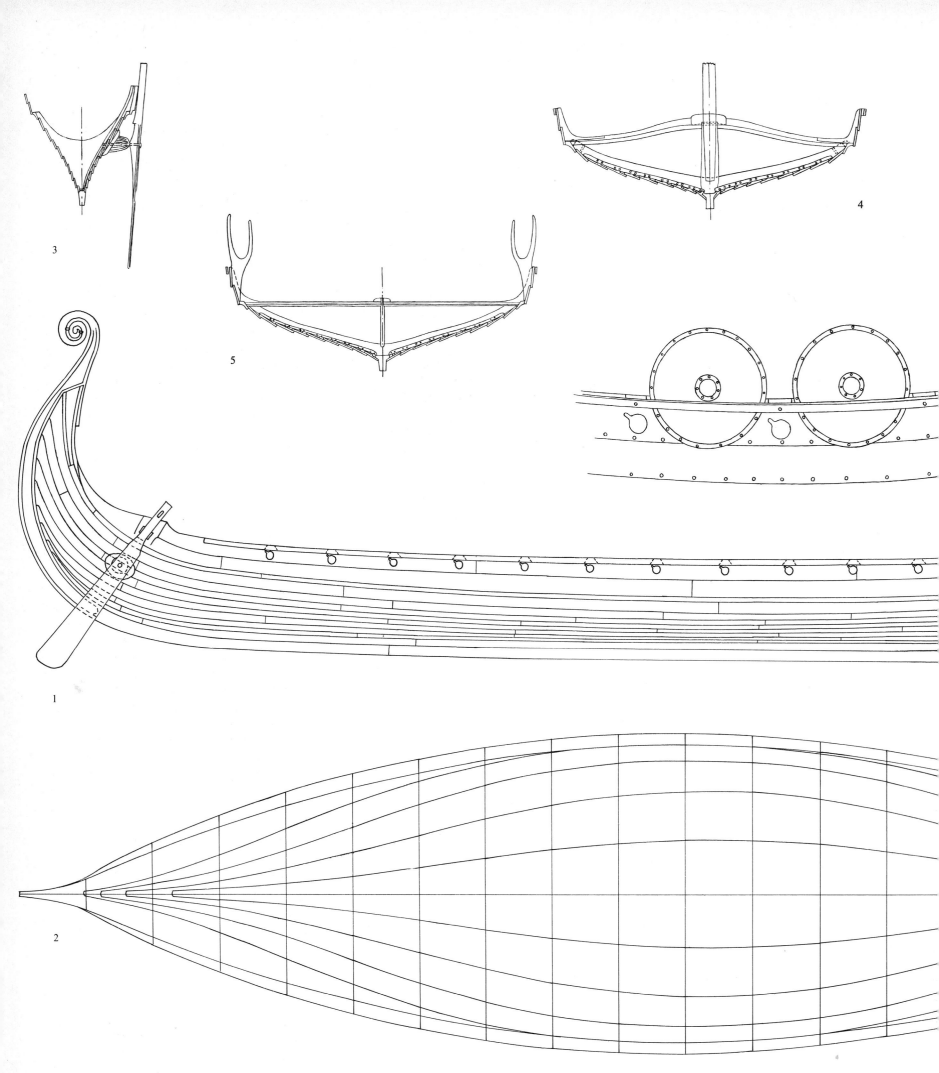

3

4

5

1

2

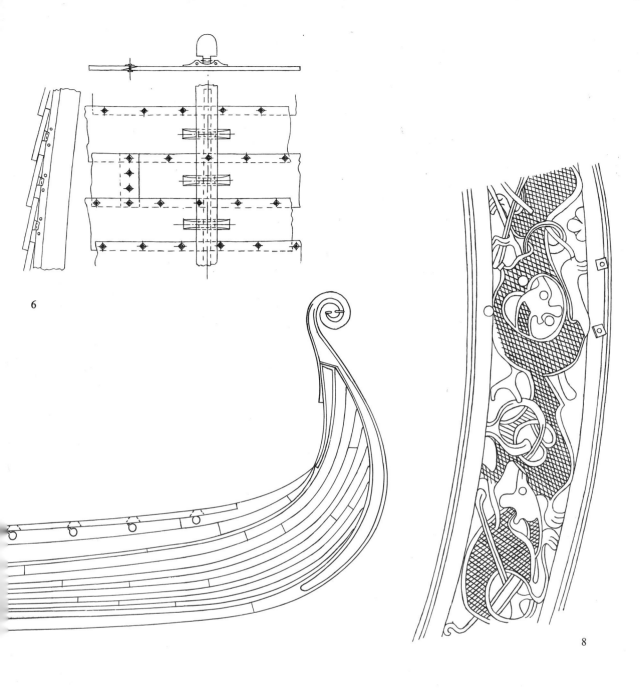

6

8

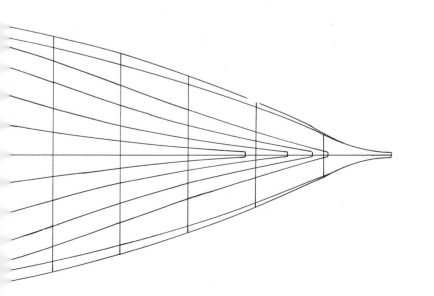

A comparison of the ships found at Oseberg, Gokstad and Tune soon reveals that the Oseberg ship differs from the other two in many details. Not only is it between fifty and a hundred years older than the others, but it was also a comparatively luxurious pleasure vessel. The Gokstad ship and the Tune ship, although of outstanding design, were nonetheless clearly intended for purely practical use.

Diagrams of the Oseberg ship (1, 2) include sections through the steering oar (3), at the mast (4) and abaft the mast (5). The ship lay low in the water and must have been a rather dangerous ship under sail. Whether this is because it was meant for use in shallow coastal waters, or because Scandinavian ships had not reached a more advanced stage of development when it was built around 800 A.D., cannot yet be decided with certainty. The timber supporting the lower part of the mast (known as the mastfish), is much less solidly built than on the other two ships, and even bears traces of old repairs. The rivets and the cleats of the planking, and their positions in relation to the rib, are illustrated in three projections (6). Evidently the oss beams of the Oseberg ship were not an organic part of its hull framework: they still show signs of having been developed from loose thwarts. The heavy plank, meginhúfr, found at the waterline, resembles in form the rail timber found in older ships. It has a projection along the outside, and in cross-section most resembles an inverted letter L (4). The two rows of planking above the meginhúfr give the impression of being little more than a pair of splashboards which were added on, but had not yet become a permanent part of the planking. Even in matters of shape alone there is a rather important difference between the Oseberg and the Gokstad ships.

The Oseberg ship has the same type of high, turned-back prow and stern which was found in the Kvalsund ship and in representations on coins and stone carvings. While very elegant, this must have been a real wind-catcher. In addition, finding suitable timber for it must have been difficult. The vertical ends of the Gokstad ship, with their more restrained curves, were undoubtedly more practical. The stems of the Oseberg ship are all decorated from the waterline to the top in a animal ornamentation — see detail (8) and photograph p. 256. The shields were fitted into a batten on the outside of the rail (7).

The equipment and gear found in the Oseberg and the Gokstad ships provide a fairly detailed picture of life on board a Viking vessel. According to the sagas the Vikings liked to moor their ships close to land at night, and pitch a tent on shore. The remains of one such tent were found in the Gokstad ship and two in the Oseberg ship. They consist of a light framework of timber over which a covering was spread. Unfortunately, the actual covering was not preserved. On the verge-boards of the Oseberg tents, magical symbols like the coiled serpent were painted. Possibly these were intended as protection against the evil powers of the night. In each of the two ships a large, splendid bed with carved posts was found, along with several simpler beds. All the beds could be dismantled and stowed on board. They may therefore have been field beds which could be set up for the use of the Viking leaders when they went ashore for the night. From the sagas it appears that during the early Middle Ages, it was usual to carry large skin bags called *hudfat* to store gear and weapons during the day and to serve as two-man sleeping bags at night. Little is known about the food the Vikings ate on long voyages. It was impossible to light even a cooking fire at sea, so that on open stretches of water the crew had to live on cold food. Dried and salted fish or meat with water, and sour milk or beer to drink must have been their staple diet. In both the Oseberg and Gokstad ships large cauldrons, perhaps for cooking on shore, were found. At Oseberg, in addition to cauldrons, a real piece of camping equipment turned up, a collapsible iron tripod for hanging the pots over a fire (see illustration page 181). The Gokstad cauldron is bronze and holds thirty-two gallons. Even assuming a ship carried as many as fifty men, a cauldron that large could supply ample portions of porridge or soup for everyone. On longer voyages large supplies of water were obviously necessary. It was probably carried in skin bags like those still used for wine in Mediterranean countries. Long, narrow boards with steps hewn out of them have been found on many burial ships, and these obviously served as gangplanks.

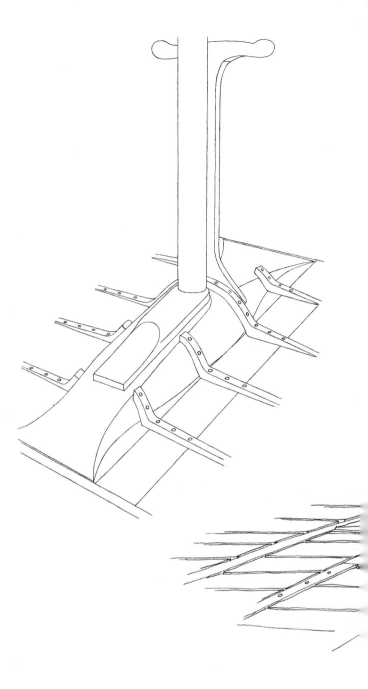

RAISING THE MAST

Raising the mast, as illustrated here, must have been heavy work. It has been reckoned that the mast of the Gokstad ship weighed about 800 pounds. While part of the crew lifted the mast bodily, walking it up, several men hauled on a stay attached to the bow of the ship, to help with the lifting and to hold the mast if the others lost their grip. When the mast was upright, the slot in the mast partner (above) was closed by the oak block lying on the decking. Then the stay and shrouds were tightened. The lower drawing shows how a short mast fitted snugly within the cross timbers in the stern of the ship when lowered.

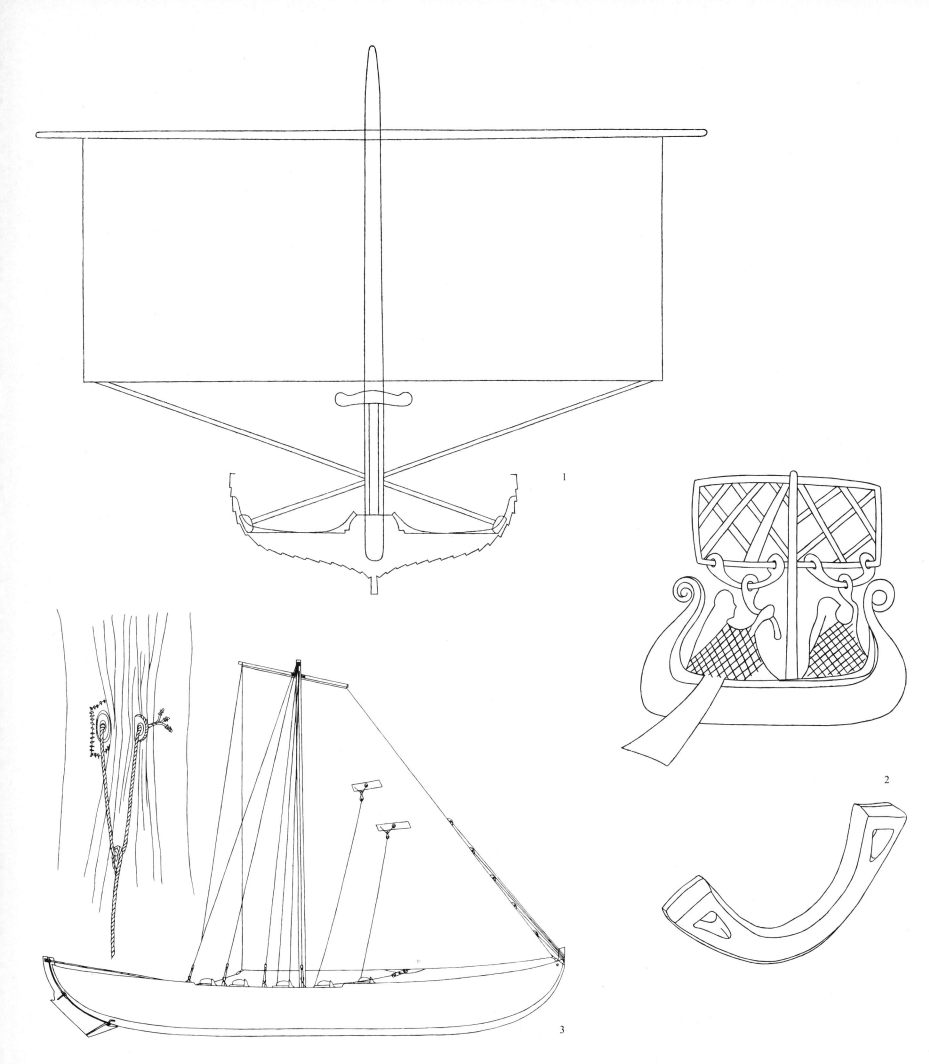

It is not known for certain when sails were first used in Scandinavian shipbuilding. It seems likely, however, that by about 700 A.D. hulls had developed far enough for ships to carry sails. Though all three Norwegian Viking ships used about the same method of mounting the mast, the mounting on the Oseberg ship, which is earliest, gives the impression of being still unsure and tentative in workmanship and design. The mounting on the Gokstad and Tune ships is fully developed.

The foot of the mast stands in a socket in the kjerringa. *In the Oseberg ship it only extends the distance between two ribs, but in the Gokstad ship it stretches over four ribs and is further strengthened by knees (see page 251). Above the kjerringa is the mastfish, a massive piece of oak laid over the cross beams at deck level. In the Oseberg ship it spans four cross beams, in the Gokstad ship, six. On the Gokstad ship it is very solidly fixed, being recessed to fit the cross beams and further supported on each side by strong knees. The mastfish of the Oseberg ship, by contrast, is fastened only by trenails at the front and the back, though it does also get some support from an extra thick cross beam in front of the mast, into which it is partly rebated. But this construction was obviously not adequate, as is shown by the fact that the mastfish split under the pressure of the sail and had to be repaired with iron bands. There is a large opening or slot in the mastfish behind the mast, so that the mast could be raised and lowered. When the mast was in position, it was held fast by a piece of oak, known as the mast-lock, placed in the slot.*

It has been said that this construction is so solid that no further support for the mast was necessary — that the Vikings sailed without stays, "on the bare timber" as the old expression has it. Indeed no physical traces of any means of securing standing rigging to support the mast have yet been found. However, there are two main objections to the "bare timber" theory. The first is that, among ships past and present about whose rigging we have complete knowledge, no ship carrying a square sail has been found where the mast is without supporting rigging. Second, all known representations of ships of the Viking Age without exception show stays and rigging helping to support the mast. It is possible, moreover, that this rigging was not fixed in any one position all the time, but moved to suit wind direction. If so, it may be that the fastening was effected by using the holes bored in the knees of both the Oseberg ship and the Gokstad ship. When sailing before the wind, the sail may have been stretched by poles (1). The U-shaped pieces seen attached to

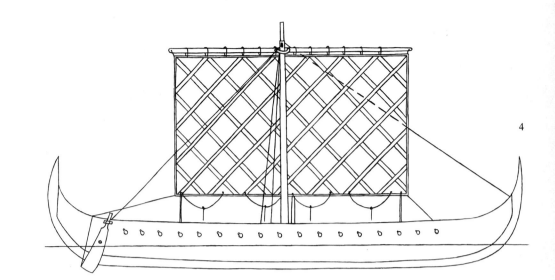

4

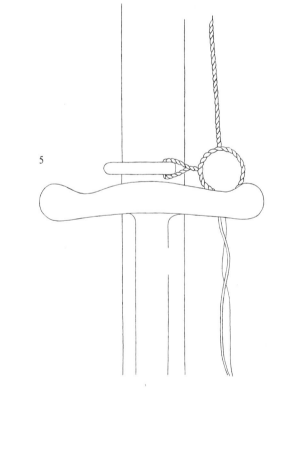

5

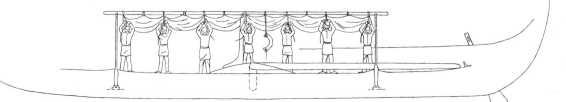

6

No known remains of sails have been found in the Norwegian ship-burials. Neither has the top part of a mast or any means of attaching rigging. But it is obvious from contemporary depictions like those on the Gotlandic picture-stones, as well as on rune-stones and coins, that Viking ships did carry a square sail. In fact what is probably a whole yard, forty-one feet long, is preserved in perfect condition at Oseberg. This large piece of timber cannot be a mast, because its diameter at both ends is much smaller than the diameter of the socket for the foot of the mast. Moreover the length of this yard corresponds well with the distance — 35½ feet — between the two outermost of the three T-shaped supports placed down the middle of the Gokstad ship. These must have been intended for carrying the yard when it was lowered. Laid along them, the yard would project about three feet at each end, a suitable margin of safety when the ship was under way. The supports are so constructed that yard and sail could be quickly hauled down on them on whatever side of the mast it happened to be. Two large spars were found lying along the three supports at Gokstad. One of these, twenty feet long, broken at the widest part, may be exactly one half of a broken yard. How broad would the sail have been? On the evidence of the existing yards, not more than forty feet. But it may have been as broad as the distance between the two outer yard supports, 35½ feet. Unhappily even the smaller of these measurements suggests that with a tall mast, Viking ships must have carried far more canvas than any of the reconstructions of Viking sails indicate. The answer to the problem lies in the height of the mast, which is difficult to determine, in view of the fact that, except for short fragments, no mast has been preserved. The mast was thick (a foot through in the case of the Gokstad ship and eight inches at Oseberg), and heavy. Yet all the evidence provided by surviving arrangements for mounting suggest that masts were quite clearly intended to be frequently and speedily raised and lowered. This being so, it is rather unlikely that they can have been so long that they stuck out backwards over the strong curves of the stern when being lowered. To manoeuvre a mast weighing 800 pounds *outside* the ship when under way would have been extremely dangerous. The mast must, therefore, have been just long enough so that it would clear the beams in the stern when lowered, that is, not more than thirty-three feet. A low sail and short mast on a Viking ship would have considerably lessened the need for special stays or ballast, because the lateral force of the wind was thereby afforded less leverage. Viking ships may therefore have been still lighter and faster than has hitherto been assumed.

the sail in picture-stones were probably used for altering the sail's profile to suit various wind conditions (2). (3) illustrates a method of reefing by gathering sail-cloth, applied to a type of ship used in Norway until recent times. Picture-stones suggest that the Vikings also used it. Little standing rigging would have been necessary when the mast was held fast by kjerringa *and mastfish. As the mast on these Viking ships was obviously intended to be raised and lowered frequently, the mastfish would have given the necessary support while the rigging was being raised.*

Judging by the evidence of the Gotland picture-stones, the mast was supported by a line to the prow and two or three lines — shrouds — from the mast top to the ship's sides, just aft of the mast (4). In addition to supporting the mast when the ship was under sail, this rigging must also have helped when the mast was being lowered and raised. When rowing or in harbour, the yard and sail, and perhaps the mast as well, could be laid along the T-shaped uprights seen on the Gokstad ship, giving more free deck space (5) and (6).

THE GOKSTAD SHIP VIEWED FROM THE HELMS-
MAN'S POSITION, AND DETAILS OF PLANKING ON
THE STARBOARD QUARTER

*In the rough oak mastfish stand the remains of
the mast, and a T-shaped trestle for raising the
yard. The ridged gang-plank is on the right, and
two wooden tubs on the left. Picture at right: the
two upper planks, the wedge-shaped repair and
the cleat are reconstructions from preserved
parts; most of the rivets, washers and planking are original.*

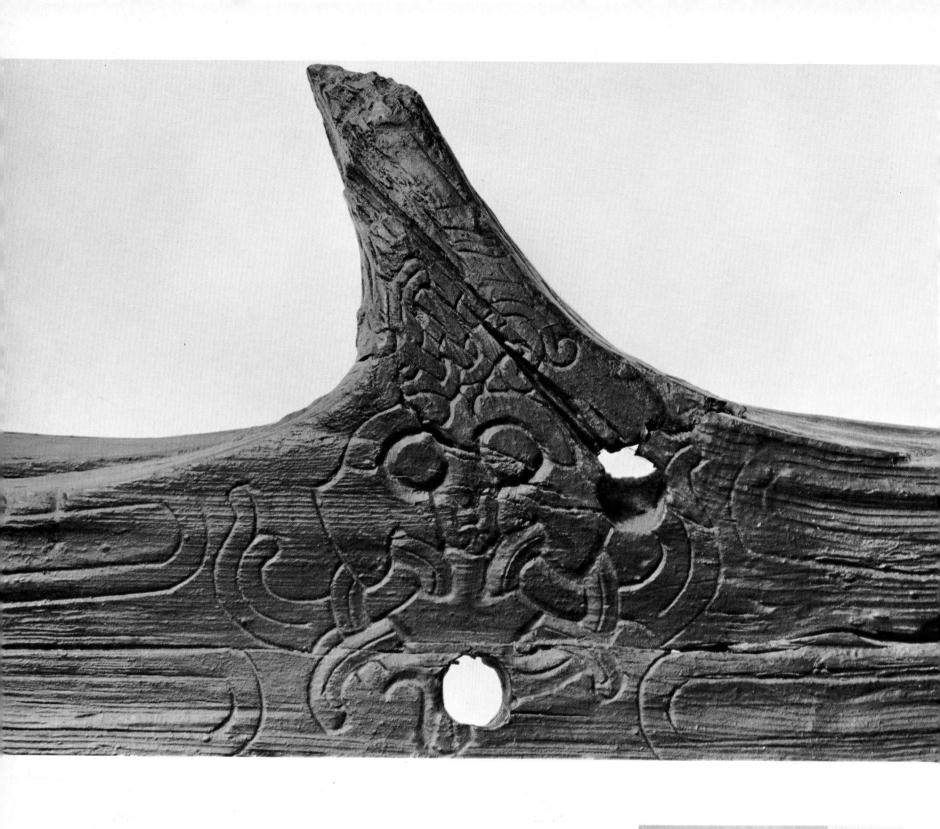

A CARVED ROWLOCK

The rowlocks of the largest of the ship's boats (left) are decorated with carved line patterns. The rowlocks acted as stops for the oars during the pull, whilst they were held in place by rope thongs which passed through the upper holes in the rowlocks.

THE LITTLE SHIP'S BOAT

Amongst the Gokstad discoveries were three small boats, thirty-two feet, twenty-six feet, and twenty-two feet long with five, three and two pairs of oars respectively. Their shape is similar to that of the large ship, with the same elegant construction and workmanship. The smallest (left), which was most suitable as a ship's boat, is built of oak with planking up to three-fifths of an inch thick. The boat is rather narrow, but fast and easy to handle.

SHIPS' GEAR

The flexible hulls of even the best-built and best-tended Viking vessels clearly shipped water sometimes, and it must have been very difficult to keep them absolutely water-tight. The crew of the Oseberg ship had a bailer shaped like a large wooden shovel. The ship carried an iron anchor, very well made (and well preserved), but rather small for a ship of its size. It is possible that it was only meant for holding the stern fast when the ship lay moored.

When it was uncovered in the burial mound, the Gokstad ship had thirty shields hanging in rows along either side outside the gunwale. They were held in position by cords drawn through the handles of the shields and through rectangular holes left for the purpose in a batten, the shield rack, attached to the underside of the gunwale on the inside. Painted alternatively black and yellow, the shields formed a continuous line from prow to stern, and overlapped each other so that one shield covered half of the shield aft of it. When hung like this, the shields completely covered the oar holes, and so they could not have been displayed when the ship was being rowed. This view is supported by the sagas, which make it clear that the shields were hung up when the ship was in harbour, but lay inside while at sea. On the other hand, several of the Gotland stone carvings show ships under sail with the shields hanging out. In the Oseberg ship they were placed in slots cut in a timber attached to the outside of the gunwale. Like this it would have been possible to row with the shields on display, and serving as a protective screen for the rowers.

269

ROWING

When the wind was unfavourable, or when making ready for battle, the ships were rowed. In the Oseberg, Gokstad and Tune ships, however, there are no fixed rowing benches. The most probable explanation is that the crew sat on their sea-chests to row (top of page). At any rate chests found in the Oseberg ship are exactly the right height for rowing. The large ships had oar-holes, but small boats were rowed with a special kind of rowlock, made from a naturally crooked piece of timber. This kind of rowlock is still used in western Norway. A loop of rope keeps the oar in place when rowing. The oars from the Oseberg ship are well-finished, with a tongue on the blade and decorative mouldings along the edges, while the Gokstad oars are rather plain.

In poems from the close of the Viking Age, and in sagas of the Middle Ages, many different names for different types of ship occur. But all these ships belonged to two main categories: merchantmen and warships.

The merchantman was designed to carry a large cargo and a relatively small crew. Built broad and deep with the emphasis on cargo capacity and seaworthiness rather than speed, the merchantman was a sailing ship with only a few pairs of oars for use during calms or when manoeuvering in narrow harbours. Warships, on the other hand, obviously had to be built for speed, with or without wind. They had places for many oarsmen, and were, in fact, most often used in sheltered coastal waters, where seaworthiness was not as essential as it was in the case of merchantmen.

No one knows when the distinction between merchantman and warship first began to be made, but by about 1000 A.D. an established difference existed. It seems reasonable to associate the origin of a special type of ship intended for commerce with the growth of the first towns. Obviously, too, there must have been a period when shipbuilders tried to combine warlike and commercial vessels in a single vessel. The Gokstad ship, for example, is probably one that had not yet acquired a distinct character, one that could be used as warship and which could also carry sufficient cargo to make sea transportation profitable.

During the tenth century the first large kingdoms were consolidated in Scandinavia, and the military organization called *ledungen* was finally established. According to this organization each district was required to build and maintain a ship, and to man her in the event of war. This allowed kings to build ships for purely military purposes, and naturally led to the development of a ship intended specifically for war.

The early medieval sagas about the last years of the Viking Age often describe very big ships. Greatest of all was the ship of Cnut the Great, reputed to contain sixty *spantrum*, as the spaces between the deck beams were called. It is probable that there is a good deal of exaggeration in these accounts of giant ships. To enable the oarsmen to use the oars properly, the oar holes should have been more than three feet apart. If the oars of Cnut's ship were spaced like those of the Gokstad ship, it would have been about 230 feet long. Knowing the Viking methods of shipbuilding, this would have meant a very weak hull. There is, therefore, reason to believe that such colossal dimensions existed only in the world of the sagas.

A VIKING CAMP FOR A LONG STAY ASHORE

All of the objects seen in the picture were actually found in a grave ship. In the foreground are several wooden tubs, a spade, a pitchfork, some washing implements, a soapstone cauldron, and a chain. Beyond are two types of portable cooking equipment. On the left preparations for baking are being carried out, and at right two tents have been put up. The foot of a bed is protruding from one of them. An oil lamp has been stuck into the ground outside the nearest tent, and the man sitting nearby is surrounded by tools and simple wooden objects, such as plates, trays, and bowls. The boats in the background have been beached.

For a long time the three Norwegian Viking ships were the only known remains of ships from the Viking period. In 1936, however, excavations at Ladby on the island of Fyn in Denmark uncovered another ship, and in 1962 five more were found in a unique "underwater" excavation in a natural channel in the middle of the extremely shallow Roskilde Fjord at Skuldelev, Denmark, west of Copenhagen. All six ships proved to be quite different from the earlier Norwegian remains. At Ladby only the iron rivets and minute fragments of timber had in fact been preserved, but by carefully recording the position of the rivets, it was possible to make a reliable reconstruction. The Ladby ship is narrow, shallow-draught, and with a less defined profile or sheer. Although probably not particularly seaworthy, it seems admirably suited to the relatively calm Danish coastal waters. It was, moreover, fast and easily propelled because of its narrow shape. That oars were not its only means of power is indicated by the presence of four large iron rings which were found on each side of the ship, fastened to the ribs aft of amidships. These rings were probably for fastening the lines that supported the mast. The ship is dated to the period 900-950 A.D. A large anchor was found with the Ladby ship, fastened to thirty feet of iron chain which was, in turn, tied to the remains of a hawser. The five ships from Skuldelev were built later than the Ladby ship and the three from Norway. They probably date from shortly after the year 1000. Three were merchantmen, but of different sizes and construction. The others were probably warships. One, shaped much like the Ladby ship, was very likely a coaster.

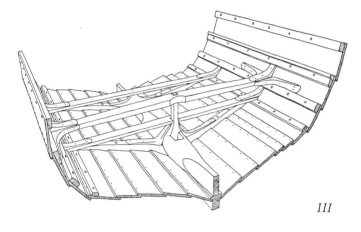

III

DESIGN DEVELOPMENTS FROM DENMARK

These drawings of the ships found at Ladby and at Skuldelev show developments in ship building and design that took place in the 150 years between the building of the Gokstad ship and the Danish vessels. In one of the later models, known as Wreck III (above and opposite page) the planking is no longer lashed to the ribs, but fastened by trenails: a rigid construction has replaced a flexible, elastic one.

The discovery of the Skuldelev ships made it possible to study for the first time, especially in Wreck III, the mounting of the mast in a merchant ship of the Viking period. The mastfish which held the lower part of the mast in the Gokstad ship has been replaced in the Skuldelev ship by a cross beam placed higher up above the ordinary cross beam (above, this page). This beam supports the mast and also strengthens the sides of the ship. The knees fastened to the cross beams on other Viking ships, and their extra ribs, have disappeared. Instead, by way of compensation, the upper planking is reinforced lengthwise on the inside. The ship

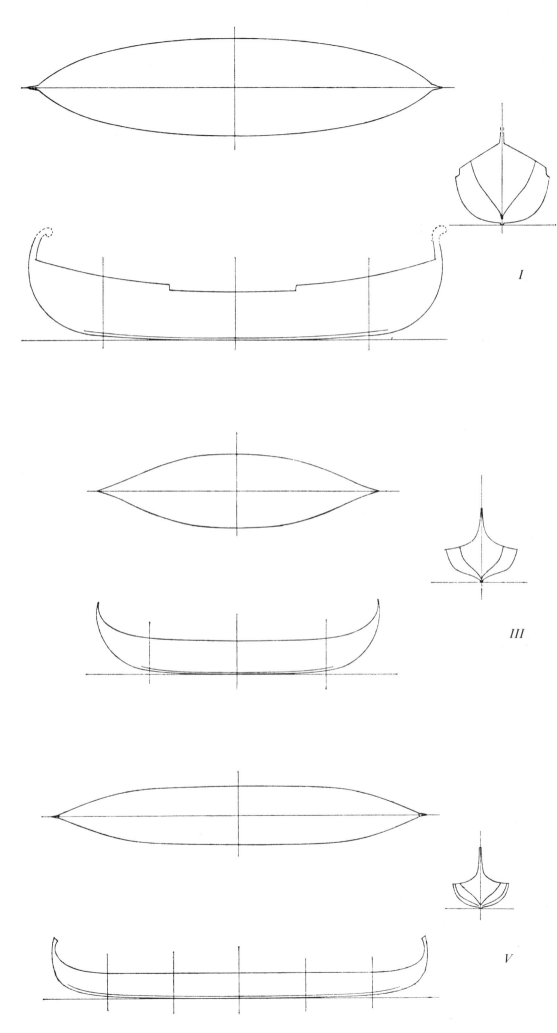

had an open hold around the mast, with decking fore and aft of it. The stern unfortunately was destroyed, so the interesting details of the bracing of the steering equipment were missing. The prow, on the other hand, was preserved intact, and it is a remarkable piece of work. The illusion of overlapping timbers is retained but, in fact, the prow is only imitation clinker-built, the whole being carved out of a single block of timber.

Although primarily a sailing ship, oars seems to have been used, though holes for them appear only fore and aft, not amidships. Wrecks I and II from Skuldelev were also merchantmen, but larger and more crudely built than Wreck III. It is probable that they are examples of the great ocean-going merchant ships from the end of the Viking Age. Because the remains of these ships are still being studied, it is not yet possible to be specific about dimensions and constructional details.

Wreck V has holes for oars along the whole length of the ship and like the smaller Wreck IV, was presumably a coastal warship.

275

THE ARCHAEOLOGICAL SENSATION OF THE TURN OF THE CENTURY.

The Oseberg grave-mound was not as impressive as most of the other grave-mounds, which were normally placed on high and open ground. It is on a flat piece of ground near a stream which runs through a valley. The Gokstad site is similar, leading to the conclusion that such places were chosen because it was comparatively easy to transport the ships to them, using the nearby stream. For both ships ditches were dug deep in the clay, which proved a very good medium for the preservation of the wood; in fact only the prow, which protruded above the clay, decayed.

At Oseberg a large pile of rocks was placed over the ships and on top of the pile the mound was built with turves; as these sank down, the mound formed an airtight covering over the ship, thus preserving it intact. At the same time the colossal weight of the rocks bore down on to the ship and the damp floor of the grave gave way, so that over the centuries the entire grave-mound sank. The ship was crushed to pieces and thus changed shape, so that the keel came to be higher than the sides of the ship. A short while after the ship had been buried, marauders managed to break into the grave-mound. They made a tunnel into the mound, destroyed the prow, which blocked their way, and broke through the ceiling of the burial-chamber. The position of the skeletons was disturbed and the bones were scattered. It is supposed that the marauders were in search of booty, for no jewels were found in the graves. But perhaps they were prompted by superstitious or religious motives, to prevent the dead man returning as a ghost. But in any case the vandals carried off all the precious metals. However, the other objects found give us an overall picture of the art and everyday life of the Vikings.

The building of the grave-mound at Oseberg was a long and arduous task, and we can imagine that the preparations were started while the Oseberg queen was still alive. Perhaps she herself decided where the grave should be. The state of preservation in the grave-mound was so good that even the grass and the plants remained intact. During the excavations it was possible to ascertain, on botanical evidence, that the grave was constructed in early spring, while the burial took place in late autumn.

THE GRAVE-MOUND AT OSEBERG, NORWAY

When the excavations were begun there in 1904, the grave-mound at Oseberg had concealed for more than a thousand years the richest burial-place of the Viking Age. It had been disturbed only once, by vandals in medieval times. The huge grave-mound rises up, just under 55 yards in diameter, an awe-inspiring monument to the respect of another age for its dead. The grave was restored after the excavations were completed and now blends with the ancient landscape.

A SHIP BROUGHT OUT OF THE GRAVE-MOUNDS
AFTER A THOUSAND YEARS

The picture on the opposite page shows the majestic prow of the ship.
Reconstruction work on the Gokstad ship lasted from its discovery in 1880 until a place was found for it fifty years later in the Ship Museum. Especially in the case of the Gokstad ship, photographic records are scarce, since photography was in its infancy in Scandinavia when the ship was discovered.

BROKEN WOODEN CONTAINERS FROM THE GRAVE-MOUND

Cooking utensils were found together in the fore part of the ship at Oseberg. There were pots and frying-pans, ladles of various sizes and several serving-plates made of wood. There was even an implement for grinding grain to make bread or porridge. Some wooden buckets had probably been used to store food. In the centre of the picture can be seen a ladle carved from a single piece of wood. The bucket has been forced entirely out of shape, as have nearly all the containers bound with staves. Originally this was a finely-made bucket, with ornamental staves made of baleen.

FRAGMENTS OF A BUCKET

The work of preparing and reconstructing all the objects found at Oseberg lasted many years. This bucket with staves is a typical detail of the world's greatest puzzle. Even if the wood had been well preserved, every single piece would have needed treatment to prevent it from shrinking or disintegrating entirely.
Before they could be reassembled the pieces had to be boiled in an alum solution and covered with linseed oil and varnish.

THE OSEBERG AND GOKSTAD SHIP EXCAVATIONS

It is difficult to imagine all the problems confronting the archaeologists in their work with these important finds. At Oseberg every single piece of the ship and of the objects found in the grave had to be marked and numbered, taken out of the grave and packed ready for transport to Oslo. The reconstruction of the ship was carried out under the direction of Ing. Fr. Johannessen, who succeeded in achieving the impossible and putting the ship together again. The oak wood used was so well preserved that it was possible to bend it back into its original shape. On the left is shown a stage in the excavation of the ship. The Gokstad ship (page 282) had disintegrated completely. The upper planks had been forced into the centre of the ship, and the extremities of the prow and the stern were decayed. Finally, the ship was divided in two and transported by cart. First of all, the ship was reconstructed only temporarily and left like that until 1930. When it was taken to the Viking Ship Museum at Bygdöy, the ship was taken to bits and the fragments steam-treated to restore their original shape; when the ship was finally reconstructed, new pieces of wood were used to replace those which were quite decayed.

THE SLEDGES OF THE OSEBERG QUEEN

The four sledges of the Oseberg queen had suffered much deterioration from their long storage in the grave-mound. One of them was broken into nearly a thousand pieces. The simple everyday sledge was so poorly preserved that it was not possible to put it together again, while the three resplendent sledges, for special occasions, could be exhibited after much careful and time-consuming work had gone into restoring them. Even after careful scientific treatment the wood was so fragile that it could hardly withstand its own weight, and extensive technical problems had to be solved before the sledges could be exhibited. In the state in which the sledges were found during the excavations, their reconstruction must have appeared practically impossible. They had been crushed to such an extent that they had quite lost their shape, and in many places the damp wood had taken on the shape of the stones which lay beneath them.

During the excavations it was possible to discern traces of paint on the box-frames. Black, brown and red had been used to emphasize the lines of the carving. The sledges were made in two parts: the box-frame was fixed on top of the lower section, consisting of the legs and runners. An examination of the ornamentation revealed that the carving had been carried out by several craftsmen, and that the box-frame and the lower section were not carved by the same person.

At one time sledges were used all the year round in Norway. The roads were bad and the sledges could run over grass as well as over snow. We can therefore presume that the Oseberg sledges were not only for winter use.

FRAGMENTS OF THE WAGON FOUND DURING THE EXCAVATIONS

Two of the wheels as they were found on the ship. Even these solid fragments, enormous and made of oak, were crushed to pieces and had lost their original shape. During the burial ceremony the wagon was dismantled. The wheels, the body and the undercarriage had been taken apart. The construction of the wagon was technically rather primitive, and it is clear that the making of wheels and carts at that time was difficult and that capable craftsmen were hard to find.

Fragments of wagons were found in various places in the graves and several wagons can be seen on the Gotland picture-stones, so that it is certain that the Oseberg wagon was not unique, but wagons were far from common in Viking times.

INSTITUTES AND MUSEUMS

Gratitude is due to many research institutes and museums in European and other countries.

Bergen Maritime Museum, Bergen, Norway.

British Museum, London, Great Britain.

Gothenburg Maritime Museum, Gothenburg, Sweden.

Gothenburg University Library, Gothenburg, Sweden.

Gotland Collection of Antiquities, Visby, Sweden.

Iceland National Museum of Antiquities, Reykjavik, Iceland.

Musée de Normandie, Caên, France.

National Museum, Helsinki, Finland.

National Museum of Antiquities, Copenhagen, Denmark.

Norwegian Maritime Museum, Bygdöy, Oslo, Norway.

Royal Library of Sweden, Stockholm, Sweden.

Schleswig-Holstein Museum of Prehistory and Protohistory, Schleswig Schloss Gottorp, Germany.

Swedish State Historical Museum and Royal Coin Collection, Stockholm, Sweden.

University of Oslo Museum of Antiquities, Oslo, Norway.

University of Uppsala, Coin Collection, Uppsala, Sweden.

Oxford University Press / Prof. Gwyn Jones, and their book The Norse Atlantic Saga.

INDEX

LITERATURE

THE HISTORICAL AND ARCHEOLOGICAL BACKGROUND

G. Arwidsson, *Vendelstile, Email und Glas.* Diss. Uppsala 1942.

— —, Valsgärde 6. *Die Gräberfunde von Valsgärde I.* Uppsala 1942.

— —, Valsgärde 8. *Die Gräberfunde von Valsgärde II.* Uppsala 1954.

A. Dopsch, *Wirtschaftliche und soziale Grundlagen der europäischen Kulturentwicklung aus der Zeit von Cäsar bis auf Karl den Grossen, I-II,* Wien 1923-24.

R. H. Hodgkin, *A History of the Anglo-Saxons, II,* Oxford 1939.

W. Holmqvist, Die eisenzeitlichen Funde aus Lillön, Kirchspiel Ekerö, Uppland. *Acta Archaeologica XXV* 1954. Copenhagen.

— —, Grävningarna på Helgö i Mälaren. Summary. *Viking* 21-22. Oslo 1958.

— —, Helgö, en internationell handelsplata. *Proxims Thule.* Stockholm 1962.

— —, B. Arrhenius & P. Lundström, *Excavations at Helgö I.* Stockholm 1961.

— —, B. Arrhenius, *Excavations at Helgö II.* Stockholm 1964.

B. Nerman, Grobin-Seeburg, *Ausgrabungen und Funde.* Stockholm 1958.

H. Pirenne, Un contrast économique: Mérovingiens et Carolingiens. *Revue belge de philologie et d'histoire,* 1922-23.

H. Pirenne, *Mahomet et Charlemagne.* Bruxelles 1935. German ed.: *Geburt des Abendlandes.* Leipzig 1939.

HISTORICAL SOURCES

Adam Bremensis, magister, *Gesta Hammaburgensis ecclesiae pontificum,* ed. H. B. Schmeidler, Hannover-Leipzig 1917.

H. Birkeland, Nordens historie i middelalderen efter arabiske kilder. *Norske Videnskaps-Akademis skrifter.* Oslo 1954.

A. Bugge, *Vikingerne, I-II.* Christiania 1904-06.

G. N. Garmonsway, *The Anglo-Saxon Chronicle.* Everyman Library 1953.

G. Jacob, Arabische Berichte von Gesandten an germanische Fürstenhöfe aus dem 9. und 10. Jahrhundert. *Quellen zur deutschen Volkskunde,* I. Berlin-Leipzig 1927.

C. H. Robinson, *Anskar, the apostle of the north. (Vita Anskarii).* London 1921.

Alexander Seippel, *Rerum Normannicarum fontes Arabici, I-II.* Oslo 1876-1928.

Johannes Steenstrup, *Normannerne, I-IV,* Copenhagen 1876-82.

H. Sweet, King Alfred's Orosius, *Early English Text Society* 1883.

V. Vogel, *Die Normannen und das fränkische Reich bis zur Gründung der Normandie,* Heidelberg 1906.

D. Whitelock, *English Historical Documents.* (500-1042) London 1955.

A. Zeki Validi Togan, Ibn Fadlan's Reisebericht, *Abhandlungen für die Kunde des Morgenlandes XXIV:3.* Leipzig 1939.

GENERAL WORKS ON THE VIKINGS

J. Adigard des Gautries, Études de toponymie normannique 4. *Études Germaniques* 15. 1960.

Jean Adigard des Gautries, *Les noms de personnes scandinaves en Normandie de* 911 *à* 1066. Lund 1954.

W. E. D. Allen, *The Poet and the Spae-Wife. An Attempt to Reconstruct Al-Ghazal's Embassy to the Vikings.* London 1960.

B. Almgren, Vikingatåg och vikingaskepp. Summary: Viking raids and viking ships. *Tor VIII.* Uppsala 1962.

B. Almgren, Vikingatågens höjdpunkt och slut. Summary: The peak and the end of Viking raids. *Tor XI.* Uppsala 1963.

C. G. Andrae, *Kyrka och frälse i Sverige under äldre medeltid.* Diss. Uppsala 1960.

H. Arbman-M. Stenberger, *Vikingar i västerled,* Stockholm 1935.

H. Arbman, *Svear i österviking,* Stockholm 1955.

H. Arbman, *The Vikings.* London 1960.

H. Arbman, Sverige och östern under vikingatiden. *Proxima Thule.* Stockholm 1962.

H. Arbman, Zur Frage der Verbindungen zwischen Ost und West in IX.-X. Jhdt. *Atti del VI Congresso Internat. Prehist. Protohist. Vol. I.* Roma 1962.

T. J. Arne, *La Suède et l'Orient.* Diss. Uppsala 1914.

T. J. Arne, Ibn-Fadlans resa till Bulgar. Résumé: Le voyage d'Ibn Fadlan à Bulgar. *Fornvännen.* Stockholm 1941.

T. J. Arne, Die Varägerfrage und die sowjetische Forschung, *Acta Archaeologica XXIII,* Copenhagen 1952.

Fritz Askeberg, *Norden och kontinenten i gammal tid,* Uppsala 1944.

F. Askeberg, La Guerche. Ett bidrag till Loirevikingarnas historia, *Namn och Bygd* 1944. Uppsala.

A. L. Binns, The Viking Century in East Yorkshire. *East Yorkshire Local Historical Society* 1963.

S. Bolin, Mahomet, Charlemagne and Ruric. *Scandinavian Economic History Rewiew* 1954.

S. Bolin, Die Anfänge der Münzprägung in Skandinavien. *Settimane di studio del Centro italiano di studi sull'alto medioevo VII. Moneta e scambi nell'alto medioevo.* Spoleto 1961.

Johannes Brøndsted, *Nordboer i Amerika før Columbus?* Copenhagen 1951.

J. Brønsted, *The Vikings.* London 1960.

A. Bugge, *Vesterlandenes indflydelse paa nordboernes og særlig nordmændenes ydre kultur, levesæt og samfundsforhold,* Christiania 1905.

P. Enemark, Om problemer vedrørende friserhandelen. *Jyske Samlinger.* Aarhus 1959-1961. (Frisian Trade, extensive bibliography.)

R. H. C. Davis, East Anglia and the Danelaw. *Transactions of the Royal Historical Society, 5th ser. V.* 1955.

R. Ekblom, Ortnamnens vittnesbörd om svenskarnas tidiga förbindelser med slaver och balter. Zusammenfassung. *Språkvetenskapliga Sällskapets i Uppsala Förhandlingar* 1940-1942.

E. Ekwall, Scandinavians and Celts in the North-West of England. *Lunds Universitets Årsskrift* 14:27. Lund 1918.

E. Ekwall, The Scandinavian Element. *Introduction to the Survey of English Place-Names I.* Cambridge 1924.

E. Ekwall, The scandinavian settlements. *An historical geography of England before A. D.* 1800. ed. H. C. Darby. Cambridge 1936.

E. Ekwall, *Concise Oxford Dictionary of English placenames.* Oxford 1960.

E. Ennen, *Frühgeschichte der Europäischen Stadt.* Bonn 1953.

K. O. Falk, Dneprforsarnas namn i kejsar Konstantin VII Porfyrogennetos' De Administrando Imperio. *Lunds Universitets Årsskrift N. F. Avd. 1, 46:4.* Lund 1951.

G. Hasselberg, *Studier rörande Visby stadslag och dess källor.* Diss. Uppsala 1953.

H. Hermansson, The Problem of Wineland. *Islandica 25,* 1936.

W. Hovgaard, *The Voyages of the Norsemen to America,* New York 1915.

Lis Jacobsen, *Svenskevældets fald,* Copenhagen 1929.

H. Jankuhn, and others. Die Zeit der Stadtgründung im Ostseeraum. *Acta Visbyensia I.* Visbysymposiet för historiska vetenskaper 1963. Visby 1965.

A. Janzén, Scandinavian Place-Names in England I-VI. *Names 1957-1963.* Berkeley, California.

E. Joransson. *The Danegeld in France.* Rock Island, Ill. 1924.

T. D. Kendrick. *A History of the Vikings.* London 1930.

E. Kivikoski, Studien zu Birkas Handel im östlichen Ostseegebiet. *Acta Archaeologica VIII.* 1938 Copenhagen.

Kulturhistoriskt lexikon för nordisk medeltid från vikingatid till reformationstid. I-XI seqq. Malmö 1956-1966 seqq.

A. R. Lewis, *The Northern Seas,* Shipping and Commerce in Northern Europe A. D. 300-1100. Princeton 1958.

H. Lindkvist, *Middle English Place-Names of Scandinavian Origin.* Diss. Uppsala 1912.

G. J. Marcus, The norse emigration to the Faroe Islands. *English Historical Review LXXI,* 1956.

I. Martens, Vikingetogen i arkeologisk belysning. Summary: The Viking Raids seen in the Light of Archeology. *Viking, XXIV.* Oslo 1960.

A. Mawer, The Scandinavian Settlement in England as Reflected in English Place Names. *Acta philologica Scandinavica 7.* Copenhagen 1932.

J. Meldgaard, *Nordboerne i Grønland.* Copenhagen 1965.

A. Melvinger, *Les premières incursions des vikings en Occident d'apres des sources arabes.* Uppsala 1955.

V. Minorksy, Rus. *Encyclopedia of Islam.* 1936.

L. Musset, Relations et échanges d'influences dans l'Europe du Nord-Ouest. (Xe-XIe siècles). *Cahiers de civilisation médievale.* 1958.

L. Musset. Les invasions: Le seconde assaut contre l'Europe chrétienne. *Nouvelle Clio XII B.* Paris 1965.

B. Nerman, Die Verbindungen zwischen Skandinavien und dem Ostbaltikum in der jüngeren Eisenzeit. *Kungl. Vitterhets Historie och Antikvitets Akademiens Handlingar 40:1.* Stockholm 1929.

P. Nörlund, *Viking settlers in Greenland and their descendants during five hundred years.* Cambridge 1936.

E. Oxenstierna, *Norsemen.* New York 1965.

S. U. Palme, Vikingatågen i väst - deras förutsättningar och samhälleliga följder. *Nordisk-Tidskrift.* Stockholm 1962.

H. Paszkiewicz, *The Origin of Russia,* London 1954.

— —, *The making of the Russian Nation.* London 1963.

S. Piekarczik, *Studia nad rozwojen structury spoleczno-gospodarczej wczesnosrednrowiecznej Szwecji.* Warszawa 1962.

B. A. Rybakov, Problèmes en cours sur la formation de la Russie de Kiev. *XIe Congrès International des Sciences Historiques, Stockholm 21-28 août 1960,* Résumés des communications. Uppsala 1960. With discussion in: *Actes du Congrès.* Uppsala 1962.

P. H. Sawyer, *The age of the vikings.* London 1962.

A. H. Smith, *The Place-Names of the East Riding of Yorkshire and York.* Cambridge 1937.

A. H. Smith, *The Place-Names of the West Riding of Yorkshire 1-8.* Cambridge 1961-1963.

Carl V. Sølver, *Vestervejen. Om Vikingernes sejlads.* Copenhagen 1954.

Johannes Steenstrup, Normandiets Historie under de syv første Hertuger 911-1066. *Det kgl. danske Vidensk. Selsk. Skrifter 7.* Række, Copenhagen 1925.

J. Stefansson, Vikings in Spain. *Saga-Book of the Viking Club,* VI, 1909.

A. Stender-Petersen. *Varangica.* Aarhus 1953.

— —, Das Problem der ältesten Byzantinisch-Russisch-Nordischen Beziehungen. *Relazioni III: Storia del Medioevo,* ed. *Comitato internaz. di scienze storiche, X congresso internaz.* Roma 1955.

— —, Varaegerspörgsmålet. *Viking, XXIII.* Oslo 1959.

F. M. Stenton, The scandinavian colonies in England and Normandy. *Transactions of the Royal Historical Society. 4th ser. XXVII.* 1945.

— —, *Anglo-Saxon England.* Oxford 1947.

— —, *The Bayeux Tapestry.* London 1957.

M. Strömberg, Neue Schwedische Beiträge zur Geschichte der skandinavisch-slawischen Beziehungen während der Wikingerzeit und das frühe Mittelalter. *Slavia Antiqua VII.* Warszawa-Poznán 1960.

V. Thomsen. *The relations between ancient Russia and Scandinavia and the origin of the Russian state.* Oxford 1877. Also in: *Samlede skrifter I.* Copenhagen 1919.

W. Vogel, *Die Normannen und die fränkische Reich.* Heidelberg 1906.

E. Wadstein, *Norden och Västeuropa i gammal tid.* Gothenburg 1925.

A. Walsh, *Scandinavian Relations with Ireland during the Viking Period.* Dublin 1922.

R. E. M. Wheeler, *London and the Vikings.* London Museum Catalogue. London 1927.

S. Wikander, Orientaliska källor till vikingatidens historia. *Historisk Tidskrift.* Stockholm 1963.

TOWNS AND SETTLEMENTS

B. Ambrosiani, Birka-Sigtuna-Stockholm. Ett diskussionsinlägg. Zusammenfassung. *Tor 1957.* Uppsala.

H. Andersen & O, Klindt-Jensen, Det aeldste Århus. Summary: Oldest Århus. *Kuml.* Århus 1963.

E. Aner. Das Kammergräberfeld von Haithabu. *Offa 10.* Neumünster 1952.

H. Arbman, *Birka, Sveriges äldsta handelsstad,* Stockholm 1939.

H. Arbman, *Birka I. Die Gräber.* Uppsala-Stockholm 1940, 1943.

Charlotte Blindheim, *Kaupang, markedsplassen i Skiringssal,* Oslo 1953.

Ch. Blindheim, En amulett av rav. Summary: An amber amulet (Kaupang). *Universitetets i Oslo Oldsaksamlings Årbok 1958-1959.* Oslo.

Ch. Blindheim, The Market Place in Skiringsal. *Acta Archaeologica XXXI* 1960. Copenhagen.

Ch. Blindheim, New Light on Viking Trade in Norway. *Archaeology 13:4.* New York 1960.

Ch. Blindheim, En barre av bly. Summary: An ingot of lead (Kaupang). *Universitets i Oslo Oldsaksamlings Årbok 1960-1961.* Oslo.

T. Capelle, Die Ausgrabungen im innern des Halbkreiswalles. (Haithabu). *Offa 21-22.* Neumünster 1964-65.

Vilh. la Cour, *Danevirkestudier. En arkæologisk-historisk Undersøgelse.* Copenhagen 1951.

Ejnar Dyggve, Gorm's Temple and Harald's Stave-Church. *Acta Archaeologica XXV.* 1954. Copenhagen.

S. Erixon (ed.), Byggnadskultur. *Nordisk Kultur XVII.* Stockholm-Oslo-Copenhagen 1953.

B. Fritz, Stadshistoria och arkeologi. *Historisk Tidskrift.* Stockholm 1965.

A. Geijer, *Birka III. Die Textilfunde.* Stockholm (Diss. Uppsala) 1938.

G. Hatz, Münzfunde aus Haithabu 1962. *Offa 21-22.* Neumünster 1964-65.

I. Heltoft, *Kongesædet i Jelling,* København 1957.

A. Herteig, Marknadsplatser-stadsbildningar. Summary: The origin of towns in the north. *Tor X.* Uppsala 1964.

Bjørn Hougen, *Fra seter til gård. Studier i norsk bosetning-historie.* Oslo 1947.

E. K. Hougen, Tinnfoliert keramik fra Kaupang. Summary: Tin-foiled pottery from Kaupang. *Universitetets i Oslo Oldsaksamlings Årbok 1958-1959.* Oslo.

— —, Kaupang-keramikken. Summary: The pottery from Kaupang. *Universitetets i Oslo Oldsaksamlings Årbok 1960-1961.* Oslo.

W. Hübener, *Die Keramik von Haithabu.* Neumünster 1959.

H. Jankuhn, *Die Wehranlagen der Wikingerzeit zwischen Schlei und Treene.* Neumünster 1937.

— —, *Die Ausgrabungen in Haithabu* (*1937-39*). Berlin 1943.

— —, Die Frühgeschichte vom Ausgang der Völkerwanderung bis zur Ende der Wikingerzeit. *Geschichte Schleswig-Holsteins III.* Neumünster, 1955-57.

— —, Zur Fortführung der Ausgrabungen in Haithabu, Probleme und Zi. *Zeitschrift der Gesellschaft für Shleswig-Holsteinische Geschichte, Band 87 1962.* Neumünster.

— —, *Haithabu. Ein Handelsplatz der Wikingerzeit. 4. ergänzte Auflage.* Neumünster 1963.

— —, Überblick über die verschiedene Grabungen. (Haithabu). *Offa 21-22.* Neumünster 1964-65.

J. Larsen. Rekonstruktion af Trelleborg. Summary: The reconstruction of the Trelleborg houses. *Aarbøger for nordisk oldkyndighed og historie.* Copenhagen 1957.

Palle Lauring–A. Hoff-Møller, Terlleborghusets rekonstruktion, *Aarbøger for nordisk Oldkyndighed og Historie 1952.* Copenhagen.

Soph. Müller og C. Neergaard, Danevirke, archæologisk undersøgt, beskrevet af tydet. *Nordiske Fortidsminder I. 1903.*

P. Nørlund. *Trelleborg.* Copenhagen 1948.

O. Olsen, Trelleborg-problemer. Summary: Trelleborg Problems. *Scandia 28.* Lund 1962.

H. P. L'Orange, Trelleborg-Aggersborg og de kongelige byer i Østen. *Viking XVI,* Oslo 1952.

K. Raddatz, Bericht über die Probegrabung auf der Südsiedlung. (Haithabu) *Offa 21-22.* Neumünster 1964-65.

H. Schledermann, Danevirkeundersögelser ved Bustrup 1962-63. *Offa 21-22.* Neumünster 1964-65.

C. G. Schultz, Vikingetidshuset paa Trelleborg, *Fra Nationalmuseets Arbejdsmark 1942.* Copenhagen.

— —, Aggersborg. Vikingelejren ved Limfjorden, *Fra Nationalmuseets Arbejdsmark 1949.* Copenhagen.

P. Simonsen, Nord-Norges bosetningshistorie i oldtiden. *Ottar 32-33.* Tromsø, 1962.

K. Skaare, Et myntfunn fra Kaupang. Summary: A coin find from Kaupang. *Universitetets i Oslo Oldsaksamlings Årbok 1958-1959.* Oslo.

— —, Nye mynter fra Kaupang. Summary: New coins from Kaupang. *Universitetets i Oslo Oldsaksamlings Årbok 1960-1961.* Oslo.

M. Strömberg, Untersuchungen zur jüngeren Eisenzeit in Schonen. (Völkerwanderungszeit-Wikingerzeit). I, II. *Acta Archæologica Lundensia.* Diss. Lund 1961.

— —, Eine siedlungsgeschichtliche Untersuchung in Hagestad, Südost-Schonen. *Meddelanden från Lunds Universitets Historiska Museum 1961.* Lund.

— —, Handelsstråk och vikingabygd i sydöstra Skåne. Om Hagestad-undersökningen. *Ale 1963:3.* Lund.

H. Wideen. *Västsvenska vikingatidsstudier.* Summary: Studies on the viking age in West Sweden. Diss. Stockholm 1955.

GRAVE FINDS

E. Aner. Die wikingerzeitlichen Kammergräber am Thorsberger Moor. *Offa 11.* Neumünster 1952.

H. Arbman, Das Årby-Fund. *Acta Archæologica XI 1940.* Copenhagen.

T. J. Arne, Ein bemerkenswerter Fund aus Östergötland. *Acta Archæologica III 1932.* Copenhagen.

— —, *Das Bootgräberfeld von Tuna in Alsike.* Stockholm 1934.

C. Bertheussen, Ei gåta frå Gokstadskipet. Summary: An unsolved problem of the Gokstad ship. *Viking 21-22.* Oslo 1958.

Ch. Blindheim, Osebergskoene på ny. Summary: The shoes from Oseberg. *Viking XXIII.* Oslo 1959.

— —, Smedgraven fra Bygland i Morgedal. Summary: The Smith's Grave at Bygland in Morgedal, Telemark County, Norway. *Viking XXVI.* Oslo 1963.

A. W. Brögger & H. Shetelig. *Osebergfundet. Resumé. Vol. I-III, V.* Oslo 1917-1928.

— —, — —, The Viking Ships. Oslo 1953.

J. Brøndsted, Danish Inhumation Graves of the Viking Age. *Acta Archæologica VII 1936.* Copenhagen.

A. E. Christensen jr, Gokstadskipets stevner. *Universitetets i Oslo Oldsaksamlings Årbok 1958-1959.* Oslo.

— —, Faeringen fra Gokstad. Summary: The Gokstad "faering". *Viking XXIII.* Oslo 1959.

E. Dyggve. La fouille par le Musée National danois du tertre royal sud à Jelling en 1941. *Acta Achæologica XXIII 1942.* Copenhagen.

E. Hinsch, Gokstadshövdingens jaktrensel. Résumé: La gibecière du seigneur de Gokstad. *Viking XXI-XXII.* Oslo 1958.

Bjørn Hougen, Osebergfunnets billedvev. *Viking IV.* Oslo 1940.

E. Kivikoski, *Kvarnbacken. Ein Gräberfeld der jüngeren Eisenzeit auf Åland.* Helsinki 1963.

S. Marstrander, Et nytt vikingetidsfunn fra Romsdal med vesteuropeiske importsaker. *Viking, XXVI.* Oslo 1963. English edition in "*Lochlann*" *Vol. III* (*Norsk tidsskrift for sprogvidenskap Suppl. VIII*).

N. Nicolayesen, *The Viking Ship discovered at Gokstad.* Christiania 1882.

O. Olsen & O. Crumlin Pedersen, The Skuldelev Ships. A preliminary report on an underwater excavation in Roskilde Fjord, Zealand. *Acta Archæologica XXIX 1958.* Copenhagen.

K. G. Peterson, Ett gravfynd från Klinta, Köpings sn, Öland. Summary: A grave from Klinta, Öland. *Tor IV.* Uppsala 1958.

Th. Ramskou, Viking Age Cremation Graves in Denmark. *Acta Archæologica XXI 1950.* Copenhagen.

T. Ramskou. Lindholm. Preliminary report of the 152-53 excavations. *Acta Archæologica XXIV 1953.* Copenhagen.

— —, Lindholm Höje. Second preliminary report for the years 1954-55. *Acta Archæologica XXVI 1955.* Copenhagen.

— —, Lindholm Höje. Third preliminary report for the years 1956-57. *Acta Archæologica XXVIII 1957.* Copenhagen.

H. Rydh. *Förhistoriska undersökningar på Adelsö.* Deutscher Auszug. Stockholm 1936.

I. Serning, *Dalarnas järnålder.* Malung 1966.

H. Shetelig, Tuneskipet. *Norske Oldfunn II,* Christiania 1917.

Thorleif Sjøvold, *Osebergfunnet og de andre vikingeskipsfunn,* Oslo 1957.

M. Stenberger, Das Gräberfeld bei Ihre im Kirchspiel Hellvi auf Gotland. Der wikingerzeitliche Abschnitt. *Acta Archæologica XXXII 1961.* Copenhagen.

H. Stolpe, *La nécropole de Vendel.* Stockholm 1927.

K. Thorvildsen, *Ladby-skibet*. Summary: The Ladby ship. Copenhagen 1957.

COINS AND HOARDS

R. H. M. Dolley, The Post-Brunnanburgh Viking Coinage of York. *Nordisk Numismatisk Årsskrift 1957-1958*. Stockholm.
M. Dolley, *Viking coins of the Danelaw and of Dublin*. British Museum, London 1965.
K. Friis Johansen, Sölvfundet fra Terslev. *Aarböger for nordisk Oldkyndighed og Historie 1912*. Copenhagen.
G. Galster, Cuerdale-fundet og de danske vikingekonger i 9. århundrede. Summary: The Cuerdale find and the danish viking kings of the ninth century. *Aarböger for nordisk Oldkyndighed og Historie*. Copenhagen 1962.
——, Möntfundet fra Kongsö plantage. Summary: The coin find from the Kongsö plantation. *Aarböger for nordisk Oldkyndighed og Historie*. Copengagen 1962.
S. Grieg, Vikingetidens skattefund. *Universitetets oldsaksamlings skrifter II*. Oslo 1929.
H. Holst. On the coins of the Hon-find. *Minor publications of the Norwegian Numismatic Society*. 4. 1931.
U. S. Linder Welin, Coins from Khwarazm and the Swedish Viking Age Hoards. *Meddelanden från Lunds Universitets Historiska Museum 1961*. Lund.
B. Malmer, Nordiska mynt före år 1000. Summary. *Acta Achæologica Lundensia*. Diss. Lund 1966.
——, Olof Skötkonungs mynt och andra Ethelredimitationer. Summary: Olof Skötkonung coins and other Ethelred imitations. *Antikvariskt arkiv 27*. Lund 1965.
E. Munksgaard, Skattefundet fra Duesminde. Summary: The Duesminde treasure. *Aarböger for nordisk Oldkyndighed og Histoire*. Copenhagen 1962.
——, Det andet skattefund fra Duesminde. Summary: The second silver hoard from Duesminde. *Aarböger for nordisk Oldkyndighed og Historie*. Copenhagen 1963.
K. G. Petersson & U. S. Linder Welin, The Slubbemåla Hoard. *Meddelanden från Lunds Universitets Historiska Museym 1962-1963*. Lund.
K. Skaare, Angelsaksiske mynter - i britisk mynthistorie og i norske vikingetidsfunn. Summary: Anglo-Saxon Coins - in the History of British Coinage and in Norwegian Viking Age Finds. *Viking XXVI*. Oslo 1963.
R. Skovmand. De danske skattefund fra vikingetid og den aeldste middelalder indtil omkring 1150. Résumé: Les trésors danois provenant de l'époque des vikings et du moyen age le plus ancien jusqu'aux environs de 1150. *Aarböger for nordisk Oldkyndighed og Historie 1942*. Diss. Copenhagen.
M. Stenberger, *Die Schatzfunde Gotlands der Wikingerzeit*. II Fundbeschreibung und Tafeln, Lund 1947; I Text, Stockholm 1958.

SITES AND FINDS FROM OUTSIDE SCANDINAVIA

H. Arbman, Hague-Dike. Les fouilles en 1951 et 1952. *Meddelanden från Lunds Universitets Museum 1953*. Lund.
——, Skandinawisches Handwerk in Russland zur Wikingerzeit. *Meddelanden från Lunds Universitets Historiska Museum 1959*. Lund.
T. J. Arne, Skandinawische Holzkammergräber in der Ukraine. *Acta Archæologica II*. Copenhagen 1931.
A. V. Artsikhovsky & B. A. Kolchin. Work of the Novgorod Archæological Expedition I-II. *Materials and researches on the archæology of the USSR. nos. 55 & 65*. Moscow 1956, 1959.
J. Böhm and others. *La Grande-Moravie. The great Moravian Empire*. Prag 1963.
P. du Chatellier-L. le Pontois, La sépulture scandinave à barque de l'Ile de Groix. *Bulletin de la Soc. Arch. du Finistère, XXXV*, Quimper 1908.
B. Dostál, *Slovanská pohrebiste ze stredni doby hradistni na Morave*. Zusammenfassung: Slawische Begräbnisstätten der mittleren Burgwallze in Mähren. Prague 1966.
B. Ehrlich, Der preussisch-wikingische Handelsplatz Truzo. *I. Balt. histor. Kongress*, Riga 1938.
K. Eldjárn, *Kuml og Haugfé*. Akureyri 1956.
J. Filip and others, *Investigations Archéologiques en Tchécoslovaquie*. État actuel des recherches et leur organisation. VIIème Congrès International des Sciences Préhistoriques et protohistoriques à Prague 1966. Prague 1966.
P. Gelling, Recent discoveries of houses of scandinavian type in the Isle of Man. *Bericht über den V internationalen Kongress für Vor- und Frühgeschichte Hamburg 1958*. Berlin 1961.
J. Hamilton, *Excavations at Jarlshof, Shetland*. Edinburgh 1956.
J. H. Holwerda, *Dorestad an onze vroegste middeleeuwen*, Leiden 1929.
V. Hruby, Staré Mesto. Velkomoravské pohrebište "na Valách". Zusammenfassung: Die grossmährische Begräbnisstätte "na Valách". *Monumenta Archæoloigca III*. Prague 1955.
V. Hruby, Staré Mesto. Velkomoravsky Velehrad. *Monumenta Archæologica Bd. 14*. Prague 1965.
H. Ingstad. Vinland ruins. Prove vikings found the New World. *National geographic Magazin*. Washington november 1964.
H. Ingstad. *Land under the pole star*. New York 1965.
H. Jankuhn, Die frühmittelalterlichen Seehandelsplätze im Nord- und Ostseeraum. *Vorträge und Forschungen IV*, Lindau 1958.
E. Kivikoski, *Finlands förhistoria*. Helsinki 1964.
Otto Kunkel-K. A. Wilde, *Jumme, "Vineta," Jomsburg, Julin: Wollin*, Stettin 1941.
P. Nörlund, Norse ruins at Gardar, the episcopal seat of medieval Greenland. *Medelelser om Grönland 76 nr 1*. Copenhagen 1930.
P. Nörlund & M. Stenberger. Brattahlid. Researches into norse culture in Greenland. *Medelelser om Grönland 88 nr 1*. Copenhagen 1934.
P. Paulsen, *Der Goldschatz von Hiddensee*. Leipzig 1936.
——, *Axt und Kreuz bei den Nordgermanen*. Berlin 1939.
J. Poulík, *Velkomoravské Hradiste Mikullcice*. Zusammenfassung: Führer durch die archäologische Grabung des Burgwalles aus der Zeit des Grossmährischen Reiches bei Mikulcice in Südmähren. Krajské nakladelstvi Gottwaldov 1959.
——, *Starí Moravané Buduji Svůj Stát*. Summary: The Old Moravians Building their State. Krajské nakladelstvi Gottwaldov 1960.
W. J. Raudonikas, *Die Normannen der Wikingerzeit und das Ladogagebiet*, Stockholm 1930.
A. Roes, Vondsten van Dorestad. *Archæologica Traiectina VII*. Groningen 1965.
Aage Roussell, *Norse Building Customs in the Scottish Isles*, Copenhagen-London 1934.
E. Schuldt, *Slawische Burgen in Mecklenburg*. Museum für Ur- und Frühgeschichte Schwerin, Sonderausstellung 1962.
H. Shetelig, ed., *Viking antiquities in Great Britain and Ireland. Vol. I-VI*. Oslo 1940-1954.
——, The Viking Graves in Great Britain and Ireland. *Acta Archæologica 1945*. Copenhagen.
M. Stenberger, ed. *Forntida gårdar i Island*. Summary: Ancient farmsteads in Iceland. Copenhagen 1943.
M. Tikhomirov. *The towns of ancient rus*. Moscow 1959.
W. Unverzagt & E. Schuldt, Teterow, ein slawischer Burgwall in Mecklenburg. *Deutsche Akademie der Wissenschaften zu Berlin, Schriften der Sektion für Vor- und Frühgeschichte, Band 13*. Berlin 1963.
H. J. Vogt, *Die Ausgrabungen auf der Wiprechtsburg in Groitzsch*. Landesmuseum für Vorgeschichte Dresden & Redaktion des "Rundblicks" Wurzen. Wurzen 1965.
D. M. Waterman. Late Saxon, viking and early medieval finds from York. *Archæologica XCVII*. 1959.
K. A. Wilde, Die Bedeutung der Grabung Wollin 1934. I. *Beiheft zum Atlas der Urgeschichte*. Hamburg 1953.
J. Ypey, Een aantal vroeg-middeleeuwse zwaarden uit Nederlandse musea. Summary: Some early medieval swords from Dutch museums. *Berichten van de rijksdienst voor het oudheidkundig bodemonderzoek 10-11*.
——, Eine Riemenzunge mit anglo-karolingischem Tierornament aus der Waal bei Rossum, Prov. Gelderland, und ein Steigbügelfragment von Huizum, Prov. Friesland. *Berichten van de rijksdienst voor het oudheidkundig bodenmonderzoek 12-13*. Amersfoort 1962-63.
——, Vroeg-middeleeuwse wapens uit Nederlandse verzamelingen. Summary: Early medieval swords from Dutch collections. *Berichten van de rijksdienst voor het oudheidkundig bodemonderzoek 12-13*. Amersfoor 1962-63.
——, Vroeg-middeleeuwse zwaarden uit Nederlandse verzamelingen. Summary: Early medieval swords from Dutch collections. *Berichten van de rijksdienst voor het oudheidkundig bodemonderzoek 14*. Amersfoort 1964.
J. Zak, Eine skandinavische frühmittelalterliche Eisenlanzenspitze aus Grosspolen. *Meddelanden från Lunds Universitets Historiska Museum 1959*. Lund.

MATERIAL CULTURE

B. Almgren· *Bronsnycklar och djurornamentik vid övergången från vendeltid till vikingatid*. Diss. Uppsala 1955.
H. Arbman, *Schweden und das karolingische Reich*. Diss. Uppsala 1937.
T. J. Arne, *La Suède et l'Orient*. Diss. Uppsala, 1916.
Gösta Berg, *Sledges and Wheeled Vehicles*. Diss. Stockholm 1935.
Gësta Berg, Sledges and Wheeled Vehicles, Diss. Stockholm 1935.
Ch. Blindheim, Drakt og smykker, Studier i jernalderens drakthistorie i Norden. *Viking 1947*. Oslo.
A. W. Brøgger, Ertog og øre. Den gamle norske vegt. *Videnskapsselskapets skrifter II, Hist.-filos. klasse no 3*, Christiania 1921.
A. W. Brøgger & H. Shetelig. *The Viking Ships*. Stanford 1953.
A. Bruhn Hoffmeyer, *Middelalderens tveæggede sværd I-II*. Copenhagen 1954.
A. E. Christensen jr, Birka-Hedeby myntene som kilde til skipets historie på 800-tallet. *Norsk Sjøfartsmuseum 1914-1964*. Oslo 1964.
D. Ellmers, Zum Trinkgeschirr der Wikingerzeit. *Offa 21-22*. Neumünster 1964-65.
A. Geijer, Var järnålderns "frisiska kläde" tillverkat i Syrien? Dummary: The pallium fresonicum of the Viking Age was it manufactured in Syria? *Fornvännen 1965*. Stockholm.
P. V. Glob, *Ard og plov i Nordens oldtid*, Aarhus 1951.
Sk. V. Gudjonsson, *Folkekost og Sundhedsforhold i gamle Dage*. Copenhagen 1941.
M. Hald, *Olddanske Textilier*. Summary: Ancient Danish Textiles. Diss. Copenhagen 1958.
M. Hoffman, The warp-weighted loom. *Studia Norvegica 14*. Kragerö Diss. Oslo.
Kulturhistoriskt lexikon för nordisk medeltid I-XI seqq. Malmö 1956.
C. A. Nordman, Vapnen i Nordens forntid. *Nordisk Kultur, XII B, Vapen*. Stockholm-Oslo-Copenhagen 1943.
A. Oldeberg, Till frågen om de ovala spännbucklornas tillverkningssätt. Zusammenfassung: Zur Frage der Herstellungsweise der ovalen Schalenspangen. *Fornvännen 1963*. Stockholm.
——, De ovala spännbucklorna ännu en gång. *Fornvännen 1965*. Stockholm.
——, *Metallteknik under vikingatid och medeltid*. Stockholm 1966.
Jan Petersen, De norske vikingesverd. En typologisk-kronologisk studie over vikingetidens vaaben. *Videnskapsselskapets skrifter. II Hist.-filos. klasse no I*, Oslo 1919.
Jean Petersen, *Vikingetidens smykker*, Stavanger 1928.
——, Vikingetidens redskaper. *Skrifter utgitt av Det norske Videnskaps-Akademi i Oslo II Hist.-filos. klasse no 4*. Oslo 1951.
——, *Vikingetidens smykker i Norge*. Stavanger 1955.
D. Selling, *Wikingerzeitliche und frühmittelalterliche Keramik in Schweden*. Diss. Stockholm 1955.
I. Serning, Vor- und frühgeschichtliches Eisengewerbe im schwedischen Järhbäraland. *Festschrift für Robert Durrer*. Schaffhausen 1965.
K. Skaare, Skipsavbildninger på Birka-Hedeby mynter. *Norsk Sjøfarts-museum 1914-1964*. Oslo 1964.
M. Strömberg, Ein wikingerzeitlicher Kumtbeschlag von Sinclairsholm in Schonen. *Meddelanden från Lunds Universitets Historiska Museum 1964-1965*. Lund.
I. Zachrisson, De ovala spännbucklornas tillverkningssätt. Zusammenfassung: Die Gusstechnik bei den ovalen Schalenspangen. *Tor VI*. Upsala 1960.
I. Zachrisson: Till frågan om de ovala spännbucklornas tillverkningssätt. Ett genmäle. *Fornvännen 1964*. Stockholm.
I. Zachrisson, Smedsfyndet från Smiss. Zusammenfassung. *Tor VIII*. Uppsala 1962.
I. Zetterberg, Furenfyndet-ett senvikingatida småländskt handelsfynd. Zusammenfassung. *Tor IV*. Upsala 1958.

ART AND RUNES

N. Aberg, Keltiska och orientaliska stilinflytelser i vikingatidens nordiska konst. *Kungl. Vitt. Hist. Antikv. Handlingar*. Stockholm 1941.
B. Almgren, *Bronsnycklar och djurornamentik vid övergången från vendeltid till vikingatid*. Diss. Uppsala 1955.
H. Arbman, *Schweden und das Karolingische Reich*. Diss. Stockholm 1937.
——, The Skabersjö Brooch and some Danish Mounts. *Meddelanden från Lunds Univ. Hist. Mus.* 1956, Lund.
H. Arntz, *Handbuch der Runenkunde*. Halle 1944.
G. Arvidsson, *Vendelstile, Email und Glas*. Diss. Uppsala 1942.
A. Bæksted, *Målruner og troldruner. Runemagiske studier*. Copenhagen 1952.
K. Berg, The cross of Gosforth. *The journal of the Warburg and Courtauld Institutes, Vol. XXI, Nos. 1-2*. 1958.
Johannes Brøndsted, *Early English Ornament*. London 1924.
H. Christiansson, *Sydskandinavisk stil*. Diss. Uppsala 1959.
J.-E. Forssander, Ireland-Oseberg. *Meddelanden från Lunds Univ. Hist. Mus.* 1943.
O. von Friesen, *Rökstenen*. Stockholm 1920.
——, (ed.), Runorna. *Nordisk Kultur VI*. Stockholm-Oslo-Copenhagen 1933.
——, Sparlösastenen. Zusammenfassung: Der Stein von Sparlösa. *Kungl. Vitt. Hist. Ant. Akademiens Handlingar 46. 1*. Stockholm 1940.
G. Galster, Knud den stores og dronning Emmas billeder. Summary: The pictures of King Canuto tho great and Queen Emma. *Aarböger for nordisk Oldkundighed og Historie*. Copenhagen 1960.
P. Gjaerder, The Beard as an Iconographical Feature in the Viking Period and the Early Middle Ages. *Acta Archæologica XXXV 1964*. Copenhagen.
W. Holmqvist, Övergångstidens Metallkonst. Summary: The metal art of the transitional period and its chronology. *Kungl. Vitt. Hist. och Ant. Akademiens Handlingar, antikvariska serien 11*. Stockholm 1963.
——, Viking Art in the Eleventh Century. *Acta Archæologica 1951*.
——, Germanic Art During the First Millennium A. D. *Kungl. Vitt. Hist. Antikv. Handlingar*. Stockholm 1955.
——, The Syllöda Silver Pin — an English Element in the Art of the Viking Age. *Suomen Museo LXVI*. Helsinki 1959.
Lis Jacobsen-E. Moltke, *Danmarks Runeindskrifter*. København 1942.
S. B. F. Jansson, *The runes of Sweden*. Stockholm 1962.
——, On Nordic Runes. *Scandinavian Past and Present*. Odense.
T. D. Kendrick, *Late Saxon an Viking Art*. London 1949.
P. Kermode. *Manx Crosses*. London 1907.
O. Klindt-Jensen & D. M. Wilson, *Vikingetidens kunst*, Copenhagen 1965.
A. Liestöl, Runer frå Bryggen. Summary. *Viking XXVII*. Oslo 1964.
Sune Lindqvist, *Gotlands Bildsteine I-II*. Stockholm 1941-42.
——, Osebergsmästarna. *Tor I*. Uppsala 1948.
E. M. Magerøy, Flatatunga Problems. *Acta Acrhæologica XXXII 1961*. Copenhagen.
Sophus Müller, Dyreornamentiken i Norden. *Aarbøger for nordisk Oldkyndighed og Historie 1880*. Copenhagen.
M. Olsen (ed.), *Norges innskrifter med de yngre runer I-V seqq*. Oslo 1944-1960 seqq.
A. Ruprecht, Die ausgehende Wikingerzeit im Lichte der Runeninschriften. *Palæstra 224*. Göttingen 1958.
H. Shetelig, Stil- og tidsbestemmelser i de nordiske korsene paa øen Man. *Opuscula archæologica Oscari Montelio dicata*. Stockholm 1918.
——, Vestfoldskolen. *Osebergfundet III*. Oslo 1920.
——, (ed.), Konst. *Nordisk Kultur XXVII*. Stockholm-Oslo-Copenhagen 1931.
——, The Norse Style of Ornamentation in the Viking Settlements. *Acta Archæologica 1948*.
——, *Classical Impulses in Scandinavian Art from the Migration Period to the Viking Age*. Oslo 1949.
——, Religionshistoriske drag fra vikingetidens stilhistorie. *Viking 1950*.
Sveriges runinskrifter. I-XIII seqq. *Kungl. Vitt. Hist. Ant. Akademi*. Uppsala 1900-1964 seqq.
E. Wessén, Om vikingatidens runor. *Filologiskt Arkiv VI*. Stockholm 1957.
——, Runstenen vid Röks kyrka. Zusammenfassung: Der Runenstein von Rök. *Kungl. Vitt. Hist. Ant. Akademien Handlingar. Filologisk-filosofiska serien 5*. Stockholm 1958.
D. M. Wilson, The Fejø Cup. *Acta Achæologica XXXI 1960*. Copenhagen.
J. Zak & E. Salberger, Ein Runenfund von Kamien Pomorski in West-Pommern. *Meddelanden från Lunds Universitets Historiska Museum 1962-1963*. Lund.

RELIGION AND LITERATURE

O. Almgren, Vikingatidens gravskick i verkligheten och i den fornnordiska litteraturen. *Nordiska studier tillägnade Adolf Noreen*. Uppsala 1904.
K. v. Amira, Recht. Paul, *Grundrisse der germanischen Philologie*, 1913.
S. K. Amtoft, *Nordiske Gudeskikkelser i bebyggelseshistorisk Belysinng*. Copenhagen 1948.
B. Arrhenius, Vikingatida miniatyrer. Zusammenfassung. *Tor VII*. Upsala 1961.
G. Dumézil, *Loki. Les Dieux et les hommes I*. Paris 1948.
V. Grønbech, *The Culture of the Teutons I-II*. London-Copenhagen 1931.
K. Hald, The Cult of Odin in Danish Place-Names. *Early English and Norse Studies presented to Hugh Smith 1963*. London.
——, *Vore Stednavne*. Copenhagen 1965.
A. Heusler, *Die altgermanische Dichtung*. Potsdam 1941.
F. Jónsson, *Den oldnorske og oldislandske litteraturs historie I-III*. Copenhagen 1920-24.
E. Kivikoski, Magisches Fundgut aus finnischer Eisenzeit. *Suomen Museo LXXII*. Helsinki 1965.
Fr. von der Leyen, *Die Götter der Germanen*. Munich 1938.
Nils Lid, Scandinavian Heathen Cult Places. *Folk-Liv XXI-XXII*. Stockholm 1957-58.
H. Ljungberg, *Den nordiska religionen och kristendomen. Studier över det nordiska religionsskiftet under vikingatiden*. Diss. Uppsala 1938.
R. Meissner, *Beiträge zur Geschichte der deutschen Sprache und Literatur 57*, 1933 (about Rigsthula).
G. Neckel, *Die altnordische Literatur*. Leipzig 1923.
M. Olsen, Farms and Fanes of Ancient Norway. *The Place-Names of a Country Discussed in their Bearings on Social and Religious History*. Oslo 1928.
——, (ed.), Ortnamn. *Nordisk Kultur V*. Stockholm-Oslo-Copenhagen 1939.
——, Hörg, hov og kirke. Summary: Horgr, hof and church. *Aarböger for nordisk Oldkyndighed og Historie*. 1965. Also Diss. Copenhagen.
F. Ström, Diser, nornor, valkyrior. Fruktbarhetskult och sakralt kungadöme i Norden. *Kungl. Vitt. His. Antikv. Akad. Handlingar, filol.-filosof. serien I*. Stock holm 1954.
——, *Nordisk hedendom. Tro och sed i Förkristen tid*. Göteborg 1961.
M. Strömberg, Kultische Steinsetzungen in Schonen. *Meddelanden från Lunds Universitets Historiska Museum 1962-1963*. Lund.
Cl. v. Schwerin, *Germanische Rechtsgeschichte*. 1936.
Jan de Vries, *Altgermanische Religionsgeschichte I-II*. Berlin 1956-57.
——, *Altnordische Literaturgeschichte I-II*. Berlin 1941-42.